The Catholic Answer Book 2

Rev. Peter M. J. Stravinskas, Ph.D., S.T.L.

Our Sunday Visitor Publishing Division
Our Sunday Visitor, Inc.
Huntington, Indiana 46750

Most of the text of this book first appeared in *The Catholic Answer* magazine between 1990 and 1993. Most citations from Holy Scripture are from the *New American Bible With Revised New Testament*, copyright © 1969, 1970, 1986 by the Confraternity of Christian Doctrine, Washington, D.C., and reprinted by permission; all rights reserved. Quotations from documents of the Second Vatican Council are taken from Vatican II: The Conciliar and Post Conciliar Documents, © 1975, 1986, 1992 by Rev. Austin Flannery, O.P. by permission of Costello Publishing Co., Inc.; all rights reserved.

Our Sunday Visitor Publishing Division
Our Sunday Visitor, Inc.
200 Noll Plaza
Huntington, Indiana 46750

International Standard Book Number: 0-87973-737-9
Library of Congress Catalog Card Number: 93-87277

Cover design by Monica Watts

PRINTED IN THE UNITED STATES OF AMERICA

Contents

Key to Abbreviations of Biblical Books
(In Alphabetical Order)

Old Testament

Am / Amos
Bar / Baruch
1 Chr / 1 Chronicles
2 Chr / 2 Chronicles
Dn / Daniel
Dt / Deuteronomy
Eccl / Ecclesiastes
Est / Esther
Ex / Exodus
Ez / Ezekiel
Ezr / Ezra
Gn / Genesis
Hb / Habakkuk
Hg / Haggai
Hos / Hosea
Is / Isaiah
Jb / Job
Jdt / Judith
Jer / Jeremiah
Jgs / Judges
Jl / Joel
Jon / Jonah
Jos / Joshua

1 Kgs / 1 Kings
2 Kgs / 2 Kings
Lam / Lamentations
Lv / Leviticus
Mal / Malachi
1 Mc / 1 Maccabees
2 Mc / 2 Maccabees
Mi / Micah
Na / Nahum
Neh / Nehemiah
Nm / Numbers
Ob / Obadiah
Prv / Proverbs
Ps(s) / Psalms
Ru / Ruth
Sg / Song of Solomon
Sir / Sirach
1 Sm / 1 Samuel
2 Sm / 2 Samuel
Tb / Tobit
Wis / Wisdom
Zec / Zechariah
Zep / Zephaniah

New Testament

Acts / Acts of the Apostles
Col / Colossians
1 Cor / 1 Corinthians
2 Cor / 2 Corinthians
Eph / Ephesians
Gal / Galatians
Heb / Hebrews
Jas / James
Jn / John
1 Jn / 1 John
2 Jn / 2 John
3 Jn / 3 John
Jude / Jude
Lk / Luke

Mk / Mark
Mt / Matthew
Phil / Philippians
Phlm / Philemon
1 Pt / 1 Peter
2 Pt / 2 Peter
Rom / Romans
Rv / Revelation
1 Thes / 1 Thessalonians
2 Thes / 2 Thessalonians
Ti / Titus
1 Tm / 1 Timothy
2 Tm / 2 Timothy

Documents of Vatican Council II
(In Chronological Order)

Sacrosanctum Concilium: Constitution on the Sacred Liturgy

Inter Mirifica: Decree on the Means of Social Communication

Lumen Gentium: Dogmatic Constitution on the Church

Orientalium Ecclesiarum: Decree on the Catholic Eastern Churches

Unitatis Redintegratio: Decree on Ecumenism

Christus Dominus: Decree on the Pastoral Office of Bishops in the Church

Perfectae Caritatis: Decree on the Up-to-Date Renewal of Religious Life

Optatam Totius: Decree on the Training of Priests

Gravissimum Educationis: Declaration on Christian Education

Nostra Aetate: Declaration on the Relations of the Church to Non-Christian Religions

Dei Verbum: Dogmatic Constitution on Divine Revelation

Apostolicam Actuositatem: Decree on the Apostolate of Lay People

Dignitatis Humanae: Declaration on Religious Liberty

Ad Gentes Divinitus: Decree on the Church's Missionary Activity

Presbyterorum Ordinis: Decree on the Ministry and Life of Priests

Gaudium et Spes: Pastoral Constitution on the Church in the Modern World

1. CATHOLIC PRACTICES

Holding hands and the Lord's Prayer

Q. What is the meaning of the people and priest holding hands during the Our Father? Where did it originate? Why do some join in, while others do not?

A. I suspect this practice began at charismatic prayer meetings and was then transferred to charismatic Masses, eventually working its way into general Sunday Masses in some places. It is supposed to symbolize the unity of the family of believers under the Fatherhood of God, addressed as such in the Lord's Prayer. While I have no theological problem with the practice, I am uneasy with it for two reasons: (1) It is not called for in the rubrics; (2) It alienates many people, and nothing should be introduced into the liturgy (especially of an optional and arbitrary nature) which would have that effect. Furthermore, when the priest gets involved in the gesture it has the effect of linking him too much to the whole Body at that point in the liturgy where his standing *in persona Christi* should be highlighted. Last but not least, in 1975 the Congregation for Sacraments and Divine Worship noted that the practice ought to be "repudiated."

May 'ex-priests' author texts?

Q. In [a recent] issue of The Catholic Answer, you responded to the question "May ex-priests teach theology?" The textbook series "This is our Faith" is authored by an ex-priest and former nun, now married to each other. Should they be allowed to author a catechetical series?

A. I do not think the ban extends to textbook writing for one reason. There is a big and important distinction between teaching in a classroom and writing a text; in the former case, one has personal influence and great latitude for expressing a host of opinions and contrary teachings, while in the latter, a catechetical text requires episcopal review and an imprimatur and no possibility for deviation from official Church teaching or the propagation of scandalous personal opinions.

I am aware of at least one catechetical text having an ex-priest for an author, and it is horrendous. The problem, of course, is how it ever obtained an imprimatur, which has sadly been given to many other bad texts, not written by ex-priests.

May 'ex-priests' teach theology?

Q. Is there a canon forbidding ex-priests to teach theology in a Catholic institution on any level? If so, why was a university in the Midwest allowed to hire an ex-priest to head its theology department? Who has the authority to enforce this law?

A. The relevant proscription is not found in the Code of Canon Law but is contained in the rescript of laicization received by men who have petitioned the Holy See to return to the lay state. The restrictions on the activities of a laicized priest usually go as follows: he may not administer the sacraments (except in an emergency) or celebrate Mass; he may not teach religion or theology at any level (that would include even CCD classes); he may not perform any liturgical role (for example, lector), even one open to other laity; he may not administer any Catholic education institution.

The local bishop is responsible for the enforcement of these norms in all cases.

A married priesthood?

Q. Our priest has printed in our bulletin that at present our seminaries are full of homosexuals and the only real way to solve the vocation crisis is to allow priests to marry. He likes to quote Father McBrien and seems to be opposed to the Pope. What can you say about these issues he has raised?

A. With no evidence for his assertion, Father Richard McBrien has caused a great deal of scandal to the faithful. His style is generally confrontational and mean-spirited, especially when he gets onto issues like clerical celibacy and the ordination of women. Your pastor has exacerbated the problem by giving a further hearing to Father McBrien's unsubstantiated charges.

Let me add but a bit more here. If anyone thinks that a married priesthood would solve our problems, either with the vocations shortage or with illicit clerical sexual activity, that person is either extremely naïve or grossly uninformed. The Eastern Orthodox have married priests, and they still have serious problems in vocation recruitment, with the average age of their priests about 15 years older than ours — hardly a striking testimony to the drawing card of marriage to alleviate the shortage of priests. Anglicans, Lutherans, and Orthodox — as well as nearly every other denomination — have married clergy and yet are plagued by the adultery, homosexuality, and pedophilia of their clergy in percentages often far greater than ours — again, a reminder that marriage is not the solution.

I never tire of saying that we have a shortage of priests and unhappy priests, as well as an unclear priestly identity to offer in many religious communities and dioceses, with the result that young men are not attracted. When that is cleared up, we'll be turning candidates away, because no sacrifice is perceived as too great when the goal is seen as worthwhile.

A widower pope?

Q. I often hear about widowed men going on to become priests. Is there anything to prevent their advancing beyond being simple priests? Could one become a bishop, cardinal, or even pope? Is it possible to have a pope who has made marriage vows?

A. Once a spouse dies, the marriage bond is dissolved, hence the surviving partner is free to remarry or enter upon a priestly or religious vocation. Once a priest, a man is eligible for any other office, regardless of his earlier commitments or vocation.

By the way, technically speaking, any baptized male can be elected pope. If he is not ordained at his election, he would have to be ordained to the diaconate, priesthood, and episcopate before being installed as Bishop of Rome and Sovereign Pontiff. That hasn't happened in centuries, but it is still possible — even if only remotely so.

Married men as priests

Q. The attached New York Times clipping of 1/24/90 describes how a married man in Brazil (married since 1947, living in celibacy since 1953) was ordained a priest in 1986 — a fact only lately publicized by Cardinal Lorscheider. Another Brazilian, having lived apart from his wife for a decade, was also ordained in 1986. Why was the need felt for four years of silence on these shocking events? Also, from whom did the "Vatican approval" referred to in the article actually come? No names are given. Was this all done without the knowledge of the Pope? Clearly, we are having a severe crisis in vocations to the priesthood when such men are being ordained. I personally believe that while Vatican II was not intended to cause such an upheaval, it certainly opened the doors to this disaster. Please comment.

A. The two cases you cite were certainly known to the Pope and needed his explicit approval before such an arrangement could be permitted. I must confess that I do not know why the Holy See maintained silence on the situation, but neither do I understand what so upsets you about this, which has nothing to do with Vatican II and the postconciliar "upheaval." As a matter of fact, Pope Pius XII had allowed Lutheran clergy who were married to be ordained Catholic priests, and those men maintained their marital rights (as do Anglican convert clergy today).

The Brazilian cases are, frankly, exceptions which reinforce the general norm. In many ways they hark back to the ancient discipline under which married men were ordained but they and their wives freely gave up their marital rights after the man's ordination. This demonstrates the esteem in which celibacy was held in the Churches of the East and West from the earliest times, disproving the allegation that a celibate clergy was a medieval invention. All of this is well documented in a new book by Father Christian Conchini, published by Ignatius Press.

Multiple Mass intentions

Q. I am enclosing a Sunday bulletin from our parish. You will note that under "Mass Intentions for the Week," there are two intentions for almost every day of the week. Is this legal or permissible?
A. The Holy See has issued a clarification on this matter, precisely because of reports of numerous abuses in this regard. While we know that one Mass is of infinite value and could thus be applied for every intention in the universe, that is not the problem here. The concern is rather one of justice, namely, a member of the faithful has given a stipend for a Mass to be offered for a particular intention, and the donor has a right to have the fruits of that Mass applied specifically for the intention. If, however, a number of people would get together and agree on several intentions for a particular Mass, that would be licit. In some parishes, it is known and accepted that Monday's Mass, for example, will be for several intentions; thus a donor realizes that in advance and goes ahead with the offering.

The Holy See's involvement with the question has to do with a desire that any semblance of trafficking in Mass stipends be avoided, and that appearance certainly is real when multiple intentions are the pattern in a parish.

Who may properly use the title 'chaplain'?

Q. In [a recent] issue of TCA, you incorrectly answered a question concerning who could be called "chaplain." I am aware of the difference between the ordained and the non-ordained, as that of being able to administer the sacraments. Perhaps you are not aware of the Clinical Pastoral Education (CPE) programs in many hospitals (including Catholic hospitals) where lay people, Religious, deacons and priests study and train to meet the needs of hospital and nursing-home patients. Are you not aware of the certification of these people as chaplains through the United States Catholic Conference? It now takes one year of study and clinical practice, as well as going before an examining board, for certification.

In today's world, when ministry is done by so many non-ordained people, it is only right to acknowledge those of us with the appropriate title "chaplain" — "a person to whom is entrusted in a stable manner the pastoral care of a particular group of Christian faithful" (Can. 564).

A. Let's start at the end of your letter and work backward. Your citation is from the Code of Canon Law, but you changed one key word, namely, "priest" to "person," and that is the whole crux of my argument. The Church is not willing to accord the title of chaplain to anyone except a priest.

Secondly, a world "when [sic] ministry is done by so many non-ordained people" is truly problematic. Again, according to the mind of the Church, both at Vatican II and at the 1987 Synod on the Laity, "ministry" is not done by the non-ordained, and the word should not be used for services performed by the non-ordained. If lay people visit the sick, teach, counsel, etc., their work is properly termed an apostolate, not a ministry. This is not my "hang-up," but the careful use of language to reflect Catholic theology. Because of our carelessness over the past decade, we find a great deal of confusion among clergy and laity alike, which has resulted in what Pope John Paul II has called "the clericalization of the laity and the laicization of the clergy."

Thirdly, whether or not the USCC calls these people "ministers" is immaterial. The USCC has no teaching authority in the Church and, in fact, has produced not a few troublesome documents over the years; even the National Conference of Catholic Bishops (which has more claim to authority) has had to have its work reviewed by the Holy See on occasion (for example, its document on the relationship of theologians and bishops, the failed pastoral on women's concerns).

Therefore, I stand by my original statement: The use of the title "chaplain" is inappropriate in a Catholic context when referring to someone who is not a priest.

One final note: CPE has come under fire from many quarters in the past few years, and many dioceses have done away with it since it is often practiced in a manner which denigrates sacramental ministry, overemphasizing psychological skills, etc.

Catholic schools

Q. If you have to economize in providing a child with a Catholic school education in a parish, which grades should be eliminated — primary or junior high?

A. It is unconscionable to me that the American system of educational funding would force a parent into choosing one level of schooling over another for one's child. Therefore, I would like to underscore the tremendous importance for Catholics and others of good will to work effectively within the political process to eliminate this horrible injustice.

That having been said, I do not think a true choice can be made for a number of reasons. The primary grades provide the necessary foundation, but the junior-high years are so critical in terms of sensitive issues (particularly related to sexuality and other values not generally shared by Catholics today with the broader culture). My advice is always to begin at the beginning; once the child is in the parochial system, who knows what else can change? He or she could conceivably continue in it all the way through. If one starts a child out in the government school system, it is highly unlikely that the child would be withdrawn later; at least that is what the statistics tell us.

One last word: If finances are truly the major obstacle, do not hesitate to talk to your pastor and seek the necessary help from your parish; in my judgment, this is a parochial responsibility — that is, if we are serious in all our talk about parishes being families, Christian communities, etc.

Education dilemma

Q. I am in a dilemma. Our children are coming up to school age. Our options for them are the local public school (with which we are very uncomfortable), an Assembly of God school, or home schooling;

regrettably, there is no Catholic school. I should note that I happen to be a certified elementary school teacher and know that I could do justice to their education, at least until the sixth grade.

A. I am glad that you understand the importance of Catholic schooling and equally regret the fact that none is available to you.

As an intelligent woman and mother, you have concluded that the local public school is problematic. Since I do not know any of the details, I think your judgment must be taken seriously here. Certainly any government school presents problems for committed believers because of the Supreme Court's insistence on a religious neutrality which all too often crosses the border into outright hostility toward traditional Christian values. When amoral or immoral sex education is thrown into the pot, the situation becomes even worse.

As far as an Assembly of God school is concerned, I would be most wary. That denomination is infamous for proselytizing Catholics and boasts of having half their membership made up of former Catholics. Were the school under the auspices of a more mainline group like the Episcopalians or Lutherans, I would have less hesitancy.

As a professional educator, my reaction is generally negative toward home schooling, not because I'm afraid this will put schools out of business but because I am concerned about children's socialization — a very important function of education. However, given the options open to you, home schooling may indeed be the best route to go, especially given your own expertise and training.

Parish schools are worth the price

Q. Our parish school keeps us in debt. I maintain we should introduce a very efficient religious-education program for the whole parish, including adults as well as teenagers and children. What are the statistics for parishes that have gone this route?

A. The historical record is clear: The Catholic school has been — and still is — the most effective form of evangelization and inculturation into the Catholic community ever invented. Parishes have spent thousands of dollars on trying to find viable alternatives, and I am unaware of any great success stories. The very fact that so many non-Catholics have gotten into the "school business" in recent years (from Fundamentalist Christians to Reformed Jews) is perhaps the best argument in favor of denominational schools. Twenty years ago these groups would not have dreamed of running a school, but they have come to see that the best chance for religious faith to come alive occurs when learning takes place in an integrated environment, where faith and secular knowledge are seen as compatible, indeed, mutually enforcing and complementary.

Schools are expensive, but I can think of no better investment, especially since they educate at least two generations at once (parents and children) if they are administered properly. Furthermore, a school need not be seen as detrimental to a program of adult education in itself; as in most things in life, this is not an either-or situation as much as a both-and. After all, Catholics in the United States are among the most affluent members of society-at-large, and if we cannot maintain the schools our immigrant forebears built, something is drastically wrong with us.

Academic freedom

Q. I had occasion for correspondence with the University of Detroit Mercy, following the Time magazine article that cited Professor Jan Schaberg regarding the interpretations of the infancy narratives in the Gospels. I do not believe that "every university has an obligation to support traditional tenets of academic freedom and scholarly research on the part of its faculty" is applicable to a Catholic university on theological studies and publications. Please comment.

A. Academic freedom is the liberty to teach the truth. If we are part of a Catholic school, that means we find the fullness of truth in Jesus Christ and the Church He founded. If we don't, our presence betrays the identity of the place and flies in the face of the philosophy on which the institution was built and should be maintained.

Catholic colleges

Q. Enclosed is a page from the "Catholic Almanac" which lists colleges and universities. You will notice that several Catholic schools are listed as "independent" and others as "private." What does that mean?

A. Catholic institutions of higher learning have generally been divided into: 1) pontifical — chartered by the Holy See; 2) diocesan — administered by a local diocese; 3) private — run by a particular religious congregation. Examples of each category would be: 1) The Catholic University of America; 2) Seton Hall University, under the auspices of the Archdiocese of Newark; 3) The University of Notre

Dame, founded by the Congregation of the Holy Cross.

The designation of "independent," I do not understand, except that, in certain instances in recent years, some catholic colleges have tried to evade ecclesiastical control and/or obtain state funding by asserting independence from religious authority. Of course, this is precisely the route taken by dozens of Protestant colleges in the last century, and who today remembers that Princeton was once a Presbyterian college? I have no problem with a college's declaration of independence, so long as it does not attempt to have the best of both worlds, by which I mean regarding itself as secular to avoid Canon Law and proclaiming itself Catholic to garner support from unsuspecting alumni and other committed believers. That is just downright dishonest.

'Independent' vs. 'private'

Q. I note . . . that you discuss the use of the word "independent" as applied to Catholic colleges and universities.

The word "independent" has been used for years by many non-public institutions to distinguish them from public institutions.

The reason for the preferred use of the word "independent" rather than "private" is that the majority of non-public institutions of higher education are open to the public, perform a public service, and, as is the case with St. Mary's College of California, are officially listed in state corporation codes as "public benefit corporations." The use of the word "private" to distinguish independent institutions from public institutions tends to indicate to the general public that independent institutions are restrictive and not open to the public. . . .

If there are Catholic institutions which prefer to disassociate themselves from the Church, I agree that in those cases such institutions should no longer be called Catholic the same way most Catholic institutions of higher education in the United States call themselves Catholic. The fact that our institutions and all other Catholic institutions of higher education in California call ourselves "independent" has nothing to do with separation from the Roman Catholic Church.
A. Thanks for the clarification.

Catholic name cause of confusion

Q. In response to a question in [a recent] issue on sterilizations in a Catholic hospital, I know of the hospital mentioned by the questioner. St.

14

Thomas Hospital in Akron, Ohio, was formerly a part of the Catholic Hospital System of the Diocese of Cleveland.

Several years ago, when the Sisters who founded it decided they could no longer staff it, it reverted to private ownership. Its board then began to make decisions radically out of step with Catholic medical practice, notably with regard to sterilization, and removed it from the Catholic system.

Bishop Sheldon, auxiliary for that region, publicly declared that St. Thomas Hospital was no longer to be considered a Catholic hospital. I seem to recall that the Blessed Sacrament is no longer reserved there.

Many people have forgotten this break with the Catholic health care system and still believe it to be one.

A. Thank you for this information. I do wonder, however, why the name remains attached to the hospital, since that is probably responsible for most of the confusion. Was it sold with that name, and is the name a permanent fixture?

The consecration of Russia

Q. Russia has not yet been consecrated to the Immaculate Heart of Mary, as requested by Our Lady of Fátima. Why are the Pope and bishops so reluctant to carry out this grave responsibility?

A. I believe that the Holy Father has indeed consecrated the whole world to Our Lady's Immaculate Heart; if that has happened, then presumably Russia has been brought under Mary's mantle. By the way, I cannot help but think that so much of what happened in the former Eastern Bloc is precisely the fruit of all those Rosaries and First Saturday devotions. Changes as startling as these cannot be the work of man; for that to occur at all, let alone with such astounding rapidity and force, can only be the work of Almighty God. Continued prayer and penance are obviously needed to bring these tentative beginnings to a happy conclusion.

Canon Law and the Roman Missal

Q. I have purchased "The Code of Canon Law: A Text and Commentary," commissioned by the Canon Law Society of America and published by Paulist Press. I have some real doubts about positions it takes; is it reliable? Second, you often quote from the General Instruction of the Roman Missal; where might that be obtained?

A. No commentary on the Code of Canon Law is authoritative, except for interpretations offered by the commission established in Rome to do just that. All other works carry only the authority of the individual authors. Like you, I am quite uncomfortable with many aspects of the work you cite because, in certain instances, it appears that some of the commentators are playing sleight-of-hand games with canonical texts to advance an agenda at odds with the rather clear and obvious intent of the law as it is written. I can appreciate the fact that there are (and always will be) disputed points of law, which is why we have lawyers to begin with. But to treat a rather recent and relatively clear document as an arcane manuscript from the prehistoric era in need of major exegesis is, in my opinion, problematic. I do recommend, however, the text and commentary on the Code published by Scepter Press.

The General Instruction of the Roman Missal is, first of all, found in the front of the missal used by the priest at the altar, but the text is also published in Volume I of the Flannery edition of the Conciliar and Postconciliar Documents (Costello Publishing Co., 49 Central Ave., Cincinnati, Ohio 45202.).

The revised Code of Canon Law

Q. Where can I obtain a copy of the revised Code of Canon Law. I think I live in a diocese where it's unknown.

A. Different editions exist, but the one I use has both the Latin and English texts on facing pages. It is published by the Canon Law Society of America, Catholic University, Washington, D.C. 20064.

Homiletic hyperbole?

Q. I have been reading a book containing sermons of St. Alphonsus Liguori dealing with "the number of sins beyond which God pardons no more." It contains some chilling examples that I find hard to understand. Can you please offer some clarification?

A. Not having the whole passage before me, I am unable to make an intelligent judgment about the text you cite. My only guess would be that the saint was engaging in homiletic hyperbole, to raise his congregation or readers to a sincere change of heart. If it says literally what you indicate, it is definitely not reflective of the Gospel and Church teaching, which teach of the infinite patience and mercy of God, willing to forgive as often as we fall and repent.

More work is needed

Q. Some nuns in our diocese have just published a "pastoral visiting manual" to help deal with the problem of proselytizing. Have you seen it? Would you recommend it?

A. Yes, I have seen it and was quite enthusiastic when I first saw it noted in the Catholic press.

The manual offers some good ideas on how to visit fellow Catholics, giving good tips on listening techniques and on proceeding in an interview in a non-threatening manner. Some practical suggestions are made on how to organize a total parish visitation program. All of this is fine, as far as it goes. And that's the problem — the program doesn't go far enough. We need to put into the hand of the average lay Catholic good tools for confronting the onslaught being made by Fundamentalists on the Catholic community, especially among Hispanics. Unfortunately, this manual does not deal with questions of doctrine and ways in which one might rebut Fundamentalist teaching or respond to their attacks. Perhaps someone else can pick up the project where these two authors left off.

Greek letters

Q. I recently purchased a door knocker that used early Christian symbols, including the fish and the letters IXOYC. Are these Greek letters? What do they stand for?

A. Yes, they are Greek, standing for *Iesous Christos Ouios Theou Soter* ("Jesus Christ, God's Son, the Savior"). It is an acronym that spells out the work *ichthus* ("fish," in Greek) and was used as a kind of password among the early Christians to gain access to their gatherings during times of persecution.

Papal document on JFK's character?

Q. For several months, I've been doing research into the character assassination of President John F. Kennedy. The enclosed document is a written statement by Pope Paul VI (the original is in Latin). I would appreciate your opinion on this document, which I obtained from the John F. Kennedy Library.

A. The document you enclosed sounds like a great deal of "overkill," profuse even for papal documents! Inasmuch as there is no seal on it and no indication of who "translated" it or where the original Latin text is, I would question its authenticity. Even if it were true, what does it prove? That Pope Paul thought John Kennedy was a good man?

Without getting into "character assassination," to use your term, the record at the time made it abundantly clear (even to the present writer, who was only ten years old when JFK was elected) that we were not going to have any Catholic crusade going on from or in the White House. In some sense, the prurient interest in the more private elements of the former president's life has taken away from the more substantive and objective questions that can be raised, not just about him but about any individual who would wish to be considered a committed Catholic and run for public office.

Capitalizing pronouns referring to God

Q. Why do so many of our readings and songs use the pronoun "he" instead of "He" when referring to God, as was formerly done?

A. Capitalization is a sociocultural phenomenon. In German, for instance, all nouns are capitalized; in most Romance languages, what we refer to as "proper nouns" in English (names of nationalities, religions, etc.) are not capitalized. In our culture, of late, there has been a tendency to downplay capitalization in general. I think it unfortunate that many liturgical books have thrown in the towel on this one so quickly, rather than leading an effort to restore some sense of the sacred in our language. It seems that some Catholics prefer to capitulate to the culture-at-large, instead of challenging it and offering it a different perspective.

The meaning of 'for private use'

Q. What does the inscription "for private use" mean on certain Catholic pamphlets?

A. That inscription most often appears on devotional literature. In other words, the devotion has not been approved by the Church for public worship (e.g., because the individual being invoked is not beatified or canonized). This type of material is intended, as might be assumed, only for individuals or groups of individuals gathered for informal, unofficial prayer.

Why all the changes?

Q. I've been away from the Church for nearly twenty years and have been shocked to discover upon my return that the altar has been replaced by a table, that the altar rail is gone, and most amazingly of all, that some people actually take the Host into their own hands. How come this has all happened? I feel like Rip Van Winkle.

A. First, welcome home — even if the furniture has been rearranged in your absence!

I don't want to come off as flippant, however, because what you describe can truly be a traumatic experience. Some explanation or clarification would seem to be in order.

The Mass is still offered on an altar, although it may have a more table-like appearance than the old altars attached to the back wall. Interestingly, though, it needs to be noted that the name traditionally given to the top of the altar in the preconciliar period was "mensa," which means "table" in Latin. Perhaps the best way to explain this is to say that when the action is an offering or sacrifice, it is best to speak of an "altar," while when the gifts are being received, we are more concerned with "the table of the Lord." The same object does "double duty," as it were.

The altar rail generally went out of use when the option to stand for Communion came in. Many churches, however, have retained the rail since it fits in architecturally with the overall design. Similarly, many churches give people the option to receive the Eucharist either standing or kneeling. Both positions have venerable traditions behind them. In the Church of the East, standing has represented one's identification with the risen Christ; in the West, kneeling is a sign of humility and adoration.

Communion-in-the-hand came into use in the United States in 1977. Having already discussed that in great detail on another occasion, I would simply refer you to that (see Vol. I). Now, in truth Vatican II never said a word about altars facing the people or the removal of altar rails, let alone Communion-in-the-hand. If you have tried to understand these things and still have problems in accepting them, find a parish which will provide you with the peace of mind you need and deserve.

The "Rip Van Winkle" syndrome you describe needs to be taken seriously by everyone, because the last thing we want is for someone to return to the Church after much time only to find himself more alienated than before he first left. Genuine sensitivity is required to ensure the reintegration of the lapsed, but also care in effecting changes, so that one does not come back to find what appears to be a whole new Church within the span of two decades.

Is 'centering prayer' a fad?

Q. I am confused about "centering prayer." I read about it in "The Life of Prayer and the Way to God," advertised in The Catholic Answer. I have also heard cautions about the use of it from solid Catholics who consider it part of the New Age doctrine. Are all these people talking about the same thing?

A. No progress in one's life in Christ is possible without good spiritual direction, given by a solid believer (who need not be a priest). Therefore, simply reading spiritual books or "trying out" various spiritualities (while noble) will probably not accomplish all that much. I say this by way of preface. Any technique of prayer can be misused (even the Rosary) if it is not used according to good spiritual principles and the mind of the Church.

I find it hard to imagine how centering prayer, at least as I understand it, can be related to New Age religion. Sometimes people latch onto certain phrases and beat them to death, so that every problem in the Church and the world is laid at the doorstep of that whipping boy. You may remember how, some years back, Fundamentalists constantly blamed all contemporary disasters on secular humanism: I don't deny that secular humanism is at the root of much American decadence, but it's surely not the only cause. And the same goes for the New Age movement.

When we tend to attribute all evils to one source in a knee-jerk and uncritical manner, we destroy our own credibility.

'Community': Is it an overused word?

Q. Is the concept of "community" emphasized, mandated, or recommended by Vatican II? It seems to me that community is stressed as a major factor in every Protestant denomination, and now in our parish we are being constantly inundated with the term.

A. "Community" is the English equivalent of the Greek *koinonia*, used frequently in the New Testament to describe the body of faithful who were, as the Acts of the Apostles tells us, of "one heart and one mind." Simply because Protestantism has something does not automatically mean that it's wrong. Remember, Protestants believe in the Trinity. Does that mean we shouldn't?

My experience suggests that today many Catholics are tired of the word because they are being beaten over the head with it, and it is being used to justify dubious practices and concepts at times. In my boyhood parish (back in the '50s), we had "community" to the nth degree; we never did anything apart from the parish: spiritual, academic, athletic, social. But we didn't call it "community," and we didn't even know we were doing anything special: it was the only way we knew how to be Catholic. In other words, it was a nonreflective (in the best sense of the word) response to our Catholic Faith.

In recent years, I have found an incredible lack of community in the Church, usually in the very places where it is most discussed. As one theologian put it, "You always talk about what you don't have!"

For all those well-intentioned priests and parochial workers, I would like to propose that we have a ten-year moratorium on the use of the word "community" — even as we attempt to live it!

Donations for private devotions

Q. In our parish, there is a sign at each side of the Blessed Mother shrine that reads, "Minimum Donation: 25 cents per candle." My husband doesn't like the signs and thinks they are wrong. What if a poor person wishes to light a candle and pray? What is your thought on this?
A. First off, I would say you're getting off a lot cheaper there than in my parish, where we ask for an offering of three dollars!

Seriously, though, if the signs are not "tacky," they simply let people know what kind of offering they should be giving. After all, candles are very expensive these days, and inasmuch as no one has to light a candle, I don't think it fair to expect the parish-at-large to carry the responsibility for someone's private devotions.

Certainly we do not want to give the impression that the Church is trafficking in sacred things or that only the well-off can indulge their devotional hearts. However, financial realism is also important, and people need to be sensitive to that aspect of church life as well.

Support for one's local church

Q. I do not want to support our church because our parish priest does not abide by the laws of the Roman Catholic Church. Am I wrong? I do donate to other Catholic programs and charities.
A. I would be cautious about making a blanket statement like your

opening sentence. If it is accurate as it stands, your bishop ought to be involved in remedying the situation. If it is correct and the bishop has failed to deal with the problem, then I think your course of action is legitimate. Many sociologists of religion have noticed that Catholics tend to "vote" a parish or pastor up or down with their feet and with their pocketbooks. What I mean is that if they don't like what's going on in a particular parish, they either go to another church or else continue attendance but cut back on the contributions.

While there is something valid here, there is also a great danger, namely, that good priests preaching the full Gospel of Christ and faithful to the teachings of the Church could get caught in the crossfire as some people become resentful of the truth. For example, if Catholic priests had been susceptible to parishioner opinion back in the 1940s and 1950s, Catholic churches and schools would never have begun the integration process, and the proof of that is simply that most Protestant churches dealt with the evil of institutional racism by waiting for a Supreme Court decision. It would be very tragic if priests today stopped preaching about the immorality of abortion or artificial contraception, for instance, out of fear of losing members of their flock or their financial support. But as you tell it, it seems you are within your rights to do what you are doing.

Knights of Malta: Who are they?

Q. Who are the Knights of Malta? What is their historical connection with the Church? What are the requirements for membership and how might one contact them?

A. The Knights of Malta began as a religious order of chivalry during the First Crusade, particularly by opening a hospice/infirmary for pilgrims in the Holy Land. Interestingly enough, members of this order eventually became the rulers of the island of Malta, until the time of Napoleon.

The order is predominantly charitable today and has a national association in the United States. For further information, see *Our Sunday Visitor's Catholic Encyclopedia*. The Knights may be contacted by writing to 1011 First Ave., New York, NY 10022.

Chick Publications

Q. Why does the Church tolerate organizations like Jack Chick Publications, which is clearly anti-Catholic, publishing all kinds of falsehoods about Catholicism ? Why doesn't the Church sue such organizations for libel?

A. I don't know exactly what the Church could do, since libel laws don't cover such situations. In Canada, I believe that Chick Publications were banned through use of their law against pornography; apparently the definition is flexible enough to include scurrilous material like Chick's. That seems rather appropriate since hate literature like his is really obscene.

The best response we can give to him and his kind, however, is being prepared with intelligent answers to the bizarre claims he makes; most people of goodwill and even those of average intelligence will be able to see the whole thing for what it is. Fundamentalist friends of mine, normally not too well-disposed toward things Catholic, have told me that even they have a hard time swallowing Chick's pamphlets that rail against the Church.

'What Catholics Believe'

Q. *The local cable station carries a program entitled. "What Catholics Believe," on the PTL channel. Much of what is presented is good, but there is also much criticism of Vatican II, certain members of the hierarchy, and even Pope John Paul II. Is this a legitimate Catholic program?*

A. It's a dreadful airing of dirty linen in public, as well as a barrage of half-truths and outright lies. The priests responsible are all involved in schismatic or semi-schismatic groups. Avoid it, is my suggestion, and write to your station asking to have it removed.

Media and bias against the Church

Q. *What can we do to get accurate information on the Church from the media? It seems that everything gets so distorted.*

A. I don't think the distortions about the Church are accidental, for the most part. Yes, at times we find sloppy reporting by incompetent journalists, but usually we are dealing in the secular press with people whose agenda is very different from that of the Church. This is not paranoia talking — it is documented in numerous attitudinal surveys (e.g., the 1986 study done by Rothman and Lichter) participated in by the media elite. For five years, I worked with the Catholic League for Religious and Civil Rights on just such issues. It seems to me that a two-pronged approach is needed: a) educate Catholics to the problem; b) train Catholics in ways to vindicate their rights in the public forum. This methodology has been used effectively by every group in this country; indeed, it is the very means by which democracies function.

A very fine organization exists to monitor the media; it is not tied to exclusively Catholic (or even generic religious) concerns, but attempts to bring before its members' eyes the way media biases affect supposedly objective reporting. The organization is Accuracy in Media, and for $20 a year, members are informed of gross examples of what we have been discussing. You can obtain further information by writing to: AIM, 1275 K Street, NW, Suite 1150, Washington, D.C. 20005.

Negative attitudes toward Opus Dei

Q. Your recent piece on the founder of Opus Dei causes me to write. My husband and I are loosely affiliated with it as "cooperators," and we are also surprised by the attitude of so many diocesan priests toward Opus Dei. After all, Opus Dei is loyal to the Holy Father. Why would this threaten so many priests?

A. It's an indication of the sad state of affairs in some places that loyalty to the Holy Father is automatically interpreted as belonging to some type of "secret society." Very often I am "accused" of being a member of Opus Dei, only because I try to represent orthodox Catholic teaching. The truth of the matter is that Opus Dei is not a secret society, nor am I a member of it. Sometimes misinformation has a way of creeping into the collective consciousness of a group, and that seems to have happened with Opus Dei and certain kinds of Catholics. A knee-jerk reaction causes such people to imagine that an Opus Dei takeover of the Church is just around the corner; it is the same brand of silliness exhibited by certain extreme Fundamentalists who talk (or talked) about Jesuit plots to destroy various governments and Protestant communities. One of the reasons I ran the article on Monsignor Escrivá de Balaguer was precisely to dispel false notions about the man and the work he began.

The politics of negative publicity

Q. What's going on with the beatification of Msgr. Escrivá of Opus Dei? I've read all kinds of stories in The New York Times and Newsweek. Has his cause been "railroaded" through by Opus Dei?

A. Like you, I have been fascinated by the amount of negative publicity being given in the secular media to the beatification of Msgr. José María Escrivá de Balaguer. Why should people who generally don't even acknowledge an afterlife be interested in this matter? The only conclusion I can draw is their desire to halt the process for political purposes. Hence, the unsubstantiated and unsubstantiatable charges of undue haste, anti-Semitism, and so on. All these allegations have been carefully handled and responded to by Vatican officials, and even by the President of Italy himself.

So, what's the real issue? Many people outside the Church, and not a few still within, are upset that the founder of Opus Dei, known for its adherence to doctrinal orthodoxy and fidelity to ecclesiastical discipline, is on his way to canonization. They realize that this will enhance the prestige of Opus Dei as its seeks to play a significant role in the postconciliar renewal of the Church.

Catholic bookstores

Q. There are several Protestant-run "family bookstores." Why, haven't we Catholics picked up on the idea? I feel uncomfortable about buying anything at these stores when I know that some of the money I spend will be going to promote anti-Catholic material.

A. I tend to agree with you. When I was a boy, at least ten whole blocks of New York City were filled with Catholic stores for books, vestments, vessels, religious articles, and the like. Almost all of them are now closed, for a variety of reasons. Catholic publishers were especially hard-hit in the years just after the Second Vatican Council because books like missals were rendered obsolete so quickly (due to a constant flood of changes) that people stopped buying things and publishers stopped printing. The Daughters of St. Paul have been singularly effective and successful in running excellent Catholic bookstores. They should be patronized whenever possible and encouraged to open stores in new areas.

Blessed salt at abortion clinics?

Q. Please explain the blessed salt that some pro-lifers spread near abortion clinics.

A. I have never heard of this, but I would be open to receiving information on the practice.

Information on blessed salt

Q. In [a recent] edition of TCA, you wrote that you would be open to receiving information on blessed salt. A pamphlet explaining the history behind this sacramental was written by Father John Hampsch, C.M.F., and is available from Claretian Tape Ministry, P.O. Box 19100, Los Angeles, California 90019.

A. Thank you.

'Pray,' not 'say'

Q. Please allow me to make a comment. Will we ever cease using the word "say" in reference to the Rosary? While we understand the thought meant, let us begin to say "pray" for our prayers, rather than simply "say" the words.

A. A point well made; thank you.

The fifteen mysteries of the Rosary

Q. If I say all fifteen decades of the Rosary on a given day (say, Tuesday), should I make all fifteen decades the sorrowful mysteries, or should they be divided among the joyful, sorrowful and glorious? I have gotten conflicting advice on this.

A. There is no absolute answer on private devotions, but it seems to me that it would make sense to meditate on all fifteen mysteries. After all, the very reason that the Church distributes the fifteen mysteries over the course of a week is just so that all of them would be covered by people who pray only five decades a day.

Information on the Rosary

Q. A charismatic Christian friend of mine is interested in some reading material on the Rosary, not to attack it but to learn about it. Any suggestions?

A. Any number of fine publications exist on the Rosary. Several papal encyclicals have been written on it. Pamphlets are available from the Blue Army Shrine in Washington, N. J., as are many from the Daughters of St. Paul. Since your friend is not a Catholic, he may be particularly interested in a Methodist minister's meditations on the mysteries of the Rosary: J. Neville Ward's *Five for Sorrow, Ten for Joy*, published by Doubleday.

Two Fátima magazines

Q. Are there two Fátima magazines — Soul and Fátima Crusader? I am confused. The second one seems to attack the Pope all the time, and we have heard that there is no record of the ordination of the priest who runs it.

A. *Soul* is the official organ of the official Fátima movement sanctioned by the Church.

The other magazine is edited by a Father Gruner; his ordination is not in doubt, but he has no priestly faculties, either from Italy (where he was ordained) or from the dioceses in the United States and Canada where he functions. The material in the magazine is often extremely negative toward the Pope and also highly inaccurate and defamatory in many instances.

Bayside messages are fraudulent

Q. Enclosed is a booklet which explains and sums up all the apparitions and messages to Veronica Leuken of Flushing Meadows, N. Y., popularly called Bayside. It's all very negative toward the Church, especially the hierarchy. However, she does make many points with which I find myself in agreement, particularly in regard to abuses involving the Blessed Sacrament. Please comment.

A. We can find ourselves in agreement on certain points with all kinds of people with whom we might otherwise disagree, and this can be the case here. Yes, terrible irreverence for the Blessed Sacrament is in evidence in many places, and that needs to be addressed by careful catechesis and solid preaching about the Real Presence. However, I would never want to use Mrs. Leuken as a source of authority for any topic; after all, she has introduced more confusion into many people's lives than enemies of the Church could ever do. Of course, the truth of the matter is that she is, in reality, outside the Church as a result of her persistence in asserting the validity of the visions which the Church has officially declared to be fraudulent.

Taking the 'higher road'

Q. It has come to my attention that Marywood College in Scranton is allowing students of the Bible Baptist College to borrow books from its library by showing their college or seminary ID card.

*I know that the Baptist college teaches that we preach a false
gospel. Do you feel this is an appropriate form of cooperation between
two opposing theologies?*

A. Under normal circumstances, I would see this as a completely
acceptable form of academic and ecumenical cooperation. What
surprises me, frankly, is not that Marywood is open to the Baptist
college but that, in spite of their negativity toward Catholicism, they
would want to use a Catholic college library. Aren't they afraid of being
tainted by the "Antichrist"?

There's an obvious inconsistency here, but I think Marywood has
taken the higher road. Perhaps the Baptist students, through regular
contact with Catholics, will come to see that we're not as bad as their
professors claim.

By the way, is the library use reciprocal?

Differing views of Church history

*Q. I have read some books written by Protestant authors who claim the
Roman Catholic Church became the most powerful of the early
Christian churches simply due to the fact that it was at the seat of power
of the Roman Empire, and that many emperors and high-government
officials joined that Church after it was legalized in A.D. 313. It then
engulfed all the other churches and forced its false doctrines on them
until God restored Christianity to its original form at the time of the
Protestant Reformation.*

*This seems to be a common view of Christian history among
Protestants. Is there any evidence of this in the Bible or other ancient
writings?*

A. What you have outlined is the standard view of history propagated by
Fundamentalists, who seek to justify their own existence by reference to
an alleged golden age of Christianity, followed by an apostasy which
became the Catholic Church. No serious secular historian, however,
subscribes to that. As a matter of fact, the anti-Catholic historian Edward
Gibbon, in his monumental work *The Decline and Fall of the Roman
Empire*, goes so far as to declare that it was the existence of the Catholic
Church which destroyed the Roman Empire.

Obviously, you can't have it both ways. But more balanced,
standard works of history likewise maintain that there never was a
Western Christian Church apart from the Catholic Church until the time

of the Protestant Reformation; in that regard, it is worth consulting Crane Brinton's *History of Civilization*. Beyond that, objective non-Catholic ecclesiastical historians also admit Catholicism as the mother church of Christianity (for example, Henry Chadwick in *The Early Church* or J.G. Davies in *The Early Christian Church*).

Did the Church form alliances with civil rulers? Certainly. Did she make mistakes in doing so? Perhaps, on occasion. However, involvement with the world is not a luxury for a Church which exists in the world. The challenge for the Church in general and for individual Christians is always the same: to be in the world but not of it.

Nostradamus and St. Malachy

Q. Please clarify the spiritual status of the writings of Nostradamus and those attributed to St. Malachy.

A. As far as I know, they have no official status in the Church, either pro or con. It seems to me that the predictions of both are general enough, like the daily horoscope, that the reader ends up providing more than either Nostradamus or St. Malachy ever did, to begin with; surely that is the case with Malachy's descriptions of various popes.

What is a 'Black Mass'?

Q. What is meant by a "Black Mass"? Does it follow the format of a regular Mass? What arenas are to be avoided to protect oneself from exposure to it? I understand it is becoming rather widespread.

A. A "Black Mass" is a "Satanic Mass" — in other words, devil worship. Many of the symbols, vessels, and vestments of the Mass are used; the rite of the Mass is followed in various contorted ways. An essential element for such a diabolical event is a consecrated Host, which has obviously been taken from a true Mass and is then desecrated. It does seem to be spreading, and the most important things to do are to stay away from any gathering which you suspect of being involved with Satanic worship and to remember that the devil is never more real than when he is denied or ignored, and hence the necessity of praying daily to be delivered from his wiles and snares.

Double duty for the baptismal font

Q. In our remodeled church, the baptismal font is used as a holy water font as well. Some of us are concerned about the sanitary aspects of this, especially for infants, if people are dipping their hands into water which will later be used for baptisms. Is our concern justified? Does the Church permit "double duty" like this?

A. The idea of using the baptismal font as a holy water font is theologically appealing because we should always see the connection between Baptism and blessing ourselves with holy water (as a renewal of our baptismal commitment). I have never seen a font, however, where the same water does "double duty," to use your expression, and I imagine some sanitary problems could exist. Talk to your pastor about the possibility of isolating the water to be used in Baptism. As a matter of fact, in most newer constructions, the water at the font is flowing, rather than stagnant.

What age for First Communion?

Q. What is the current teaching of the Roman Catholic Church on the reception of First Holy Communion? Can the parish priest or bishop change the age at which children customarily receive their First Communion?

A. The 1983 Code of Canon Law notes that children's reception of First Holy Communion should take place when they "have sufficient knowledge and careful preparation so as to understand the mystery of Christ according to their capacity, and can receive the Body of the Lord with faith and devotion" (Can. 913). Canon 914 goes on to speak of this time as the age of reason (usually given as seven years old), noting also that First Eucharist is to be "preceded by sacramental confession." That same canon observes that it is the responsibility of the pastor to determine if children are indeed suitably prepared and knowledgeable to receive the Eucharist.

The norm, then, is the age of reason (which would be a diocesan guideline), with the possibility of deviating from it based on the judgment of parents, teachers, parish priest, and so on.

A mandatory time for confessions?

Q. Our parish is in a rural setting, and our priest just comes on Sundays. We used to have confessions before Mass, but this priest likes to play the organ and sing hymns before Mass, so he has transferred confessions to the time after Mass. Does he have the right to do this?

A. Yes, he does. There is no mandatory time for confessions; however, I would see great value in hearing confessions before Mass (especially in a parish where the priest is only present once a week), so that those who felt the need to confess could then receive Holy Communion at that very Mass.

Selection of a Confirmation name

Q. I am a recent convert, coming into the Church through the local RCIA program. I was looking forward to selecting a Confirmation name, but my pastor told me that since Vatican II that is no longer done. I later learned that a friend's child had taken a Confirmation name. Which is it?
A. The adoption of a special name at Confirmation is possible, and is the choice of the candidate. Sometimes the continuity between Baptism and Confirmation is stressed, so that a new name is discouraged. However, a good case can be made for assuming a second patron when the celebration of the two sacraments is separated by several years. It would also make sense for someone who is coming into full communion with the Catholic Church, as a special way of marking this important transition and to seek the heavenly patronage of a particular saint, perhaps one he or she wishes to emulate especially.

How to convert to Catholicism

Q. I am an Episcopalian and have always felt close to the Catholic Church. What would I have to do to convert to Catholicism? What are the requirements, and how long would it take? Would my Baptism and Confirmation in the Episcopal Church be taken into consideration?
A. Assuming that you are well-educated in your faith, the process would be quite simple. You should go to your Catholic parish priest and inform him of your desire to enter into full communion with the Catholic Church. He will then determine what gaps might exist in your religious education and decide on a course of action (e.g., readings and discussions with him on papal primacy, Marian devotion, eucharistic theology). Of course, if you come from a "High Church" background, you may already know and believe everything required of a Catholic.

Once the catechetical questions are dealt with, you would need to be received into the Church. Your Baptism as an Anglican is certainly valid and could never be repeated. You would be required to go to confession, make a profession of faith and be confirmed by the priest receiving you into the Church. On that same occasion, you would make your First Holy Communion as a Catholic.

Some pastors might invite you to participate in the RCIA program, but that is strictly optional for someone in your position and totally your own decision.

Never too old to convert

Q. I grew up in a "federated" church and was stopped by my father from becoming a Catholic. Presently, I attend Mass and say the Rosary. Can I still become a Catholic even though I'm in my forties? Please tell me what I am allowed to do and not to do while attending Mass without being a baptized Catholic.

A. Anyone can become a Catholic at any time. Emperor Constantine did so on his deathbed, and the famous British journalist and biographer of Mother Teresa, Malcolm Muggeridge, came into the Church on his eightieth birthday. Just go to see your local priest, tell him of your interest and that you wish to begin instructions for reception into the Catholic Church.

I don't know exactly what you mean by belonging to a "federated" church, and so I can't say whether or not you were validly baptized. But if you bring a copy of your baptismal certificate to the rectory, the priest should be able to make a determination of that rather easily.

In the meantime, continue going to Mass and saying the Rosary, read and study about the Catholic Faith. Of course, until your reception into the Church (which may involve the full sequence of Baptism, Confirmation and Eucharist — or just a profession of faith with Penance, Confirmation, and Eucharist), you cannot receive the sacraments or perform any liturgical function. But all other avenues of grace are open to you, and you should use them well and wisely. May I suggest you read or reread the parable of the workers in the vineyard, who come to labor at different times and all end up with the same pay (cf. Mt 20:1-16).

In advance, let me welcome you to the fullness of truth and life, found in the one true Church of Jesus Christ. May the Holy Spirit guide your journey.

A dress code for Church weddings?

Q. Are women who have had a child outside of wedlock required to wear something other than a white dress for a Church wedding?

A. The Church has no requirements about attire for a wedding. I should note that wearing or not wearing white is a social custom having nothing to do with childbirth but with virginity. In other words, wearing white (and especially a veil) is the customary sign that the bride is a virgin — a remnant of an age that valued virginity more than contemporary society.

A Catholic funeral for a Protestant?

Q. My husband is a Presbyterian who goes to the local Catholic parish with me. We asked our priest if he can become a member of our parish, even though he has no interest in converting. Is this possible? Frankly, the main concern is that if anything should happen to him, I would want him buried from my church, rather than the Presbyterian church.

A. It might be a good idea for your husband to take a course in the basics of the Catholic Faith, so that he can see the important differences between his own denominational tenets and those of the Catholic Church. If he is not persuaded of the truth of the Catholic Faith, it would make little sense to become a member of a church with which he disagrees on fundamental dogmas, even if such membership were open to non-Catholics.

That having been said, if his (or your) only concern is his burial with Catholic rites and in consecrated ground, that is already possible. While I could understand a man wanting to be buried with his wife, I would find it difficult to see why a non-Catholic (who consciously remained outside the Catholic Church) would want to have a Catholic Funeral Mass.

Parish registration and burial

Q. My brother-in-law was married outside the Church, gave up practicing his Faith, and never registered in a new parish when he moved. In the hospital before his death, a priest heard his confession, anointed him and gave him Holy Communion. When he died, the pastor said he would not bury him because he wasn't registered in the parish. The old parish wouldn't take him, either, because he had moved. Is this Church law?

A. Aside from notorious public sinners, I cannot imagine a priest doing this today, especially for a reason like non-registration. The bad will engendered among distraught family members lingers in people's minds and hearts for years to come. Centuries ago St. Augustine reminded us that a Funeral Mass is as much for the family as it is for the deceased, and a guiding principle of ecclesiastical law is encapsulated in the maxim, "*Salus animarum lex suprema*," that is, "The salvation of souls is the highest law." Certainly people should register in parishes for any number of reasons, but if that wasn't done, I don't think a man's funeral is the time to teach that lesson.

How new bishops are appointed

Q. Nearly a year ago now, our bishop was transferred to another diocese, and we have been without a bishop. The following questions arise:

Who transfers a bishop? Why is a bishop transferred? Why does it take so very long to get a new bishop? Who selects the new or transferred-in bishop? Who promotes the new bishop if one is promoted? What exactly is an archbishop?

A. Ultimately, it is the Holy Father himself who appoints a bishop; however, there is an intricate process designed to obtain the best information possible on a particular diocese and a particular candidate.

When a see (the technical name for a diocese) becomes vacant due to the resignation, death, or retirement of a bishop, the process begins under the direction of the nuncio, the Pope's representative in a given country. A profile of the diocese is drawn up through consultation with various bodies of the faithful (including clergy, religious, and laity) and selected individuals as well. The purpose is to determine what the assets and liabilities of the see are and then to come up with a profile for the type of leader who could be effective in responding to the local needs. Since great care is given throughout, it usually takes at least one year to come up with specific recommendations. The nuncio then puts together a list of his top three candidates (called a "terna") and submits it to the Congregation for Bishops in Rome, which, in turn, offers its recommendation to the Holy Father, who makes the final choice.

A bishop must be a priest a minimum of ten years and must be at least thirty-five years of age. He should have an earned doctorate in one of the sacred sciences and should be known as a priest who is devout, thoroughly orthodox, and loyal to the Holy See, and a strong promoter of the Catholic Faith in the areas of responsibility already given to him.

An archbishop is a bishop who presides over an ecclesiastical province, which is a number of dioceses joined by geographical nearness and a common culture. In the heavily Catholic northeastern part of the United States, most ecclesiastical provinces are coterminous with the various states (e.g., the five dioceses of New Jersey form the Province of Newark, under the Archbishop of Newark; all the dioceses of New York State form the Province of New York, under the Archbishop of New York). While the suffragan bishops (that is, the ordinaries of the other dioceses) are answerable only to the Pope or his representative, the archbishop or metropolitan sets a tone for a province and is most influential in the selection process for a new bishop when a see becomes vacant.

The bishop as a bridegroom

Q. At a recent Mass for schoolchildren, the bishop asked if they knew he was their bridegroom. Aside from Christ, I had never heard that title given to anyone else. Any explanation?

A. The Second Vatican Council, picking up on a theme hit upon by the Fathers of the Church very frequently, referred to the bishop as fulfilling the role of Christ for a local church (diocese). The bishop traditionally wears a ring because it symbolizes his marriage to that local church, and so, yes, he relates to the diocese as his bride. I am sure that is what your bishop had in mind.

'Pastor' and the English language

Q. In reading the documents of Vatican II and other ecclesiastical texts, I often find references to the pastors of the Church. I know what a pastor is, but these references sound as though they apply more to bishops.

A. You are correct in your evaluation. The problem is related to our English usage. In ecclesiastical documents (in Latin), the word *pastor* (shepherd) means "bishop," while the word *parochus* refers to the parish priest, whom we call "pastor" in English. You may have noticed since the promulgation of the revised Code of Canon Law that priests formerly called assistants or associate pastors are now spoken of as "parochial vicars," that is, those who take the place of or assist the "parochus."

The other problematic expression in English is "local church." In technical parlance, "local church" is a diocese, not a parish, as some might think.

Why kiss the bishop's ring?

Q. Why do Catholics kiss the ring of a priest or bishop?

A. Kissing the ring of a bishop (not a priest) is a sign of one's acceptance of the apostolic authority of the bishop and of one's willingness to obey him as one would Christ, whose place the bishop takes in the local church (diocese).

The priesthood and the religious life

Q. I know that once a man is ordained a priest, that is forever, even if he should leave the active ministry. Does the same hold for a woman who has taken perpetual vows?

A. Consecrated religious life is not a sacrament; therefore, the same standards do not always prevail for both priesthood and religious life. A woman in perpetual or final vows may be dispensed from those vows, either by her diocesan bishop or by the Holy See, depending on the particular congregation to which she belongs; the same holds true for male Religious. Dispensations from the active ministry for priests can only be handled by the Holy See (although they are processed through local chanceries), and are personally signed by the Holy Father himself — which tells you how seriously the Church takes such requests.

Religious and their assignments

Q. Is it permissible for a religious order to have only one Sister stationed at an assignment?

A. Technically, Religious (male and female alike) are to live in community. For serious reasons (e.g., parental illness requiring the presence of the child, unique needs of the Church which only this person can address), a Religious may be permitted to live apart from his or her community for a set period of time. However, a second aspect of the question is whether a Religious can, let us say, live with her community but maintain an assignment where she would be the only Religious. The answer to that depends on the particular community, since policies differ greatly. Canonically, there is no problem with this, but the constitution of a specific religious congregation might well stipulate that the only assignments considered are those with which a number of Religious from that community would be involved. I know many fine Religious, for example, who live with their own religious community but work as principals and teachers in nearby parochial schools, in which they are the sole Religious, providing a wonderful service to those institutions which would otherwise be deprived of their witness and talents.

Clergy and Religious need special attire

Q. Why might a priest or Religious choose to wear civilian clothes, instead of clerical attire or the habit?

A. The norm for all clergy and Religious is that they be identifiably attired at all times, unless common sense dictates otherwise (athletic activities, for example). The drive for secular dress bespeaks an unhealthy attitude toward one's vocation, which comes to be seen as something that can be put on and taken off at will.

Equally unhealthy is the assertion heard all too often of late that one cannot "relax" in clerical garb or habit. I cannot imagine why a priest or Religious would have to go incognito to dinner or a movie or play, unless something were wrong with the form of entertainment. Seeing the Church's full-time workers in the secular city is an important form of evangelization — one too little in evidence in the past twenty years.

The presumption of the questioner is that clergy and Religious are normally attired in a distinctive manner. It goes without saying that those who have abandoned clerical or religious garb on a permanent basis are in defiance of both the letter and the spirit of the Church's law. Please, readers, do not write in to ask me why bishops allow this to go on if the law forbids it — I have no answer to that!

Seminarians and clerical garb

Q. In our seminary, we have been told we cannot legitimately wear clerical garb until we have gone through the Rite of Admission to Candidacy; furthermore, we may never wear the collar off-campus. However, I know of at least five other seminaries where such a policy is not in effect. Would you care to comment?

A. The Rite of Candidacy has nothing to do with becoming a cleric or of wearing clerical garb. In reality, it seems to be a ceremony is search of a meaning. Let me explain.

When I was a seminarian, my class was the last to become clerics while still unordained. The ceremony was a revision of the old tonsure rite (in which the candidate's hair was clipped in the form of a cross), whereby a seminarian became a cleric and a member of a particular diocese.

The following year saw the introduction of the rite to which you refer; it is intended to be a formal and public declaration of the candidate's desire to go on for Holy Orders and is, to some degree, the diocese's acceptance of that decision.

Clerical status, however, is now delayed until diaconal ordination. Even under the old system, though, seminarians always wore clerical garb, whether or not they were clerics.

Several years ago, Pope John Paul II issued a policy for the Diocese of Rome, requiring seminarians to wear what he termed "ecclesiastical garb" (defined as a cassock, religious habit or Roman collar and suit), perhaps to deal with the question of whether or not non-clerics should wear "clerical" garb. Certainly, the new Rite of Candidacy should not be treated as if it in some way makes one a cleric.

As far as wearing the collar off-campus, just a few observations. The ban on this has uniquely American origins. Back in the '40s and '50s, American seminarians were given as an "off-campus uniform" the black suit and tie, which many fellows have come to refer to as "the mortician's outfit"; the intent was to enable seminarians to "blend into" the overall culture somewhat, even while setting them off at the same time. If it ever worked, it surely does not seem to do so today, so much so that most seminarians tell me they would prefer either clerical garb or lay clothes, but not the no-man's-land of a black suit and tie, which offers little immediate recognition and simply invites joking and long explanations. The Church in Europe, and especially in Rome, never had the fear of having seminarians identified with priests and certainly never had one dress code for school and another for other times and places.

Of course, in Rome particularly, seminarians always lived "off-campus" and left their residences ("colleges") to attend classes at the university, thus making very normal and natural their appearance all over the city of Rome in clerical attire. In the United States, seminaries were traditionally self-contained institutions, from which the students departed only infrequently; therefore, the concern about what to wear in other locations was not seen as requiring much attention. With seminarians often away from seminaries today (for pastoral work, days off, classes at universities, and even some less-than-worthwhile engagements), the question bears some interest and attention.

Colored clerical clothing

Q. Very often our priests wear blue or grey clerical shirts. Is this permitted by Rome?

A. Funny you should phrase the question as you did because, believe it or not, colored clerical clothes are permitted in Rome but not in the United States! Perhaps an explanation is in order. Back in the late '70s, some bishops had petitioned the National Conference of Catholic Bishops to consider colored clerical clothes, but the American bishops voted to maintain black, presumably so that our clergy would not be confused with Protestant clergy, who are wearing clerical collars more and more. In the early 1980s, when the Pope repeated his desire that clerical garb be worn by all priests and seminarians living in Rome, he also acknowledged the rather long-standing practice of colored clerical shirts in Europe. There is no problem with confusion in most of Europe for one of two reasons. The first is that Europeans tend to live in religiously homogeneous communities or even countries. Hence, if you saw a cleric on the street in Munich, he would most likely be a Catholic; in the north of Germany, a Protestant. The second is that Protestant clergy in Europe are not as likely to wear clerical garb as are their counterparts in the States, except for Anglicans and Lutherans.

I must admit that I wish we had the option for grey, at least during the summer, in the same way that many communities of Sisters have a summer habit. Some bishops have permitted their priests to adopt grey or blue, and they are within their rights to do so.

The Third Order of St. Francis

Q. My foster grandmother was a member of the Third Order of St. Francis. Does such a society still exist? How might I obtain information on it?

A. The simplest procedure is to contact the nearest house of Franciscan friars or Sisters; they would be able to refer you to a local Third Order group (now called Secular Franciscans) in your vicinity.

May Religious have bank accounts?

Q. I am acquainted with several men in the religious life who have larger personal bank accounts than most of the lay people I know. Why don't their superiors remind them of their vow of poverty?

A. To be perfectly honest, they shouldn't have personal bank accounts at all, if I understand the vow of poverty correctly. When people find that living a vow like poverty is not working in their lives, two options suggest themselves: First, go through a conversion experience and relearn the meaning of the vows and how to live them afresh. Second, if that is not happening, then be honest enough to be dispensed from one's vows and, for the ordained Religious, join the presbyterate of a local diocese, where a vow of poverty is not at stake.

At the same time, it would be good to mention that although secular or diocesan clergy do not profess a vow of poverty, all clergy and Religious are called upon to live lives of Gospel simplicity.

Faithful women religious

Q. I am a young woman, just graduated from college, and am most interested in religious life in an active community. The nuns who taught me in grammar school, high school, and college came from communities which either hate men or the Pope or are into all kinds of goddess worship, as well as the usual dissent from Church teaching. Needless to say, I want nothing to do with that kind of community. Do you know of any congregations which are faithful to the Holy Father, pray and live together, wear a habit, and engage in the teaching apostolate?
A. There are several faithful communities of women Religious. Let me note just a few from my own experience:

Franciscan Sisters of Christ the Divine Teacher
2605 Boies Avenue
Davenport, IA 52802

Apostles of the Sacred Heart
265 Benham Street
Hamden, CT 06514

Dominican Sisters of Divine Providence
137 Metlars Lane
Piscataway, NJ 08854

Sisters Servants of the Immaculate Heart of Mary
Villa Maria House of Studies
Immaculata, PA 19345

Dominican Sisters of Nashville
St. Cecilia's Convent
801 Dominican Drive
Nashville, TN 37208

Sisters of Charity of Our Lady, Mother of the Church
Holy Family Motherhouse
Baltic, CT 06330

Sisters of Christian Charity
Mallinckrodt Motherhouse
Mendham, NJ 07945

Sisters of the Resurrection
Mt. St. Joseph
Castleton-on-Hudson, NY 12033

I am sure I am going to get into trouble because there are many others, but this is a start at least. If you want a more complete listing, write to the Institute on Religious Life, 4200 N. Austin Avenue, Chicago, IL 60634 (phone: 312-545-1946). The Institute serves as a center for traditionally oriented religious congregations, both female and male.

Women as pastors and co-pastors

Q. I am in receipt of an invitation to "celebrate and congratulate" a nun of my acquaintance on becoming "co-pastor" of her parish church. If a woman cannot be a "pastor," how can she be a "co-pastor"?
A. You are quite correct.

At times we can become rather sloppy in our common parlance. An unordained person (male or female) cannot be appointed a pastor, and thus, logically, such a person cannot be a co-pastor. In all likelihood, the religious in question has been named to serve on a pastoral team and so might be appropriately referred to as a pastoral assistant, but certainly not a co-pastor. What we name people is important because it says what we expect of them; what people ask to be called is also crucial because it tells us what they expect to be in our regard.

Why no Pope Peter II?

Q. A non-Catholic friend has inquired as to why the popes do not take the name of "Peter" since he was the first pope. Is there any ecclesiastical rule prohibiting the choice of that name?

A. No, there isn't, but custom prevents it, a custom born out of reverence for the first pope, who carried that name. A legend (or better, superstition) maintains that the man who would take Peter II for a name would be the last pope, having ushered in the last days.

Is it OK to fly the papal flag?

Q. I am a woman Religious who lives in a convent near the U.S. Catholic Conference's new headquarters and teaches in an inner-city parochial school. I pass the building every day and I have often wondered why they fly the American flag but not the papal flag. I called up one day and someone told me that it's forbidden by American law. That sounds fishy to me.

A. First and most importantly, thanks for continuing your indispensable work in Catholic education.

I, too, have noticed the absence of a Vatican flag. After your letter, I checked out the protocol on this and was told that there is nothing to prevent the flying of any foreign flag, so long as the American flag is present and flies higher than any of the others.

Religious brothers

Q. Recently, I have come across a book that mentions several religious orders with "Brothers." What is a "Brother"? I asked our parish priest, and he did not know.

A. I find it hard to believe that your parish priest did not know what a Brother is!

A Brother is a male Religious (one who lives a consecrated life according to the three traditional vows of poverty, chastity and obedience). Like women Religious, or Sisters, Brothers live in community, have a local superior and generally have a community apostolate (for example, teaching, care of the sick, and so on). Brothers are not ordained and will never be priests (sometimes they become permanent deacons, but rather infrequently).

There are also male Religious who are priests, sometimes both groups belonging to the same community. For instance, the Jesuits,

Franciscans, and Dominicans all have both priests and Brothers. Other communities, like the Christian Brothers, are composed exclusively of Brothers.

Seminarians turn to tradition

Q. We had a seminarian in our parish this summer, and I thought we had taken our time machine back to the Middle Ages, or at least to my childhood. He wore a cassock, bowed his head at the name of Jesus, genuflected all over the sanctuary and before receiving Communion, which he always took on the tongue. What's happening? Are we returning to the '50s?

A. In one of the seminaries on the East Coast, they have a saying, "If you liked the '50s, you'll love the '90s!" I don't want to treat your question flippantly, but I think most observers realize that there is a real swing of the pendulum in the Church, especially among younger clergy and seminarians. Some of that is good and necessary; some of it is a reaction to the nonsense they have been fed for the past twenty years — a kind of reaction formation, which presupposes that since they got a lot of misinformation through the so-called renewal process of the Church in the United States, anything new is bad and anything old is good. This is an unfortunate correlation to make, but quite understandable under the circumstances.

That having been said, the things which upset you are all good and praiseworthy, for not one of the items which caused you concern was changed in any way by the Second Vatican Council. Everyone is supposed to bow his or her head at the name of Jesus; everyone is supposed to genuflect whenever passing the tabernacle; the cassock (or at least a clerical shirt) is the appropriate garb of any seminarian; receiving Communion on the tongue is the norm for the universal Church. Rather than being worried, I would rejoice if I were in your shoes; it sounds as though your parish was graced this past summer by a seminarian who has a keen sense of the sacred and a healthy self-identity. If everything else is in place in his life, he will be a great asset to the Church upon ordination.

For readers who would see all this in a more positive light than our inquirer, be encouraged and know that many more young men like the one in question here are being prepared to serve God's People as priests completely in tune with the Church's Tradition, yet conscious of the needs of the world in which they live at the very same time.

Major and minor seminarians

Q. I am a college seminarian, and many of us get tired of being told that we are "only" college seminarians, not major seminarians. And, to be perfectly honest, it's also rather confusing. What are we? Neither fish nor fowl. What is the Church's position on this?

A. The distinction, between major and minor seminarians does not exist in Church law. Prior to many of the changes in priestly formation, minor seminarians were candidates for the priesthood in high school and the first two years of college. After that, they began their formal study of philosophy (two years) and theology (four years). The breakdown was an attempt to fit a European educational model into the American system of schooling. Today, college seminarians begin their study of philosophy in their freshman year, with those courses spread throughout their college career. So the distinction between major and minor has no significance, either in terms of the law or reality. Finally, in the mind of the Church, the only distinctions among seminarians surface in regard to the various ministries they have received: lector, acolyte, deacon — and these offices have nothing as such to do with their standing in the Church in general, but rather with the particular functions they are permitted to perform in the celebration of the liturgy.

Although my college seminary years are more than twenty years behind me, I still empathize with these young men. It seems to me that priests — and especially those involved in formation work — need to be very sensitive to questions of identity, lest seminarians become disheartened over being "neither fish nor fowl." The Church officially acknowledges the unique identity of all seminarians and tries to give them the support needed for a rather long haul, with rights, privileges, and obligations essentially the same for them all.

May non-clerics teach seminarians?

Q. The seminary I attend has two Sisters teaching us. One teaches liturgy, and the other teaches preaching. Is this permitted?

A. Yes, it is permitted for non-clerics to teach in seminaries, provided they have the appropriate background for the courses they are teaching. The courses you mention could be taught by any qualified person from an academic point of view; I would have questions about practical aspects.

For example, can a Sister convincingly teach seminarians how to baptize or anoint, inasmuch as she has never done these things? Similarly with preaching; although a lay person or Religious might have much to offer in terms of public-speaking techniques, being incapable of preaching oneself hardly adds credibility to one's presentation.

Aside from considerations about the seminarians' education, I would also wonder about the advisability of placing people in positions which could set them up for frustration. It seems to me that it would take an extremely rare person to prepare young men to perform actions which one is unable to do oneself. While any qualified person may teach in a seminary, spiritual direction is limited to priests. Apparently, some American seminaries were not observing this norm and Rome was required to intervene, reminding all of the limitation.

Non-clerics as seminary teachers

Q. In [a recent] issue of TCA, it is stated that non-clerics may teach in seminaries. However, the Ratio Fundamentalis Institutionis Clericalis of 1970 states that as a general rule professors of all sacred subjects should be priests. Kindly explain your position.

Q. In discussing whether non-clerics can teach in seminaries, you noted that you find it strange for them to be assigned to teaching courses in preaching since they are "incapable" and "unable" to preach. I am a seventeen-year-old girl, and I would like to set you straight on some things, which you have obviously not learned to this date. I am quite capable of preaching and speaking about spirituality because of my involvement in forensics and my personal attempts to strengthen my bond with God. Do not term me or any other person "incapable of preaching," unless you have heard them (sic) speak. I know that I could give a far better sermon than many I hear on Sunday mornings, for I love to write and speak in order to share God's message to His people. The insinuation you have made is therefore rude and uncalled for. Had you used the words "not allowed to preach," you would have been correct. Though it may be only a few words, this really matters to me and to many others, I am sure.

A. Damned if you do, and damned if you don't!

To the first writer, I must say that while he is correct in regard to the document he cited, that norm is superseded by the 1983 Code of Canon

Law, in which we read: "Only those persons are to be appointed by the appropriate bishop or bishops to teach the philosophical, theological, and juridical disciplines in a seminary who, being outstanding in virtue, have obtained a doctorate or licentiate from a university or faculty recognized by the Holy See" (Canon 253.1). No mention is made of a professor having to be a priest, nor is the professor's sex stipulated. Hence, anyone who fulfills the requirements given above could teach in a seminary.

To the second writer, I have a number of comments. First of all, when a seventeen-year-old wants to "set straight" an elder, let alone a priest, that is "rude," to say the least.

What I said was not rude; it was a simple statement of fact, which I repeat: The non-ordained are *incapable* of preaching at Mass. That does not mean they are ignorant of spirituality or lacking in forensic skills. They are deficient in one crucial area, however, and that is the sacramental character of Holy Orders — and that deficiency makes them *incapable* of preaching in a liturgical setting.

You see, one of our problems in the postconciliar Church of the United States is a refusal to admit spiritual realities as decisive. As a result, we view everything in exclusively humanistic terms. Divine grace is a powerful reality which transforms people's lives. No one is ever the same after being baptized, nor after being ordained. And the grace of those sacraments is so strong that it actually changes people at the very core of their being. Does that mean that, by virtue of sacramental ordination, a man is automatically turned into another Fulton Sheen? Hardly, and personal experience tells us that. It does mean, however, that every sermon of an ordained minister becomes a sacramental encounter because the grace of Christ present in the preacher calls forth a response from the person possessed by Christ through the grace of Baptism.

People concerned more about rights than truth will miss out on all this, but that is not a new reaction to Christian teaching. St. Paul found his words described as absurdity and folly, but also felt compelled to remind his readers that people who viewed things that way were headed for destruction (cf. 1 Cor 1:18—2:16).

An important role for Thomas Aquinas

Q. My spiritual director tells me that St. Thomas Aquinas is supposed to play an important role in the theological training of seminarians. He is rarely mentioned in our classes, except to be held up to ridicule. Is there any documentation on my spiritual director's claims?

A. Yes, there most certainly is. The Vatican II decrees on Christian education and priestly formation speak of the centrality of St. Thomas in contemporary theological study. The 1983 Code of Canon Law asserts that theological students should be given "St. Thomas as their teacher in a special way" (Canon 252.3).

I should also cite here the appearance of a new *Summa Theologiae*, which is easy to consult and convenient to handle. This work condenses St. Thomas' masterpiece into one readable volume for all who are interested in the core of Christian thought. It is available from Christian Classics, P.O. Box 30, Westminster, MD 21157. I recommend it very highly.

Questions asked about vocations

Q. Which of the following statements are true?

1. The number of seminarians in the United States is dwindling, but increasing elsewhere.

2. Contemplative orders of women in this country are growing.

3. Traditionally oriented communities (that is, those whose members wear habits, practice poverty, and so on) are also on the upswing.

If these are true assertions, do you have any theories to explain them?

A. 1. Overall, the number of seminarians in this country continues to decline. Asia, Africa and Eastern Europe (as well as parts of Latin America) are experiencing a vocations boom. In certain American dioceses and seminaries, all-time highs are reported, contrary to the general trend, but fitting a pattern of a traditional orientation.

2. Many contemplative communities are doing extremely well.

3. Active congregations with an identifiable, unified lifestyle and apostolate seem to be doing reasonably well, while those lacking such elements are clearly headed for extinction.

Why is this happening? Very simply, what young man or woman would want to enter the priesthood or religious life when confusion abounds? In certain instances, the anti-institutionalism (and specifically, antipapal sentiment) is so strong as to border on the pathological. Anger and hostility do not breed vocations; love for the Church and pursuit of holiness do. Twenty years ago, I used to worry a great deal about the future of religious life in our country. I now realize that the Holy Spirit has a plan, which will not include dissenters and rebels, and they themselves are willynilly executing God's plan by putting themselves out of existence!

Bowing heads at things sacred

Q. Why don't priests and people bow their heads at the name of Jesus anymore?

A. I don't know. The General Instruction of the Roman Missal, for example, reminds the celebrant that he is to bow his head at the name of Jesus, Mary, and the saint of the day or patron of the parish. Furthermore, all are directed to bow at the words of the Creed which recall the mystery of the Incarnation (and to genuflect at those words on March 25 and December 25).

Given the casual attitude toward sacred things in society today, I think this is a much-needed witness which should be restored to general practice.

Are diaconate programs optional?

Q. There is much confusion among many of us here in our parish concerning Archbishop Hunthausen's action canceling the diaconate program in our diocese since women cannot be ordained deacons. That sounds like blackmail to us. Can he do this?

A. As our longtime readers know, I am not a great fan of the permanent diaconate, but for very different reasons from the Archbishop's. I think most permanent-diaconate training programs are poorly constructed; that once a man is ordained, no one knows what to do with him; that it gives the impression that one must be ordained in order to serve Christ and His Church.

Having a permanent-diaconate program in a diocese is an option, up to the discretion of the diocesan bishop. A bishop may decide he has enough deacons, and so he declares a moratorium for five or six years; or he may not be interested in having any permanent deacons (for any number of reasons), and so he never institutes the ministry at all. I regret that Archbishop Hunthausen has acted as he has, because it will bring about great polarization not only in his own diocese but throughout the nation; but his own comments indicate he wants to make a cause célèbre out of the issue of women's ordination.

2. DOCTRINE

Cannibalism in the Eucharist?

Q. A nearly Catholic friend recently objected to the Eucharist as sounding like "cannibalism." I know the adverbs "sacramentaliter" and "spiritualiter," but I also know the text, "Unless you eat my flesh and drink my blood . . ." and didn't want to water down the doctrine. What should I have said?

A. The presence of Jesus in the Eucharist is, as you note, a sacramental and spiritual presence but nonetheless real: Body and Blood, soul and divinity. The problem of your "nearly Catholic friend" is not new or unique. In the sixth chapter of St. John's Gospel, we find the first objections raised to the doctrine of the Real Presence, and Jesus' response must be ours as well. He attempted to explain the doctrine but never backed off the apparently scandalous truth of it, even to the point of inviting people to leave His company should they be unable to accept the teaching.

One of the charges consistently brought against the early Christians by the pagan Romans was that of cannibalism. And although it got the Church into great difficulty, she always remained faithful to Christ's eucharistic doctrine. While we must eschew any kind of eucharistic explanation which borders on a gross physicality or bizarre notions of receiving parts of Christ's Body, we must do our best to explain the Lord's presence in the Blessed Sacrament in a manner which is faithful to divine revelation and capable of being understood by people of normal intelligence and goodwill.

Baptism of desire

Q. As a young nurse, I participated in a Caesarean delivery. The Jewish doctor asked me if I knew how to baptize, which I said I did and proceeded to do so. Later on, I realized the baby was in the amniotic sac and that the baptismal water never really touched the child. To this day, thirty-five years later, I am in agony when I think that I gave the baby a "limbo" existence. I once told this story to my parish priest, who said it was all my fault. Tell me: Was the baby baptized or not?

A. I can't believe that a priest could be so insensitive as to blame you for having tried your best to perform a good act.

As you know, baptism by water is the normal means by which one is incorporated into Christ. But I am sure you also recall that there is such a thing as baptism of desire. If parents, for instance, intended to have their baby baptized and the child died before the ceremony, the parental intention constitutes a kind of baptism of desire. I think one could see something similar in your efforts. Therefore, I would encourage you not to worry about the infant and leave him to the love and mercy of the God Who created him.

Is it a sin to be baptized twice?

Q. I was baptized a Methodist and later in life was rebaptized in the Baptist Church. Is it sinful to be baptized twice?

A. I imagine that your second "baptism" was demanded by the Baptist minister, probably because you were baptized in the Methodist Church as an infant. As most people know, Baptists regard infant baptism as invalid because they believe that full, conscious faith must be operative. The Church, from the very beginning, however, has never subscribed to that theory because it makes God's activity entirely too dependent on us. Infant baptism conveys in a powerful way the primacy of divine initiative and grace in God's relationship to man. Therefore, God calls even an infant, so great is God's love and power. The faith necessary for any sacrament is, at that point, a "borrowed faith," but one which will necessarily be claimed as the child matures.

Repeating a sacrament like Baptism is indeed sinful, since it implicitly denies the effectiveness of God's grace; in doubtful circumstances, the Church administers "conditional baptism" if she is not sure whether or not someone was once validly baptized. In your case, I doubt that serious sin was committed, because you seem to indicate that you merely wanted to do what was right and did not realize the implications.

Mormon baptism: Is it valid?

Q. Could you please comment on whether or not baptism as performed by the Mormon Church is recognized by the Church as a valid baptism.

A. Mormon baptism is not a valid Christian baptism for the simple reason that Mormons are not Christians, and they do not intend to do what the Church intends in the Sacrament of Baptism. What keeps them outside Christianity, for starters, are their Trinitarian doctrine and their

50

Christology — Arian at base, with the result that humans who die and go to heaven end up as gods equal to Jesus.

Were baptisms valid?

Q. I thought it was necessary for the godparents at baptism to be practicing Catholics. In my family, some of my grandchildren have a non-Catholic as one of the godparents. Has the Church changed this requirement? Are my grandchildren really baptized?

A. Godparents must be Catholic, but only one is needed. Sometimes, parents ask that a non-Catholic be allowed to stand in as a godparent, but the person is really considered only a "Christian witness," being unable to promise to provide a Catholic example and environment for the child since he or she is not Catholic to begin with. When the priest accepts a "Christian witness," both parents and godparents should be told the difference and not be left in confusion or ignorance.

As far as the validity of a baptism is concerned, all that is required is the pouring of water over the forehead in the name of the Trinity by someone intending to do what the Church wants done. So don't worry.

Is there Baptism for aborted babies?

Q. I am told that the Church will not permit aborted babies to be baptized. Doesn't this contradict our teaching that they are human beings?

A. Some pro-abortion activists in the Church have been passing off that statement as truth, but it is patently false. Unfortunately, most abortions are so "successful" that the poor little victims are killed; if they are dead, they obviously cannot be baptized since only the living may receive a sacrament. In spite of that, if the baby survives the procedure, for however short a period, it should indeed be baptized, as is pointed out in Canon 871.

Furthermore, it should be recalled that in many cities funeral services have been held (and presided over by bishops) for aborted babies whose bodies were found in trash receptacles and the like, and surely we only do this for human beings.

Mary as the co-redemptrix

Q. Enclosed is some material that I received in the mail which I find disturbing. In it Mary is referred to as the co-redemptrix. As I understand it, the redemption of mankind is found in the paschal mystery of Christ's passion, death, and resurrection. While I honor Mary, I have never thought of her as sharing equally with Christ in the redemption of mankind. Please share your thoughts on this.

A. The term can have an acceptable meaning, but since confusion can arise from its use, I tend to avoid it. I would understand Mary as co-redemptrix in this manner: Christ is the sole Redeemer of the human race; however, He deigns to associate all of us with Him in His work of salvation as we cooperate on our own behalf with the grace offered and as we work to bring others into a relationship with Him and His saving death and resurrection. St. Paul clearly envisioned the participation of believers in the salvation of the world: "In my own flesh I fill up what is lacking in the sufferings of Christ for the sake of his body, the church" (Col 1:24). If that can be true of sinful people like you and me, that is certainly true of the sinless Virgin Mary.

Lumen Gentium of Vatican II discussed a variety of titles by which Our Lady is invoked by the Christian people; the Fathers of the Council did not mention "co-redemptrix" but did include Advocate, Helper, Benefactress, and Mediatrix, adding this caution: The attribution of these titles should be "so understood that it neither takes away anything from nor adds anything to the dignity and efficacy of Christ the one Mediator" (n. 62).

Imitate Mary's faithful love

Q. A friend of mine insists that Our Lady was an "unwed mother." I disputed this but need to know more about the Jewish marriage rites of the period.

A. When people use that expression for the Blessed Mother, they are generally attempting to highlight the trying circumstances surrounding the conception and birth of Jesus and to the fact that St. Joseph, to whom Mary was wed, was not the father of the Christ Child. While it places Our Lady in solidarity with unwed mothers today who need an example of protecting unborn human life, even in the midst of difficulties and embarrassment, to the extent that the image is inaccurate, it does not really help over the long haul. Far better, it seems to me, to make the correct point: namely, that in today's culture Mary would have been an apt candidate for abortion, but faith and respect for human life did not present these as viable options for her, just as they should not for anyone who follows her Son today. By seeking her intercession and attending to her example, girls and women can imitate her faithful love.

The Immaculate Conception

Q. As a priest for many years, I have tried to instruct congregations on the difference between Mary's Immaculate Conception and Jesus' virginal conception. I must say that the Gospel reading assigned for the day does not help. If the passage were limited to the greeting of the angel ("Hail, full of grace. . ."), that would be fine, but the passage goes on to talk about Jesus' conception — and that's where the confusion comes in. I would be interested in your thoughts on this.

A. I think most priests would share your difficulty in differentiating the two conceptions for the average Catholic. The Gospel reading for the Solemnity of the Immaculate Conception continues with the conception of the Lord, precisely because Our Lady's Immaculate Conception was granted her solely so that she might be a worthy vessel for the One Who would be conceived in her. And maybe using that Gospel passage would be the very way to make both points at the same time.

Mary and the Church as sacraments

Q. Someone giving a talk at a Cursillo weekend referred to Mary and the Church as sacraments. My old Baltimore Catechism spoke of only seven, and all of them as rites of the Church. Was this heresy?

A. At Vatican II, the bishops spoke of Christ as the first sacrament (that is, sign); He is the sign of the Father's love abroad in the world. Representing Him, in turn, is the Church; therefore, she may be properly referred to as a sign or sacrament as well. From Christ and the Church come all other sacraments, including the seven sacramental rites of the Church, which are the visible signs of Christ's invisible grace working within us. Used loosely, one could also call Mary a sacrament, but I would be cautious, especially if a clear explanation would not be forthcoming or there would be potential for misunderstanding.

Sickness, death and the Blessed Mother

Q. I always thought that our Blessed Mother, because of her Immaculate Conception, was not subject to sickness and death, the results of original sin. What is the Church's official teaching? Recently two priests stated that she suffered both; one said that there is a tomb where she was buried and that theologians are still "arguing" this matter.

A. Theologians debate the state of humanity before the Fall: Would man have had to work if Adam had not sinned? Would man have died?

Immunity from work and death is an element of what are known as the preternatural gifts, those endowments of Adam and Eve lost to their descendants through original sin. I am not so sure that freedom from work and death, as such, would have been a part of the life of men if the original sin had not been committed. It seems to me that work is a part of human personality and its fulfillment; in fact, it is our means of being co-creators with God. Death is an intimate part of what it means to be a finite human being. I think that the result of original sin was not that the need for work and death entered the world but that they were now seen as dreadful, fearsome realities. In other words, the punishment was that they would no longer be viewed by man as natural, normal parts of human existence.

As far as Our Lady is concerned, you are correct in connecting her Assumption to the privilege of the Immaculate Conception; her sinless body should not undergo corruption in the grave, but should be brought to the full glory of her Son's Resurrection. The Eastern Church speaks not of Mary's death but of her "dormition" (that is, her going to sleep). The Church of the West has generally believed that Mary did die but was then assumed, body and soul, into heaven. When Pope Pius XII defined the dogma of the Assumption in 1950, he carefully refrained from taking sides in the two approaches by declaring that the Assumption occurred "when the course of her earthy life was finished," thus allowing for either possible interpretation.

Yes, there is a grave for Mary in Jerusalem, over which is located the Church of the Dormition, but the grave is empty, as is Christ's grave in the Church of the Holy Sepulchre. Mary's bodily assumption is tied into the Resurrection of Christ and must be believed by every Catholic. Her Assumption is likewise the promise of our own bodily resurrection, a privilege granted to her in advance of the rest of humanity by virtue of her being the Mother of Christ and Mother of the Church.

The doctrine of purgatory

Q. Must a practicing Catholic believe in purgatory? What does the Council of Trent (Session 25) have to say?

A. The doctrine of purgatory is part of the Deposit of Faith and must be believed by all Catholics. Several ecumenical councils have dealt with the topic. The Council of Florence (1439), for instance, taught that the souls of those who die "truly penitent" "are cleansed after death by purgatorial penalties," going on then to encourage works of intercession on their behalf on the part of Christians still living. The twenty-fifth session of the Council of Trent, as you correctly noted, discusses the issue from more of a disciplinary stance than a doctrinal one (although Canon 30 on justification touches on it as an *obiter dictum*): "Therefore, this holy Council commands the bishops to strive diligently that the sound doctrine of purgatory, handed down by the Holy Fathers and the sacred Councils, be believed by the faithful and that it be adhered to, taught, and preached everywhere."

Purgatory exists despite disbelief

Q. Is it possible for Christians who do not believe in purgatory to go there? What about Catholics who no longer believe in purgatory?
A. Objective reality exists, independently of my knowing or wanting. Hence, even if I have not seen China or perhaps even if I am not convinced that Uranus is in the universe, those realities exist. Similarly, with purgatory — or hell, for that matter.

Just because someone chooses not to believe in it, does not mean he may not end up there! I'm sure many dead atheists have had quite a surprise when face-to-face with the God Whose existence they habitually denied.

Catholics who no longer believe in purgatory should study the Church's teaching on this carefully and pray for an increase in the supernatural virtue of faith, in order to believe what the Catholic Church teaches under divine inspiration.

Limbo and purgatory

Q. What is the difference between limbo and purgatory?
A. Limbo is a theological theory and was never defined as Church teaching. The idea behind it is to suggest a place for unbaptized people who never committed personal sins; it became particularly popular as an explanation of where unbaptized infants go. I must repeat, however, that although this may have been common teaching, it was never official teaching.

Purgatory, on the other hand, is officially taught to be the place where people go who, although not in mortal sin at the time of death, are not yet ready to behold God, due to venial sins and the punishment due to sins already forgiven. We have dealt with this topic (as well as prayers to and for the dead) on numerous occasions in TCA.

A dangerous religion

Q. Please comment on the religion called "Santeria." Supposedly a mixture of Catholicism and African voodoo, it is said to be spreading rapidly. Would you consider this a dangerous religion?

A. It is most definitely dangerous and sadly attracts many poorly educated people, especially in the Hispanic cultures. These folks should be advised by pastoral workers (priests, Religious, teachers, etc.) on a consistent basis of the problems entailed in such syncretism. Particular attention ought to be given to the young, to forestall the forward movement of this strange religion in yet another generation.

Hierarchy, unity, and Communion

Q. You have said that "the liturgical documents make it clear that the hierarchical nature of the Church is to be demonstrated in the reception of Holy Communion." Are you sure this is the case? The Eucharist is my primary link to the Catholic Church; it's the single most important reason I keep coming back — even though I find much in the Church that I cannot in good conscience reconcile with the Gospel, such as the hierarchical pattern by which authority has been structured. Now if you and others insist that "the chain of command" must be made clear at the Breaking of the Bread, then I must object. Aren't we all one because of the Eucharist, with no one lording it over the others? Please explain fully and precisely why the hierarchy is an essential structure for the Church, and why this should be clear at Holy Communion.

A. Vatican II's Dogmatic Constitution on the Church, *Lumen Gentium*, as well as the Liturgy Constitution, *Sacrosanctum Concilium*, make clear the points with which you take issue.

First, *LG* states in numerous places, especially in the third chapter, that the Church by her very nature is hierarchical; in other words, the structure is not superfluous to the life of the Church. In fact, the Council teaches that the spiritual and hierarchical elements of the Church are joined to one another essentially and inextricably, just as Christ's humanity is to His divinity, so that one cannot exist without the other (cf. *LG*, n.8).

Second, *SC* reminds us that the Church is never more the Church than when she gathers to celebrate the liturgy, and that liturgical norms are to be "drawn from the hierarchic and communal nature of the liturgy" (n.26). Now, does that mean that some "lord it over" others in the Church and even in the liturgy? Not at all, for our divine Savior made it clear that those who exercise authority in His Church cannot behave like the pagans.

However, authority is an essential aspect of Catholic life, and, yes, people must be able to see authority in the celebration of the Church's rites. Therefore, the priest should, by his demeanor, position, and role, be visible as the Person of Christ within and at the head of His Church. And so, liturgical norms call for the distribution of the Eucharist in hierarchical order, not so as to honor individual human beings, but to highlight and venerate the presence of Christ in our midst in the unique person of the priest who, again in the words of Vatican II, has been configured to Christ by means of sacramental ordination.

Are we all one at the time of Holy Communion? By all means. Are we all the same? No. From your question, I get the impression that your greatest difficulty with all this is that you seem to have imposed secular political models on life in the Church, so that you evaluate these things by way of categories like democracy, monarchy, etc. But such concepts are out of place in ecclesial life, which is, at root, beyond all such categories. The Church lives according to the Gospel and grace, which comes to us from Christ's cross, whereon the Victim was never more a King. To secular ears, that sounds like a contradiction in terms; faith, however, perceives a paradox or mystery to be lived and celebrated.

When do Catholics leave the Faith?

Q. Does joining a non-Catholic church constitute a formal departure from the Faith? If not, what does?

A. I am not exactly sure of what you have in mind. However, let me take a stab at it.

If a Catholic deliberately ceases to attend his local parish, consciously begins to worship with a non-Catholic community, and then formally registers with that congregation, that would constitute "a formal departure from the Faith," in my opinion. Lately, pastors report that people of this kind often specifically notify their Catholic parish of this disaffiliation and ask to have their names removed from the roster.

Valid Orders in the Church of England

Q. You have indicated on several occasions that the Eastern Orthodox, Old Catholics, and Polish Nationals have valid Orders. Since each of the above churches must have had a bishop with valid Orders at the time of the break with Rome, as did the Church of England, why does the Catholic Church not consider the Church of England to have valid Orders, too?

A. The validity of the Sacrament of Orders depends on two things: correct intention and proper rite. After Henry VIII's break with Rome, various people (most notably Archbishop Cranmer) began to tamper with the liturgy. This became extremely problematic in regard to the ordination rite, in which words pertaining to the sacrificing priesthood were eliminated. The fact that they were dropped indicated a failure to believe that Holy Orders conferred the power to offer sacrifice. Therefore, the Anglican celebration of the sacrament was deficient because the words were lacking, but even more so, because the intention to ordain a sacrificing priest was lacking. The two defects combined to create a serious doubt in the mind of the Holy See that the Church of England had the priesthood as we know and understand it; that conclusion was formally reached in Pope Leo XIII's Apostolicae Curae.

Many "Anglo-Catholics," that is, "High Churchmen," have expressed distress over that judgment of Rome, especially since many of them sought ordination only from Anglican bishops who had been consecrated by Eastern Orthodox bishops, thus guaranteeing (in their minds) the validity of their Orders. As a result, should an Anglican clergyman come into full communion with Rome and desire to serve as a Catholic priest, he must show the "pedigree" of his Orders. If absolute proof of a valid ordination is not forthcoming, he must be ordained as a Catholic priest. The difficulty has been compounded since 1976, when Anglicans in this country began to ordain women as priests and now even as bishops.

Some readers might think this all sounds either snobbish or esoteric, but the validity of the sacraments, the truth of the Gospel, and the salvation of souls are all at stake here — rather high stakes, which reach into eternity.

Definitions of 'heretic' and 'schismatic'

Q. Could you please define "heretic" and "schismatic." How do the definitions apply to modern Catholics, particularly those with a "Protestant" mentality?

A. A heretic is one who denies one or more truths of the Catholic Faith.

A schismatic is one who has cut himself off from union with the Bishop of Rome.

Your question raises the matter of baptized Catholics who, by their attitude and/or conduct, demonstrate that they fall into one or both categories. The Church distinguishes between formal heresy (a conscious, deliberate act) and material heresy (in which falsehood is believed, but without the degree of consciousness of the former). While I would be slow to apply such titles to people, it is regrettably true that not a few individuals exhibit heretical and/or schismatic tendencies. The charitable thing to do, in my judgment, is to point these weaknesses out to them as a genuine act of fraternal correction so that they can get back on track with the Church in their minds and hearts.

Indulgences and their application

Q. Our parish priest has said that Church teaching on indulgences changed after Vatican II, but said no more. Could you explain?
A. The teaching has not changed, but the application has, and I guess that's what he meant.

Formerly, we could obtain either a plenary or partial indulgence. A plenary indulgence is the full remission of all temporal punishment due to sin (not forgiveness of sin), and that remains intact. A partial indulgence, however, had a specific time period attached to it (e.g., 300 days), so that one's temporal punishment is lessened by the same amount as would have been received by performing the public penances in the early Church for the specified number of days, weeks, etc. It is this second area where the change has occurred.

The old approach was an attempt to be concrete with a topic which is spiritual — always a necessary effort but also one fraught with difficulties. For instance, since purgatory exists in the world beyond time, how can we speak of days, months, or years? It was decided, therefore, to eliminate any discussion of precise amounts of time and to limit ourselves to talk about a partial remission of punishment.

Catholic Church isn't the Antichrist

Q. Although I am not Catholic, I am a baptized Christian. How can I explain to my Protestant friends that the Catholic Church is not the Antichrist?
A. As someone once remarked, "For those who believe, no explanation

is necessary; for those who do not, none is possible." I think that epigram applies very well in the case you bring.

Those who wish to engage in weird biblical interpretation because of preconceived notions are merely using Sacred Scripture for their own purposes. For you to tell them that the Book of Revelation, for example, has nothing to do with the Roman Catholic Church but with the Roman Empire will probably accomplish little, even though any respectable exegete (Protestant, Orthodox, or Catholic) would tell you the same thing. Having discussed this particular matter in earlier issues of TCA. I would simply refer you to them but warn you in advance that you are most likely embarking upon an exercise in futility.

Proof of Church's hierarchical nature

Q. In [a recent] issue of TCA, a reader asked for proof of the hierarchical nature of the Church. I have always seen a witness for the hierarchical nature of the Church in the Gospel's use of the word "apostle." This word, taken from the Greek, means "one who is sent." But one who is sent has authority from above. Hence, the structure in the Church and its hierarchical nature are seen from the very beginning in the Gospel's use of the word "apostle."
A. Absolutely correct. Thank you.

Archbishop Lefebvre and schism

Q. Why are Archbishop Marcel Lefebvre and the four bishops he consecrated accused of being excommunicated because of being in schism. Canon 1382, which I understand was used to excommunicate him, doesn't say anything about schism, only about consecrating a bishop "without a pontifical mandate." Why, then, does everyone say he is in schism if he really isn't?
A. The late Archbishop Lefebvre was in schism long before he was excommunicated. He fell into schism when he ordained priests even after Pope Paul VI directly ordered him not to do so. That deliberate act of disobedience constituted an act of schism (from the Greek word meaning a break [of unity]). His whole subsequent behavior pattern was schismatic as well. I should underscore the point here that the use of Latin had absolutely nothing to do with his falling from Catholic unity, since any priest or bishop can celebrate a Latin liturgy any time he wishes or the people desire it. Although the Archbishop's priestly

ordinations were illicit, they were valid. Episcopal consecrations, however, are a different story; since the Church is founded on the apostolic college, disunity in that body destroys the total unity of the Church. That is why a papal mandate is needed to ordain bishops, and that is why failure to obtain one and to proceed regardless is such a grievous fault, so as to merit *automatic* excommunication. In other words, simply to perform the act brings about the penalty — with no notification necessary and no juridical process. In short, Archbishop Lefebvre may have had many legitimate complaints about the nature of some of the postconciliar reforms; he killed his effectiveness, however, by illicit ordinations and even more so by illicit episcopal consecrations.

The Old Catholic Church

Q. A friend of mine has begun studies for the priesthood in something called "the Old Catholic Church." He says they have valid Orders and differ from the Roman Catholic Church only in that they do not accept papal infallibility and certain ecclesiastical disciplines. My friend continues to attend Mass and receive Holy Communion in his former parish, with the full knowledge of his pastor. He also wants me to attend his ordination when that occurs; my pastor says he would see nothing wrong with that, either. What's your advice?

A. From reading the literature which your friend sent you, two things seem clear: His group has split from the main body of Old Catholics; they differ with us on much more than papal infallibility. Anyone who has formally left the Catholic Church has excommunicated himself and can hardly consider himself eligible for Holy Communion. Besides that, why would someone like that have a desire to be a part of his old parish? How his pastor could countenance such a dishonest arrangement is beyond me, let alone your pastor's seeing nothing wrong with your participation in his ordination liturgy.

The Bayside apparitions

Q. I find your treatment of the Bayside apparitions most unfair. No official ecclesiastical pronouncement has ever been made on this topic, surely not from the Pope, at any rate.

A. I beg to differ. On Nov. 4, 1986, the following statement was issued by Bishop Francis Mugavero: "I, the undersigned Bishop of Brooklyn, in my role as the legitimate shepherd of this particular church, wish to

61

confirm the constant position of the Diocese of Brooklyn that a thorough investigation revealed that the alleged 'visions of Bayside' completely lacked authenticity . . . [and are] contributing to the confusion which is being created in the faith of God's people." I think that is as official as anyone could want it. By the way, it is not the task of the Pope to pronounce upon such alleged visions, but the responsibility of the local bishop. Of course, one could always appeal the decision of the local bishop to higher authority, but that has never been done with Bayside; therefore, no Catholic desiring to be in communion with the Church should frequent that spot.

Catholics are Christians

Q. My husband left both the Catholic Church and me. Now he tells me that Catholics can't go to heaven. What should I say in reply?
A. If your husband is so concerned with matters of salvation, why not ask him how he justifies leaving his wife when the Gospels are so clear on Jesus' position on divorce?

Regarding the question of your damnation as a result of your association with the Catholic Church, apparently your husband subscribes to the theory that Catholicism is a non-Christian religion. When one has said that this is sheer nonsense, one has been as charitable as possible under the circumstances. No respectable scholar (Protestant, Catholic, Jew, or even atheist) who has studied the history of religion would ever make so irresponsible a claim, yet this kind of statement is not all that uncommon among the more extreme expressions of Fundamentalism. I think your best answer is to ask your husband to pray for you and to assure him of a remembrance in your prayers as well, reminding him that both you and he have to face the same Judge and that you would prefer to leave your case in His hands.

Appearances can be deceiving

Q. A friend of mine came back from an Episcopalian First Holy Communion and couldn't believe how similar everything is to ours. She asked me just what the real differences are between us, and I was hard-pressed to identify them. Can you help?
A. Appearances can be deceiving. There are Anglicans who would believe everything the Catholic Church teaches, with the exception of an acceptance of papal infallibility. And there are others who, although

liturgically oriented, would eschew many traditional Catholic positions from birth control to abortion, homosexual activity, divorce and remarriage, women's ordination. It is sad but true that, in many ways, Catholics and Episcopalians were closer to each other twenty-five years ago than today because of the slow but sure drift of so many Anglicans into trendy forms of theology which are uprooted from Christian Tradition. This is not said in a condemnatory or triumphalistic manner, but with some degree of sadness, an emotion affecting many Episcopalians who remain in the Anglican Communion with great distress. Of course, this is the very reason so many Anglican clergy and laity alike have come into full communion with the Catholic Church in the past fifteen years.

An explanation of apostolic succession

Q. Can you explain apostolic succession, why it is necessary, and give its biblical roots? Also, can a bishop today trace back his episcopal line to the Apostles? Just how reliable are those records?

A. The Church is apostolic because she is built on the foundation of the Apostles (cf. Eph 2:20) and to this day professes the Apostolic Faith. Catholics believe that the bishops are the successors of the Apostles. The doctrine of apostolic succession was explained at the Second Vatican Council in this way: "Bishops have by divine institution taken the place of the Apostles as pastors of the Church." Or again: "The apostolic tradition is manifested and preserved in the whole world by those who were made bishops by the Apostles and their successors down to our own time" (*Lumen Gentium*, n.20).

This doctrine, however, is not a creation of twentieth-century theologians but has been a constant feature of Catholic life since the time of the Apostles, with ample scriptural support, as well as historical reliability. In the very moment when Jesus commissioned the Apostles to teach and make disciples of all nations, He likewise gave them the promise of His presence and assistance to accomplish the task (cf. Matthew 28:20). Since God is always faithful to His promises, one can be certain that Christ's guarantee of His presence did not die with the last Apostle, for the Lord had promised never to leave His people orphaned (cf. Jn 14:18).

Authority in the Church exists to safeguard the integrity of the Gospel message and to foster the unity of the Church. That the Apostles chose successors for themselves is clearly attested to throughout the New Testament, but most especially in the Pastoral Epistles.

The process of tracing back one's episcopal lineage can be done with confidence, and many bishops actually have their whole "genealogy" traced out in great detail.

Base communities: religious or political?

Q. Can you tell me something about "base communities" in Latin America? Are they commonly associated with liberation theology? Are they usually sponsored by the Church? Are they religious, political, both?

A. Base communities are small gatherings of Christians, often subdivisions of a large parish, whereby believers get together on a regular basis for prayer, study, reflection. At a certain point in time, these groups were taken over in many instances by clergy and Religious seeking to inculcate a Marxist approach to social reform (which does not include all of liberation theology). Inasmuch as social change, from a Christian perspective, involves both religious values and political action, it should not be surprising to find them mixed (in a healthy way) in base communities.

When I worked in inner-city parochial schools, for instance, I constantly urged the parents to lobby for their interests to obtain government assistance for the Catholic education of their children. I do not think I was engaging in any kind of improper activity, but simply bringing the Gospel message of justice to bear on the formation of public policy. The problem with some activism is that it goes beyond the bounds of connecting religion to real life and gets into partisan politics and even violence, as well as the completely unacceptable Marxist doctrines of class struggle and an earthly utopia devoid of hope for eternity.

The reality of Christ's Church

Q. What is meant in the Vatican II "Decree on Ecumenism" when it says that the fullness of Christ's Church "subsists" in the Catholic Church? Is that more or less than "is"? What does that statement do to the traditional teaching that the Catholic Church is the one, true Church?

A. A standard Latin dictionary reveals that the verb "*subsistere*" is merely a synonym for "*esse*," which is to say that both mean "to be." *Lumen Gentium* thus teaches: "The Church, constituted and organized as a society in the present world, subsists in the Catholic Church, which is governed by the successor of Peter and by the bishops in communion with him" (n. 8).

The conciliar documents are very careful to maintain the traditional teaching, as you can see, while recognizing at the same time — as the Church always did — that elements of the reality of the Church exist outside the visible boundaries of the Catholic Church. That is why, for example, the Church has never rebaptized anyone coming to Catholicism from another Christian community which properly administers Baptism. In fact, *Lumen Gentium* maintains that whatever other Christian communities do validly (e.g., baptize, preach the Word), they do in virtue of their relationship to the one Church of Christ.

When the Church considers her relationship to another Christian body, she always does so with her own ecclesiality in view — that is, another body's "churchliness" is judged by how much of "the Church" has survived in its own life and structure. Thus Orthodox Christianity embodies all the essential elements of what it means to be a Church, except for the doctrine of papal primacy, and is therefore to be regarded as a Church with valid Orders, valid sacraments, Scripture, Tradition, etc. On the other hand, the Baptist denomination falls seriously short on dozens of scores, and hence cannot be officially acknowledged as a Church. Vatican II took account of such differences by referring to "Churches" (which would include the Orthodox, Old Catholics, Polish Nationals, etc.) and "ecclesial communities" to describe those Christian bodies that lack full identity as Churches (cf. *Redintegratio Unitatis*. n. 22).

Anglo-Catholics

Q. What is the difference between a Roman Catholic and an Episcopal Catholic, if any?

A. I think you mean an Anglo-Catholic. Such a person belongs to the Anglican Communion (called Episcopalians here in the United States) but has decidedly Catholic tendencies, certainly in liturgy and generally also in doctrine, as well as a favorable mind-set toward corporate reunion with Rome. An Anglo-Catholic is still not in full communion with the Holy See but can fulfill an important role as a kind of bridge between Rome and Canterbury.

On second thought, perhaps you are referring to an Anglican who has come into full communion with the Catholic Church. A few years back, the Holy See offered a "pastoral provision" to Episcopalians who wished to enter the Church, whereby they can maintain elements of their Anglican Tradition (like the Book of Common Prayer) in a fully recognized "Anglo-Catholic" parish. Several such parishes have been formed in this country; probably the most famous aspect of their existence is the fact that many of their pastors are former Anglican priests who were married and permitted to remain so upon reception of Catholic ordination.

'Ecumenical era' has its limits

Q. In our parish, a Baptist man and his Catholic wife and children come to Mass every Sunday, which we think is wonderful. However, lately he has been receiving Holy Communion, doing the readings, and even serving as an extraordinary minister of the Eucharist. Someone said he has also applied to the Knights of Columbus. Is all this possible for a non-Catholic? The man in question says the parish priest told him this is all permitted since the coming of the ecumenical era.

A. "Ecumenical era" or not, every single activity you mention is forbidden to a non-Catholic. Speak with the pastor personally, just to be sure that he does in fact realize the man in question is not Catholic. If your priest still persists in permitting this man to exercise these functions, then simply contact the dean or vicar of your area; if nothing is achieved there, write to your bishop.

Please understand: We do not keep people from performing certain roles in the Church out of mean-spiritedness but out of concern for the individual (who should not be deceived into imagining that he is some kind of "quasi-Catholic") and out of respect for the truth of the sacramental signs (which must never be allowed to be administered in a confusing manner). If this man is so favorably disposed toward the Church, why is he not invited to come into full communion with that Church? Of course, if he is allowed to reap all the benefits of membership without any of the burdens, that might explain his decision to remain outside the visible unity of Christ's Church.

The Byzantine Catholic Church

Q. What is the difference between the Byzantine Catholic Church and the Roman Catholic Church?

A. The Catholic Church is Christ's Body reflected in a diversity of local churches or dioceses, all held in union by adherence to a common creed and in loyalty to a common father, the Bishop of Rome. Most Catholics throughout the world belong to what is called the Roman Rite; that is, they celebrate the liturgy and observe the discipline of the Diocese of Rome.

Other rites exist, however, equal in dignity and in fidelity to the fullness of the Catholic Faith (e.g., Byzantine, Ukrainian, Greek, Russian, Ruthenian, Coptic, etc.). These Catholics celebrate the liturgy in a manner somewhat different from that of the Roman Rite and live under different regulations (for example, many of them permit married priests). For most Eastern rites, there is generally a corresponding Orthodox Church, which is not in union with the Pope.

When we use the expression "Roman Catholic," we can mean one of two things, which is where the confusion comes in: First, all Catholics (of whatever rite) who accept the Bishop of Rome; second, only those Catholics who follow the Roman Rite.

To answer your question as succinctly as possible, Byzantine Catholics are those who live under the Eastern Code of Canon Law, celebrate the Divine Liturgy of St. John Chrysostom and St. Basil, and accept the Holy Father as the visible head of the Church on earth.

Teachers of sacred subjects

Q. In [a recent] issue of TCA, you stated that the norm of the "Ratio Fundamentalis Institutionis" was superseded by the 1983 Code of Canon Law.

I presented the matter to the Pontifical Council for the Interpretation of Legal Texts in Rome, which forwarded my letter to the Congregation of Catholic Education. . . . In their answer the Congregation indicated that the provision of 1970 requiring teachers of sacred subjects in general to be priests was reaffirmed in their new edition (1985) of the "Ratio."

A. Thank you for the clarification. Let me make the point, however, that it is possible to have non-clerics teach even sacred subjects, but that this should not be the norm. The Latin text, which you kindly provided, says these professors "*sint communiter sacerdotes*" (that is, "should in general be priests"). As I said in my original response, this only makes sense.

Studying the Faith at home

Q. Are there any truly Catholic programs of home study for adults?
A. One with which I am very familiar and which I highly recommend is the Catholic Home Study Institute. It is officially approved by the Congregation for the Clergy and makes the catechetical diploma available by correspondence. It also offers the option of earning undergraduate college credit. The courses are produced by respected theologians, and qualified personnel grade lessons and are available for additional help. For further information, contact the Institute at: 5 Loudoun Street, SE, Leesburg, Virginia 22075; 703-777-8388.

Serious errors in Confirmation program

Q. A very popular Confirmation preparation program by Sister Kieran Sawyer, published by Ave Maria Press in 1982, offers a chart which implies that the Roman Catholic Church began in the sixteenth century. Even though this is obviously untrue and very misleading (especially to unsuspecting young adults), the book is "Published with Ecclesiastical Permission." How could this happen?
A. I have surveyed the chart you enclosed, and it gives the impression that Christianity (whose origins the author posits at the beginning of the Christian era) is distinct from Roman Catholicism. Interestingly enough, Eastern Orthodoxy is listed as beginning in the eleventh century, but from what? Even they would assert unequivocally that their break was with the Church of Rome, and no one else! Other historical information is in error, as the chart places the Methodist, Baptist, and Presbyterian denominations as all beginning in the sixteenth century, too.

The error in history is directly related to Catholic doctrine; namely, that the one Church of Christ subsists in the Catholic Church, as clearly taught by Vatican II. Therefore, I am in a quandary to hazard a guess as to how the book was ever published with ecclesiastical permission.

Where to find the Didache

Q. Probably the earliest Christian writing was the Greek manual entitled "The Didache." Was this writing ever translated into English? If so, where is it available? None of the book catalogs I have list it.
A. One can find it in several anthologies. Perhaps the easiest to find is in the sixth volume of Paulist Press's series *Ancient Christian Writers*.

Does the 'Index' still exist?

Q. Does the Vatican still publish a list of censored books?

A. In 1966, the Congregation for the Doctrine of the Faith, in effect, did away with the Index of Prohibited Books. However, prudence and common sense dictate that one not read works which will cause one to question or deny matters of faith and morals.

The sacraments and grace

Q. A priest was recently invited to speaik in our diocese and has caused a debate in our area about the Catholic teaching on grace. According to Father Himes, the celebration of the sacraments makes us aware of the grace of God, which is always with us; it has nothing to do with saying the right words or performing certain actions, which he disparages as superstition. I wrote to our bishop, who referred my letter to the Liturgical Commission, which told me to watch the priest's video to learn the answer! Please tell me, do sacraments give grace?

A. Whether or not your lecturer says it, the Church teaches that the sacraments give grace. For instance, one who is not yet baptized has no life of grace, and the relationship with the Blessed Trinity (which is what grace is) is begun with the reception of the Sacrament of Baptism and grows through the other sacraments and through a pious life. Let just one of dozens of possible textsfrom official Church teaching suffice, this one from Sacrosanctum Concilium, the Second Vatican Council's Constitution on the Sacred Liturgy: "From the liturgy, therefore, and especially from the Eucharist, grace is poured forth upon us as from a fountain. . ." (no. 10).

Out of character?

Q. How do we know that Christ was tempted by the devil? Everything else about His life was witnessed by someone else. It seems out of character for Jesus to have revealed this to anyone. And if so, to whom?

A. Presumably Jesus told others about His temptation. Why would you say this "seems out of character"? Don't many people share with others temptations they have experienced, especially when such declarations could be of assistance to someone who might be enduring the same difficulties?

Directors need proper training

Q. What is the Church's view of Catholics involved in charismatic covenant communities who receive pastoral and spiritual direction from untrained (but appointed) "pastoral leaders"? Are there other groups in the Church involved with this shepherding/discipleship movement?

A. While the Church has never maintained that spiritual directors need be ordained, she has always held that such persons must be properly trained in theology; today, I think we would agree on the value of some basic grasp of good psychology as well. I also happen to believe that spiritual direction works best when the counselee freely chooses his or her director. A further point to note is that direction can never be coercion; therefore, if one does not have confidence in the advice of his spiritual director, that would seem to be a good indicator that a less-than-perfect match has occurred and a change is called for.

The best way to determine if procedures used in a particular group are good or not is to discover if the group in question is related to and obedient to the local bishop, who should have someone responsible for the oversight of such communities or movements.

Church safeguards Christ's divinity

Q. In the last article in your excellent series on "Rubrics of the Sacred Liturgy," you related that you once heard a very fine, solid priest make the mistake of saying, "Jesus, Son of the living God, pray for us." You used this as an example of theological error, albeit unintentional: that is, denying the divinity of Christ.

How can this possibly be construed as denying His divinity?

A. While it is true that the Epistle to the Hebrews states that Jesus lives to make intercession for us (and that is, in fact, praying for us), the Church, in her liturgy especially, is most careful to ascribe intercession to the saints, in order to safeguard the divinity of Christ. As the Son of God and Second Person of the Blessed Trinity, Jesus is more appropriately asked to "have mercy on us" (see, for example, the beginnings of all the litanies, as well as the entire Litany of the Sacred Heart).

Can a layperson bless water?

Q. Regarding your answer to "Tampering with the baptismal rite," I couldn't find your reply to the part, "And is it true that anyone can make holy water?"

A. The ordinary procedure for blessing water involves a priest or deacon. In extraordinary circumstances (in mission lands, for example), a layperson may do so, following the rite as given in The Book of Blessings for a non-ordained person.

The sin of Adam

Q. Why are we being punished for Adam's sin? Isn't the concept of hereditary transmission of sin a Manichaean heresy? Adam's posterity might presuppose that human souls are derived from the parents, like the bodies. Wouldn't it be better to say that we sin by a voluntary imitation of Adam's sin of disobedience?

A. To speak of imitation of Adam's sin begs the real question. I can make a conscious decision to imitate someone, so that there is no necessary connection between an act he performed and one which I perform, except my own desire to emulate. That is not what the Church says about original sin and its effects.

If we might use the language of science, we are talking about genetics or heredity. Because I am descended from a particular set of parents, I have a set of characteristics (hair and eye color, pigmentation, and so on) that is mine, whether I want it or not. Part of the inheritance each of us receives from our first parents is a proclivity to sin. G.K. Chesterton commented that the one dogma of Catholicism which is totally provable from human experience is that of original sin. In other words, even the nicest baby, raised by the nicest parents, in the nicest environment, is prone to sin, resulting from the sin of Adam. And even after that sin is "washed away" in baptism, the aftereffects remain, as witnessed by a disordered desire for autonomy and concupiscence.

By the way, the doctrine of original sin has nothing to do with Manichaeism — a philosophy/religion which despised the human body as evil. One can believe in original sin without despising the body and also despise the body without believing in original sin.

Catholics and the 'Filioque doctrine'

Q. I heard a theologian say that the "Filioque doctrine" is not binding in faith. I thought several councils had dealt with that, and all my source books say that it is "de fide" teaching. I do know, however, that Eastern-Rite Catholics are not required to include it in their profession of faith in the Divine Liturgy, but mustn't they believe it?

A. Yes, all Catholics must accept the *"Filioque* doctrine" — namely, that the Holy Spirit proceeds from the Father *and* the Son. The Eastern Orthodox prefer to speak of the procession of the Holy Spirit from the Father *through* the Son. Although the addition of this phrase to the Creed was problematic for the Orthodox at one time, most of their theologians now acknowledge that there is a sense in which it is acceptable to their traditional understanding. At the same time, Eastern-Rite Catholics need not recite that line in the Creed (the decision is usually left to the local Eastern bishop), but they must believe what the doctrine entails.

It is interesting to note that on Pentecost of 1981, Pope John Paul II (in an ecumenical gesture toward the Orthodox) led the Nicene Creed in St. Peter's Basilica, omitting the one-time troublesome *Filioque.*

Acts by priests were gravely illicit

Q. My wife and I attended an ordination for a Presbyterian minister. Two Catholic priests present at the service took communion and also went up to the altar to pray for his ministry, while touching him as he knelt. Kindly comment.

A. The two acts the priests performed were gravely illicit. First, intercommunion is strictly forbidden; for priests to do this, however, is a source of particular scandal since the act takes on a semi-official note of disobedience or becomes a kind of doctrinal declaration that there are no problems regarding Protestant Orders and Eucharist, as well as the deep divisions among Christians. If by "touching him," you mean that they imposed hands on the candidate, this is truly shocking; to do this implies a complete acceptance of the validity of Presbyterian Orders, and not even the most starry-eyed ecumenist is ready to discuss that question when Lutheran and Anglican Orders are still problematic.

Self-appointed ambassadors of Christian unity inflict great harm on the whole Body of Christ, Protestant and Catholic alike, by "jumping the gun"; what may be motivated by goodwill or even a "holy impatience" is ultimately destructive of the real goal of Christian unity, namely, full, corporate union of all believers in the visible Body of Christ — His one, holy, catholic and apostolic Church.

How should a Christian pray?

Q. I have a great deal of trouble praying. Can you offer some advice on how to talk with God, particularly through intercessory prayer?

A. Prayer is merely conversation with God. Talk to Him as you would to any friend; tell Him how you feel about Him and His creation and about your relationship to Him and others. Praise and thank Him for what He has done in the world and in your own personal life. Express sorrow for your sins, which break or weaken your relationship with the Lord. And then do not be afraid to tell Him what you need, always in full confidence but also in the humility which acknowledges the need for your will to be conformed to His, should there be a conflict between the two.

No one can teach another person to pray, any more than one can really teach another how to teach — and that's coming from a professor of education! Nonetheless, it is possible to pick up some good pointers from those who have mastered the art of praying, and many have done so. I would suggest, however, that you go first to *the* master of prayer, our divine Lord Himself. Read passages like the Sermon on the Mount or St. Luke's many wonderful parables on the nature of Christian prayer. When everything is said and done, though, the only way to learn how to pray is to begin to pray.

One last point: Do not be discouraged if you do not reach great spiritual "highs" or do not achieve what you think you should (especially at an emotional level), remembering the marvelous insight of Blaise Pascal — "The desire to pray is prayer." I think that's how God looks on our feeble but best efforts to communicate with Him.

May Catholics believe in polygenism?

Q. *I am enclosing a part of Father Raymond Brown's book "Responses to 101 Questions on the Bible," in which he states a Catholic can believe in polygenism. I am also enclosing a part of Pope Pius XII's encyclical* Humani Generis *(concerning some false opinions threatening to undermine the foundations of Catholic doctrine). I find paragraph 37 in* Humani Generis *at odds with Father Brown's statement that the Pope did not condemn polygenism. Please give some guidance in this matter.*
A. I am quite familiar with the Holy Father's statement in *Humani Generis*, and I do not read it the way you do and am inclined toward the interpretation of Father Brown.

I think Pope Pius was saying that monogenism (the descent of the entire human race from one set of parents) is the preferred explanation, but polygenism (the descent from multiple sets of parents) is possible if one can reconcile it with the doctrine of original sin. To date, I am not aware of anyone who has successfully met the challenge of the Pope on that score; if someone came up with a theory that could safeguard the doctrinal concerns, it would then be the responsibility of the Magisterium to pass judgment on it. As I say, that has not happened yet and may actually be a moot point because scientific consensus seems once more to be favoring monogenism over polygenism.

The charismatic contribution

Q. What legitimate claims does the charismatic branch of the Church offer to all Catholics?

A. I'm not completely sure what you are asking. But if you mean, "What does the charismatic movement have to offer by way of a unique spirituality," I would answer thus.

When the charismatic movement first came into the Catholic Church, many problems existed, not the least of which was the lack of priestly leadership, as well as no small lack of docility on the part of many members of the movement, who regarded themselves as spiritually mature, if not elite. Several years into the life of the charismatic renewal, many began to discover that what they had originally imagined to be signs of great spiritual progress (speaking in tongues, for example) were not necessarily so, and that they ought to pursue what St. Paul, in his First Letter to the Corinthians, terms "the higher gifts" (*charismata* in Greek). Furthermore, because so many charismatics ended up leaving the Catholic Church in the '60s and '70s, those who remained sought out strong direction from the Church. The Holy See even appointed a prelate specifically to relate to the movement.

The result has been rather positive, in most instances: a powerful devotion to the Holy Spirit: a healthy commitment to the reading and study of the Bible; love for the very "Catholic" elements of the Christian life, such as the Eucharist, Our Lady, the Holy Father.

A fine instance of this type of lifestyle is found at the Franciscan University of Steubenville, in Ohio, which offers a quality education in a thoroughly Catholic environment, along with significant outreach programs dealing with evangelization and other aspects of Christian living.

Different definitions of salvation

Q. Could you discuss the difference between the Protestant and Catholic views on salvation?

A. In engaging in any kind of ecumenical dialogue, it is good to define terms before launching into the deep. The word "salvation" is a case in point.

Most Catholics treat redemption and salvation as synonyms; most Protestants do not. But the difference in terminology does have a parallel in Catholic usage. Let me explain.

We speak about objective and subjective redemption (or salvation), which translates in this way for Protestants: You and I and the entire human race were redeemed on Good Friday afternoon (objective redemption); you and I were saved when, to use their language, we asked Jesus Christ to come into our lives as our personal Savior (subjective redemption). Catholics would put a little finer face on subjective redemption, so we would say that, while here below, we are saved in hope and are not totally saved until the day Christ declares us so in judgment.

As you can see, this is a very complex topic, with many facets, and extremely important to understand. Hence, the necessity for clear definitions.

No changes to Trinitarian formula

Q. May the priest give a blessing "in the name of the Creator, the Redeemer and the Sanctifier," instead of using the traditional formula?
A. No, he may not.

While it is true that the Father is the Creator, the Son is the Redeemer and the Holy Spirit is the Sanctifier, something different is happening in using the different terminology. In the traditional Trinitarian formula, the focus is on how the Persons of the Blessed Trinity relate to one another from all eternity. In other words, the stress is on God *in se*. In the alternative wording, the emphasis is on Who God is *pro nobis* (for us), switching from an ontological reality to one which is functional: How does God relate to *me*? Furthermore, the specific revelation of Christianity is the fact that God is our Father; Jesus is His only-begotten Son; the Holy Spirit is the loving Gift of the Son to His Church.

Teilhard de Chardin; ICEL translations

Q. Two questions for you. First, I've enclosed a poem by Teilhard de Chardin, given in Volume 1 of the Liturgy of the Hours. How is it

*possible that this French priest's works, which were condemned by the
Church six times, can now be incorporated into the mandatory reading
of priests? Second, the prayer for the Feast of the Chair of St. Peter
says, in English, "You have built your Church on the rock of St. Peter's
confession of faith." This sounds very Protestant to me. Is this another
shining example of unscholarly ICEL translation efforts?*

A. As far as Teilhard is concerned, I am not aware of his poetry having
been condemned but rather certain theological propositions, which I
doubt would find their way either into his poetry or the breviary.
Furthermore, the poetry section of the American breviary in no way
constitutes "the mandatory reading of priests" since that is all in the
Appendix and is really there more as inspirational material, in no way
part of the Liturgy of the Hours proper.

Regarding the collect for St. Peter's Chair, let me note that the Latin
text (which is, of course, the official text) does not mention Peter at all.
Rather, it prays for those whom God "[has] firmly established on the
rock of the apostolic confession." A similar prayer, used for the
anniversary of the Pope's election, does indeed speak of the Church as
having been established on Peter himself. The problem that you
discovered is, sadly, only one of many deficient translations.

Maximilian Kolbe, saint and martyr

*Q. I have a problem with Pope John Paul's declaration that St.
Maximilian Kolbe is a martyr; a saint, for sure, but not a martyr. After
all, doesn't one have to die for the Faith, not just to save another
person's life (which is what Kolbe did)?*

A. I suspect the Holy Father's reasoning in all this was that while the
proximate cause of St. Maximilian's death was his offering his life in
place of another (which in itself is a heroic witness), he was placed in the
extermination camp initially because he was a priest. He was there
precisely to be killed. Had he not come forward to save the married
man's life, he would undoubtedly have been murdered anyway, and
explicitly out of hated for and rejection of the Catholic Faith and all that
it represented to the Nazi regime. And that constitutes martyrdom.

Wording of the Creed

*Q. Where has the word "men" gone in the line of the Creed which says
(or said), "for us men and for our salvation"? In my area of New Jersey,*

parishes just say, "for us and for our salvation." However, on recent trips to Pennsylvania and Florida, the Creed was still being recited in the old way. Is the dropping of "men" a local option, left up to the discretion of the local bishop?

A. No. there is no local option on Mass texts. And no, the text is the same as it has been since this translation was first accepted by the National Conference of Catholic Bishops. For changes in translations to occur, the whole episcopal conference must vote and then have their decision ratified by the Holy See. Undoubtedly, you will recall that some years back, "men" was dropped from the prayer of consecration over the wine, so that it now reads, "for you and for all." That change was made by the bishops' conference and approved by the appropriate congregation in Rome. I am told that there was some agitation at that time to make the change you discuss, and that the Congregation for the Doctrine of the Faith specifically intervened and ruled out such a change. Why, you ask? Because the line "for us men and for our salvation" is intended to be a parallel and balance to an earlier line, "He became man." In other words, these two elements of the Creed are in dialogue with each other, in the same way that humanity and divinity are, precisely in and through the mystery of the Incarnation affirmed in the Creed. As you can see, liturgical translation work is a multifaceted endeavor, which cannot be engaged in lightly or by theological lightweights since the essence of the Catholic Faith is at stake at times. Apparently, some priests in your area are so taken up with the alleged necessity of using "inclusive" language that they are prepared to be disobedient to the Church and even risk robbing the Church of the very doctrine which makes her life possible.

The Trinity

Q. Since the doctrine of the Trinity appears nowhere in the Bible, nor in the words of Jesus, how, when and why has it come about that the Catholic Church declares the Blessed Trinity to be a doctrine necessary for salvation?

A. It is not true that the doctrine of the Trinity is not taught in the New Testament. Granted, it is not stated in the precise terms in which subsequent theology spoke of it and the word itself is not used, but that does not mean the concept is not taught. Literally dozens of passages speak of the Father, Son and Holy Spirit, and their interrelationships; I

77

would suggest you consult a concordance to discover just how extensive this list is.

While the scriptural evidence for the Blessed Trinity is indeed massive, I would caution against a kind of "biblicism" which would hold that if a doctrine is not categorically taught in the Bible, it cannot be held by the Church or taught by her; that is Fundamentalism, not Catholicism. Interestingly enough, however, even though Fundamentalists would generally subscribe to this type of approach to the formation of doctrine, they do not do so in the case of the Trinity.

Are aborted babies considered martyrs?

Q. Are unbaptized aborted babies considered martyrs receiving the baptism of desire?

A. Martyrdom generally implies a conscious desire or willingness to die for God, the Gospel, the Church or some other spiritual reality. As such, those below the age of reason cannot technically be classified as martyrs. While the Church does celebrate the Feast of the Holy Innocents (Dec. 28) as a day of martyrs. I think the exception proves the rule here and may also be an example of some poetic license.

As for the fate of unbaptized aborted babies, the best we can do is commend them to the providential care of a loving Father, Who does not allow even a sparrow to escape His loving concern (cf. Mt 6:26). The God Who created them can likewise redeem them, and such matters are best left in His hands.

Catholic doctrine on human life

Q. Is the infallible declaration on the Immaculate Conception to be interpreted as an infallible statement by the Church regarding the beginning of human life?

A. No, I don't think so. When exegeting doctrinal statements, it is necessary to determine the fundamental point being addressed; other statements made might be interesting, but one could not assign infallible status to every sentence in such a declaration.

The key passage is as follows: ". . . the most Blessed Virgin Mary was, from the first moment of her conception, by the singular grace and privilege of almighty God and in view of the merits of Christ Jesus the Savior of the human race, preserved immune from all stain of original sin. . . ." I think it would be safe to say that Pope Pius IX was defining not when human life begins but that Our Lady was free from the stain of original sin from the first moment of her existence.

Over and above that, several doctrinal documents of the past few years (including *Donum Vitae*, the 1987 instruction on life in its origin) carefully avoided settling the issue as to the precise moment when human life begins, in the sense of when the human being (whether embryo, fetus, etc.) receives the immortal soul. Even without that definition, the Church has never hesitated to say that life in the womb — from the first instant — must be cherished and protected. Therefore, Cardinal Joseph Ratzinger in the above-mentioned document declared: "The Magisterium has not expressly committed itself to an affirmation of a philosophical nature, but it constantly reaffirms the moral condemnation of any kind of procured abortion. This teaching has not been changed and is unchangeable." Similarly, even St. Thomas Aquinas who, following the biological data of his day, accepted the theory of delayed hominization (which is, that the soul is not implanted until the fetus is fully recognizable as human), nonetheless taught that abortion at any stage of development is a grievous sin.

The Baptist and original sin

Q. I quote from "The Prayer Book," with the imprimatur of Samuel Cardinal Stritch: "Saint John the Baptist, forerunner of the Messias, was beheaded for preaching against the immorality of Herod's marriage with Herodias. Because of the teaching that he was sanctified in his mother's womb and thus free from original sin, the Church celebrates his birthday, rather than the day of his death, as his principal feast."

Is this true?

A. No official teaching of the Church exists on this matter. However, the author of the prayer book has latched onto something: namely, that the Church does not usually celebrate a saint's date of natural birth but his or her date of birth unto eternal life. The fact that the nativity of Our Lord, Our Lady, and St. John the Baptist are commemorated liturgically is evidence of an intuition on the part of the Church that the Baptist shared a sinless birth in common with Jesus and Mary.

When the conception of Mary is discussed, the concern is to demonstrate that she was *conceived* without original sin. When people speculate about John the Baptist's freedom from original sin, it is suggested that he was *born* free from original sin but not *conceived* without it; in other words, John would have been sanctified in his mother's womb (some say this in reference to the encounter between the Baby Jesus in Mary's womb and John in Elizabeth's — cf. Lk 1:39-44). The reason for the interest in his sinless birth is related to his future role as the precursor of the Messiah.

By the way, to anticipate the question of some readers, "Why did this prayer book spell the word 'Messias,' instead of 'Messiah'?" let me note the following. Until we started using Hebrew as the starting point for translations of the Old Testament (rather than Latin or Greek), our English spellings of Hebrew names and titles reflected Latin and Greek usage, rather than Hebrew (thus, "Isaias" for "Isaiah," "Jeremias" for "Jeremiah," and so on).

The phenomenon of the stigmata

Q. Please explain stigmata. Exactly what is it? How do people who appear to have it control their bodies so that only the five particular areas are affected? How does the medical profession explain this phenomenon?

A. The stigmata is a phenomenon whereby certain individuals bear on their bodies the five sacred wounds of Jesus Christ. Sometimes these wounds are permanently visible; for other stigmatists, the wounds become visible only on certain occasions (e.g., the first Friday of the month, Good Friday, etc.). At these times, there is usually a flow of blood from the wounds, and the pain (usually both physical and psychological) experienced by Our Lord during His passion becomes that of the stigmatist.

Before declaring these manifestations to be of supernatural origin, the Church insists on extensive physical and psychological testing of the supposed stigmatist. When natural explanations are ruled out and the holiness of the person's life is clear, the Church is willing to consider the possible supernatural nature of the experience.

Many people in history appear to have been recipients of the Lord's wounds. Perhaps the most famous is St. Francis of Assisi; in modern times, Padre Pio would seem to have been the most prominent stigmatist. Such people are known for their devotion to Christ's passion, identifying with Him so much that they actually enter into those events in a very real and personal manner.

God as Father and Mother

Q. I recently attended a Mass at which the celebrant referred to God, during the eucharistic prayer, as "Father and Mother." I asked him why he did this and he sent me the enclosed list of reasons, entitled "Rationale for Naming God as Father and Mother." I sent a copy to my bishop and received the enclosed reply from his director of worship, but I wanted to know what you thought also.

A. Being as charitable as possible, I would have to say that the "rationale" is not rational. Its author does not grasp basic biblical concepts, misunderstands and misuses psychology, has a very poor command of the English language, and nowhere states by what right he can arrogate to himself the authority to change the prayers of the Mass. Such failings are not unique to the author of this memo, and that is one of the strongest arguments against arbitrary changes by self-appointed experts.

The one point I would highlight, however, is that although God is a pure Spirit in Whom there is no gender, and although there are scriptural passages which ascribe both masculine and feminine qualities to God, there is not a single indication of God's ever being addressed by any feminine title, including "Mother." If one wishes to continue in the Judeo-Christian Tradition, he or she must come to grips with that basic fact of revelation and probe its significance for our lives today. Failure to do so will find us creating a new religion not in continuity with the historic faith of either Judaism or Christianity.

With all that having been said, I am astounded at the reply you received from your diocesan liturgy office. I cannot believe that a diocesan official would ever countenance this kind of behavior, let alone asserting that he hopes "this helps in allaying any fears that may arise when Father X or any other priests or bishops may make some 'adaptations' in the wording of the eucharistic prayers."

Does Jesus forgive sins?

Q. At Mass, we pray, "Lamb of God, you take away the sins of the world. . . ." Can Jesus do this on His own, or can only the Father forgive sins?

A. Jesus and the Father are one in the unity of the Trinity. Therefore, whatever the Son does is done equally by the Father and the Holy Spirit. Where the Father is present, so too are the other Persons of the Trinity.

During Our Lord's earthly life and ministry, one of the most shocking things He did was to forgive sins, leading His detractors to accuse Him of blasphemy and arguing, "Why does this man speak that way? He is blaspheming. Who but God alone can forgive sins?" (Mk 2:7). However, as we assert in the Nicene Creed every Sunday, Jesus is "one in being with the Father" and hence capable of forgiving sins, and the Church absolves from sin in His Name.

Former priests can return

Q. There is a man in our parish who many years ago left the priesthood to get married. His wife died about two years ago. Now he wants to become a priest again. He says the local bishop won't permit it, so he's moving to another state where the bishop will allow it. Is this possible? Wouldn't permission have to come from the Pope for such a thing? Has this ever been done before? Can he become a priest again? If not, why not?

A. In general, a man who left the priesthood and married could return (under some very stringent conditions) but not usually in the diocese (or even the area) where he functioned as a priest, due to the scandal that would have been caused initially. Yes, direct permission of the Pope is necessary for the process to advance. And yes, many men have been reconciled with the Church and readmitted to the clerical state. I am told that thousands of such requests presently sit on our Holy Father's desk. The rationale for the Pope's openness is that many of these men left the priesthood in haste (in fact, were even encouraged to do so by religious superiors and bishops) and now realize that they made a tragic error. Holy Apostles Seminary in Cromwell, Conn., has a program to assist returning priests with their entry process.

By the way, he does not "become a priest again" since he never lost the priesthood but only the use of his priestly faculties.

Why the Christian Sabbath is on Sunday

Q. What are the details surrounding the decision to change the Sabbath observance to Sunday for the early Christians? Similarly, how did the apostles justify eliminating the Jewish holy days, if Jesus Himself was a Jew?

A. The early Church came to the conclusion that it was empowered to speak for Christ, under the guidance of the Holy Spirit. Thus did they decide to make several changes in religious observance, among them being the celebration of Sunday as the Lord's Day and the elimination of many of the kosher regulations of the Old Covenant. They put it this way: "It is the decision of the Holy Spirit and of us not to place on you [Gentile Christians] any burden beyond these necessities. . ." (Acts 15:28).

The justification for the switch in the Sabbath observance was very simple, namely, that the greatest event in history [the Resurrection] had occurred on the first day of the week, and thus that day should be honored accordingly. Of course, it is also good to mention that in the first years of the life of the Church (that is, before the Christians were formally excommunicated from Judaism), the disciples of Jesus went to either the synagogue or Temple on the Sabbath as usual and then celebrated the Eucharist on Sunday in their own homes. It was only after the definitive break with Judaism that the Liturgy of the Word from Jewish worship was tacked onto the front of the Eucharist, giving us the Mass as a service in two parts, as we have had it ever since.

3. SCRIPTURE

The lineage of Jesus

Q. How is Jesus the "son of David" since both Mary and Elizabeth belonged to the tribe of Levi? The Gospels give only the genealogy of Joseph, and he is of the lineage of David. Can you comment please?

A. It is Joseph who descended from the lineage of David, for sure; we have no certain data about Mary — although certain Fathers of the Church held to an oral tradition which maintained that Mary too came from the line of David. Although Joseph was merely the foster father of Jesus, or His putative father (that is, supposed to be the father of Jesus by outsiders), ancestry was traced and passed on through the father's side, even the adoptive father's.

Did Adam and Eve have daughters?

Q. I am confused. The Book of Genesis says that God created Adam and Eve. They had two sons, Cain and Abel, but did they have any daughters? How did they reproduce?

A. In the patriarchal culture of the Hebrews, very little discussion revolved around female children. And so, Genesis 4 tells us about the conception of Cain and Abel, and then later about a wife of Cain.

Presumably, the first humans had numerous children, both male and female. Genesis 5:4 specifically alludes to both sons and daughters of Adam. Furthermore, it is logical to conjecture that these children married one another, with divine blessing and protection, in order to begin and propagate the human race. We see that in the early days of the earth, polygamy was also countenanced by God for the same reason but gradually was phased out as it became unnecessary for the fulfillment of God's plan.

Dating of biblical texts

Q. All pre-Vatican II Bibles indicate that the Synoptic Gospels and Acts were written before A.D. 65. Recent Bibles give dates as late as A.D. 80. What is the reason for this change in dates?

A. Dating of biblical texts is, at best, engaging in "guesstimation" at any time. Using linguistic, historical, and archaeological evidence available, determinations are made regarding place and time of composition, as well as authorship. It should be noted that none of those questions affects the inspiration, inerrancy, or canonicity of biblical texts. Whether the Gospel of John was written in A.D. 50 or 100, it is still part of the inspired Word of God. Dating can help us appreciate the process of development which went into the writing down of God's revelation.

Differences in Bible translations

Q. I have both the Douay-Rheims Bible (DRB) and the New American Bible (NAB), and I am amazed at the differences between the two. As you know, the DRB is the English translation of the Old Latin Vulgate, which the Church has adopted as its official translation for centuries now. In studying the two translations, I have noticed numerous discrepancies between the two. Could you offer some explanation?

A. "New" is not always "improved," regardless of what the detergent commercials may tell us. Nor is "old" always superior.

I would be the last to detract from the genius of St. Jerome in producing the Latin Vulgate; his work is mind-boggling by any stretch of the imagination, but that does not mean his work was perfect. Pope Pius XII understood that very well and, therefore, called for a revision of the Vulgate to deal with inadequacies of the work. The completed edition is now available.

The Douay translation of the Scriptures was lovely and poetic; its greatest flaw, however, was that it used the Vulgate as its base — a scholarly weakness. Why? Because that made the Douay text yet another step removed from the original text. In *Divino Afflante Spiritu*, Pope Pius also indicated that future vernacular translations of the Bible should use the Hebrew or Greek texts as their points of departure. As a result, the Confraternity of Christian Doctrine edition of the Scriptures began to be translated for the United States in the late 1940s, with the project completed as the New American Bible in 1972. The New Testament of that version was, in turn, refinished in 1986.

Who made Paul an Apostle?

Q. Where in Scripture does it indicate that Paul was proclaimed an Apostle? We know he is referred to as such, but did he take the title for himself? If so, when and where did this first occur? If he didn't, who gave him the title of Apostle?

A. St. Paul refers to himself as an Apostle on more than a dozen occasions in the New Testament (for example, Rom 1:1; 1 Cor 1:1; 1 Cor 9:1; 2 Cor 1:1; Gal 1:1). He also spoke of himself as the "Apostle to the Gentiles" (Rom 11:13). He admits that he was one born out of the normal course of events but links his apostolic identity to the special call of the Lord to him on the road to Damascus, citing a special revelation from the Jesus Whom he was persecuting as he harassed the Church of God.

In this, however, we should not see Pauline lust for power and prestige. On the contrary, Paul would have thought of this as part of the divine revelation of his identity and mission.

The miracles of Jesus

Q. I have heard homilies that questioned the miracles of Jesus — for example, saying that He did not really multiply the loaves and fishes to feed the multitude, but merely convinced them to share with one another the food they had brought with them. Can you tell me where these strange ideas originated and whether or not the Magisterium has made any official pronouncements regarding them?

A. A lot of this is rehashed '60s nonsense. The example you cite, for instance, I heard back in high school from a nun (who not long afterward left religious life) who had just come back from one of those summer sessions trying to make theologians out of everyone in six short weeks. The man responsible for that particular piece of biblical demythologizing was a French priest by the name of Louis Evely.

When the nun gave this explanation for the multiplication of the loaves and fishes, I blurted out that if that was indeed what happened, then getting the people to share was an even greater miracle than multiplying the loaves and fishes! My speaking out of turn caused her no small amount of embarrassment and got me a detention!

Seriously, however, after the Enlightenment in the eighteenth century, miracles began to be questioned, especially in liberal Protestant circles, slowly but surely catching among some Catholics, too. To deny the possibility of miracles is to deny the omnipotence of God, arrogantly asserting that if man can't do such things, neither can God. Or as the philosopher Voltaire wittily put it, "God made man in His own image and likeness, and man has never ceased to return the compliment!"

Now, it is important to observe that the Church does not look for miracles all over the landscape, either now or in biblical times, generally seeking much simpler, human explanations for events first. But neither is she averse to accepting divine interventions into human affairs, then or now.

Finally, the miracles of Christ were, according to the Evangelists (and St. John in particular,) His "calling cards," declaring His identity as the Son of God. This point is made in a very important document of the Holy See issued in 1964. "On the Historical Truth of the Gospels," which I would recommend most highly, available from the Daughters of St. Paul (50 St. Paul's Ave., Boston, MA 02130).

Gentiles

Q. Why are Christians called Gentiles? I read that "Gentile" means "pagan," and I don't consider myself a pagan.

A. "Gentile" comes from the Latin word "gens," which means "nation." The ancient Jews, inasmuch as they were a wandering people and not a nation, referred to the other peoples of the world as "the nations" or "the Gentiles." To this day, that designation has stuck as the world, at least from a Jewish perspective, is made up of the Jews, or the Chosen People, and the Gentiles. Coincidentally, before the beginnings of Christianity, all Gentiles were also pagan; hence, the connection or the thought, in the minds of some, that "Gentile" and "pagan" are equivalent.

Christmas prayer of the angels

Q. As this Christmas season passed, I was struck again by the difference between the two versions of the prayer of the angels: "Glory to God in the highest, good will toward men" and "Glory to God in the highest and peace to men of goodwill." Which is correct?

A. The line in question, of course, comes from the Gospel account of the angels' visitation to the shepherds. The revised New Testament of the New American Bible puts it this way: "Glory to God in the highest and on earth peace to those on whom his favor rests" (Luke 2:14). As you suggest, there is a big difference between the two renderings. What I have quoted reflects the second of your citations, while the first of yours is based on the King James version, which is, in this instance (as in many others), inaccurate.

The New American Bible is translated into English from the original languages of either Hebrew or Greek. Although some people object to its lack of poetry, few would question its accuracy. And the recent revision is greatly improved on both counts, as well.

To explain very briefly the difference between the two translations of that familiar Christmas text, let me say that "peace on earth to men of goodwill" calls for God's peace to be granted to those who are disposed to receiving it, while the other version suggests some kind of external imposition of a fond hope for peace on people who may or may not even be interested. After all, God's peace can only become a reality in human affairs when people take seriously God's will and law in their daily lives; any lesser peace is not really peace.

Discrepancies in Bible versions

Q. In my 1957 edition of the Bible (Confraternity-Douay Version), the Old Testament passage from Tobias 6:17-22 contains beautiful teachings regarding sex in marriage, especially verse 22. In the New American Bible all those teachings have been eliminated, and only the burning of the fish's liver has been retained. Why is there such a major discrepancy between the two translations?

Also, I have always heard that it was the woman, Mary, who would crush the head of the serpent. Even the statues of Mary showed this. Yet both of my Catholic Bibles read: "He shall crush your head. . ." (Gen 3:15b). Was this verse always translated "he" or was it at one time translated "she"?

A. Several passages in the Wisdom Literature of the Old Testament have been disputed for years, and it appears that the editors of the New American version opted to exclude these verses from their work.

In regard to your second question, you are correct in noting that frequently in the past it was suggested that Mary would crush the head of the serpent (surely that is the image on the Miraculous Medal). A better understanding of the Hebrew text, however, leads to the conclusion that it is the seed of the woman and not the woman herself who will crush Satan's head.

Events of Jesus' 'hidden life'

Q. I have been reading many fascinating facts about St. Joseph, Our Lady, and the Infant Jesus in various devotional books. In what works are these events recorded? Why do we never hear about any of this at Mass?

A. Sometimes information like this comes from the apocryphal gospels, that is, those works attributed to various ancient (and even apostolic) authors but never accepted by the Church as canonical. At other times, certain visionaries have claimed to obtain particular revelations about the infancy of Our Lord or His Blessed Mother. None of this is reliable, although much of it has found its way into popular piety over the centuries. It is not an accident that we generally refer to the period of Our Lord's life between the ages of twelve and thirty as His "hidden life." I see no reason why we have to try to discover more than the Holy Spirit deemed necessary for our salvation.

However, if nothing in those works contradicts the doctrine of the Faith, then one can use the material for private prayer and meditation, if one finds it helpful.

Jewish dietary regulations

Q. Several passages in the Scriptures seem to forbid us to eat or cook with the blood of animals. I am anxious about this, as a favorite delicacy of mine, traditional in my culture, has blood as an ingredient. Is this a problem?

A. The Jewish dietary regulations (kosher laws) were extremely important under the Old Covenant, and still are for observant Jews today. However, very early in the Church's history, the apostolic community faced this issue and decided that such customs were not at the heart of the Christian life and that, in fact, Christ had freed us from most of those laws (cf. Acts 15). That initial position was modified even further by St. Paul in such noteworthy epistles as those to the Galatians and Romans.

Imprimaturs and explanatory notes

Q. What is the formal position of the Church regarding the footnotes and introductory matter in the different Catholic translations of the Scriptures? Much of the revised material in the St. Joseph Edition of the New American Bible appears contrary to traditional teachings.

A. When a bishop grants an imprimatur to a new translation of the Bible, it extends to the explanatory notes and other study aids in the volume, not just to the translation proper. I use the edition that you question, and I must say I have never found anything problematic in it. Unless you can cite specifics, I would not be in a position to give you an answer.

Warning against lukewarm faith

Q. Did Jesus ever state that "either you are with me or you are against me?" If so, where can I find this statement?

A. You are probably thinking of the verse: "Who ever is not with me is against me," which appears in Matthew 12:30 and has a parallel in Luke 11:23. The point of the verse, of course, is Christ's call for people to take a stand for or against Him, similar to the Book of Revelation's condemnation of the lukewarm, whom Jesus will vomit out of His mouth (cf. Rv 3:16).

Judaism and the afterlife

Q. In 2 Maccabees 12:42-46, we read about prayers for the dead and offering sacrifices for them. Was that customary in Judaism, and is that practice retained in contemporary Judaism?

A. You may recall that Judaism, even in the time of Jesus, was divided on the whole question of the resurrection of the dead. If one did not believe in a life after death, obviously prayers for the dead would make no sense. However, the school of thought that did hold for an afterlife (reflected in many passages in the wisdom literature of the Hebrew Scriptures) likewise prayed for the happy repose of the dead.

A similar division over this matter exists in contemporary Judaism, with the Orthodox believing in life after death and the attendant necessity of praying for the purification of the dead so that they might enter into eternal bliss. The common practice is to pray the "Mourner's Kaddish" for a deceased relative or friend for eleven months, the time assigned in Jewish tradition for final purification. As one can readily see, this corresponds totally with the Church's teachings on the same topics, or actually vice versa.

Christians and biblical curses

Q. The New Testament says Christians should not curse anyone, but the Book of Psalms has many curses in it. Please comment.

A. This is a very good question. The Church has traditionally had difficulty with many of the so-called "cursing" or "imprecatory" psalms, which is one reason why many of them were removed from the Liturgy of the Hours when the Divine Office was revised, or at least had the more problematic sections deleted for liturgical use.

How do I look at these texts? First, the psalms convey the very depths of human and religious emotion. Hence, one should not be surprised to find passages which are, at times, more human than profoundly religious. Second, the psalms were composed by individuals living hundreds of years before Christ. The fact that we find their sentiments unacceptable today is an indication of how far the Gospel has moved us from our forefathers in the faith of Abraham.

Can a Christian pray lines that ask that the children of one's enemies have their skulls smashed against the rocks (cf. Ps 137:9)? Perhaps the best way to do so is to thank Almighty God for the gift of His Son, Who taught us and indeed commanded us to love all, even our enemies.

The Bible and future events

Q. What exactly is the value to be attached to the Bible as a predictor of future events?

A. If the Bible is the Word of God and if past, present, and future are equally present to God, then predictions of future events would be no difficulty either for God or for His Word. At the same time, it is important to remember that interpreting the Sacred Scriptures needs to be done according to some basic principles. Therefore, it is necessary to determine the type of literature one is reading. Hence, the genre of literature (poetry, history, sermon, narrative, and so on) will dictate the fundamental stance one takes in approaching a particular passage.

People tend to get themselves into problems with the Bible when they read certain pericopes in isolation from the rest of the Scriptures or when they try to get the Word of God to do things it was not intended to do. Obsession with predictions about the future is a preoccupation of people in every age as they seek to eliminate the uncertainties of life on earth by claiming to have divine guarantees (or at least, indicators) of what is coming.

The Bible exists far more to tell us how to live in the present than it does to inform us about the future. Both Our Lord and St. Paul had to challenge people to be less concerned with what's on the horizon and when "everything" would happen and instead to concentrate on living the Gospel with conviction and enthusiasm.

In short, while we accept the fact that the Word of God can transmit information about the future, we also acknowledge the fact that this is not its primary purpose, and thus it should not be a priority for us, either.

List of prophecies concerning Jesus

Q. Jesus was the only founder of a religion Who was preannounced. Can you tell me how I can find a complete list of all the prophecies that deal with His coming?

A. Archbishop Fulton Sheen has a wonderful talk on this topic. I am unaware of any single place in which such prophecies are assembled; however, St. Matthew's Gospel quotes the Hebrew prophets as foretellers of Jesus' coming on dozens of occasions. St. Paul in Acts invites his Jewish hearers to search the Scriptures for the truth of his claims that Jesus is truly the Messiah of God. Following up on that lead, Jews for Jesus today have many booklets dealing with that theme.

Which translation of the Bible?

Q. When one is choosing a translation of the Bible, are there any guidelines to follow, or critical characteristics to be known, or scholarly reviews available? I know there is no "perfect" translation, nor one Bible suitable for everyone's needs or abilities. But because there are so many translations available, a layperson like myself needs some assistance in choosing.

As far as I know, the following translations are approved for Catholics: New American Bible (1970); NAB, with revised New Testament (1986); Jerusalem Bible (1970); New Jerusalem Bible; New English Bible (1970); Revised English Bible (1989); Revised Standard Version (1952), with New Testament (1971); New Revised Standard Version (1989); Good News Bible, Today's English Version (1976).

Also, is the NAB Old Testament being revised?

A. You certainly know your English translations of the Bible! To take your last question first, I am not aware of any move to retranslate the Old Testament of the NAB, probably because most people seem rather satisfied with it as it is.

My favorite English translation is the Revised Standard Version — even though I rarely use it for teaching and the like, the reason being that the New American Bible is most frequently used in parishes for the liturgy. Therefore, I try to maintain some consistency for students. I like the RSV because it combines accuracy with felicity of expression. The New American Bible with the revised New Testament is a rather accurate translation, but it lacks a poetic quality (but it is far superior, in my opinion, to the earlier edition). The Jerusalem Bible has excellent study notes, but its weakness resides in the fact that it is a translation of a translation, that is, a rendering from the French, rather than from the original Hebrew and Greek.

One edition you missed is the Navarre Bible, available from Scepter Press, which I have reviewed in TCA on occasion. The text is RSV, with some of the finest study notes I have ever encountered.

I should also highlight the point you made, namely, that no translation is ever perfect because of the difficulties inherent in the process. That does not mean, however, that we should not strive to produce as nearly perfect a product as possible, nor continue to seek out the best translation on the market.

What is the Rapture?

Q. Recently, a friend mentioned "rapture." I asked her what that is, and she said I should read the Book of Revelation, but I see nothing in there about rapture. Could you explain?

A. Some Protestant denominations, particularly those of a more fundamentalistic stripe, have very carefully worked-out theories of what will happen at the end of time and/or at Christ's Second Coming. Truth to tell, most of them end up contradicting one another, precisely because the scriptural evidence for their positions is rather weak. Some maintain that the Lord will come again and take the elect (the Rapture) to the kingdom, where they will reign for a thousand years (millenialism). Others hold for the Parousia (the Greek word for the Second Coming) to be followed immediately by the end of the world and the final judgment.

I find it difficult to get excited about these various theories for at least two reasons. First of all, Jesus Himself said that these things would not be known to men. Second, He urged people to be prepared to meet Him whenever He should come. That second point should be the priority of our lives, not trying to second-guess God on mere trivial mathematical calculations. For a scriptural example of the ambiguity on this matter, let me refer you to a passage like 1 Thessalonians 4:16f; but then read on into the fifth chapter's first three verses!

God as 'Mother' in Scripture

Q. Father, where in the Scriptures is God described with "feminine" qualities, as your response in [a recent] issue of TCA seems to suggest?

A. Several times the prophets speak of God's love as the love of a mother (cf. Is 49:15; Is 66:13). In St. Matthew's Gospel, Jesus compares His concern for Jerusalem to that of a mother hen (cf.23:37).

As I recall my point at that time, it was very simply that: (a) God has no gender, masculine or feminine; (b) humans need to talk about God in human terms, so as to be comprehensible, and that necessarily means positing sexuality of God in speech — always with the understanding that this is mere metaphor; (c) while the Scriptures speak of God as having both female and male characteristics, the Bible never once calls God "Mother" or "Her," while it does regularly refer to God as "Father" and "Him"; (d) Jesus clearly instructed His disciples to invoke God as "Father."

My position, then, is somewhat nuanced in this regard, in an effort to do justice to the biblical data which provides us with divine revelation. Put starkly, we cannot say either more or less than the Word of God does on this matter.

The Immaculate Conception

Q. How does the Church justify the doctrine of the Immaculate Conception in light of Paul's statement in Romans 8:12?

A. The doctrine of the Immaculate Conception of Mary holds that no stain of Adam's sin touched the Blessed Virgin. That says something about Mary, to be sure, but it points in two other directions as well. First, it says that this privilege accorded to her was in virtue of her role as Mother of the Messiah, in order to make her a worthy dwelling for Him. Second, it is a reminder that through Christ's redeeming death and resurrection, all believers have the stain of original sin washed from their souls in the waters of Baptism.

Fundamentalists become nervous with this doctrine because they think it removes Mary from the rest of humanity and raises her to the level of a goddess. They point to the fact that in her Magnificat Mary sings of "God my Savior" (Lk 1:47), thus implicitly acknowledging her own need for redemption. Catholic theology explains this by asserting that Mary was indeed redeemed by God through "prevenient grace." This term of scholastic theology simply means that God spared Mary from sin, crediting to her in advance the benefits of her Son's redemptive sacrifice, so that she could sinlessly bear the sinless Son of God.

It is important to remember that the concept of time is a human construct and that God lives in an eternal present. Therefore, what sounds so strange to us is, in fact, not at all strange for Him. To deny this possibility is to limit the power of God.

Jesus and disciples spoke Aramaic

Q. Where can I find historic confirmation that Jesus and His disciples spoke Aramaic? This is important since it relates to Jesus' calling Simon "Kephas."
A. Any standard encyclopedia will indicate that the common language of Jews in Palestine at the time of Our Lord was Aramaic and that Hebrew was reserved for Scripture and liturgy.

You are correct that it is helpful to know that Jesus spoke Aramaic in regard to the passage in Matthew in which Jesus names Simon "Kephas"; the pun is complete in Aramaic but slightly less so in Greek. Nevertheless, Catholics do not deal with doctrinal matters exclusively from Scripture, although Fundamentalists might wish us to do so; that approach was a novelty of the sixteenth century.

Protestants and Bible interpretation

Q. Private interpretation of Scripture has always been a hallmark of Protestantism. How can Fundamentalists proclaim a literal interpretation of the Bible and also advocate private interpretation?
A. The contradiction you mention is very real and became recognizable even to Martin Luther. After a short time, Luther saw that unqualified people were trying to place their judgment on a par with his, which development he found quite unacceptable. Their logic was flawless, however: "If you can place your interpretation of Scripture over that of the Pope and the entire Christian Tradition of sixteen centuries, then why can't we question you?"

In reality, Fundamentalism in particular leaves very little room for private interpretation of Scripture. For instance, if someone said that he believes the passages in St. John's Gospel on the Eucharist teach the doctrine of transubstantiation, I don't think that interpretation would be tolerated. Nor is there as much literalism as we are led to imagine. If there were, how could Bible-believing, literal interpreters practice divorce and remarriage or not believe in Christ's Real Presence in the Eucharist?

The Constitution on Divine Revelation of Vatican II makes clear that a good reading of Sacred Scripture requires a believer to take into account not only the text and context, but also how the Church's

Tradition and Magisterium have understood a particular passage throughout the ages.

A creature of both body and soul

Q. For one who suffers from the translation of the New American Bible (its triteness turns me off), I offer this translation to prove my point: Douay-Rheims version: For what shall it profit a man, if he gains the whole world, and suffer the loss of his soul? (Mt 16:26); New American Bible: What profit would there be for one to gain the whole world and forfeit his life?

Is there not a big difference between "soul" and "life"? Isn't there a concerted effort to do away with the use of the word "soul," thus subtly undermining the absolute truth of man as a creature composed of body and soul?

A. Yes, there is a difference in meaning, but I think in this instance the New American Bible is closer to the truth. Let me explain.

Of course, man is composed of body and soul. Unfortunately, at times in our past, some people so tried to stress the "soul" of man as the seat of intelligence, will, etc., that a kind of dichotomy was created in the human person that was much more in keeping with Plato's philosophy than with Aristotle or the biblical view of man. The Hebrews likewise regarded human beings as composed of body and soul, but it was a body/soul unity. Today there is an effort (quite legitimate) to recapture that lost unity.

For my own translation of that passage, I would probably have used "self," instead of "life". Why? "Self" implies the totality of the person, body and soul, while "life" can sound as though it is limited to the natural or temporal spheres of existence.

While we cannot abandon the use of the concept or word "soul" and still be faithful to biblical revelation, we must be careful that we do not imagine that we must save only our "soul," as though we are Platonic, disembodied spirits. To be fully human, man requires both body and soul. When Christ came back from dead, He had a body as well as a soul. Mary, the Assumed One, has a body and a soul, as shall we after the general judgment.

'The land of milk and honey'

Q. What is meant by "the land of milk and honey"?

A. The expression is found in Scripture dozens of times, especially in the Pentateuch. It signifies a garden of earthly delights, that is, the Promised Land.

John the Baptist

Q. In our Bible-study group, we are going through the Gospel of Matthew. Today we had a question we couldn't resolve: How is the least born into the kingdom of heaven greater than John the Baptist (cf. Matthew 11:11)?

A. I am sure you realize that the Church does not pronounce definitively on the meaning of every verse of Scripture; as a matter of fact, she has done so in fewer than a dozen instances. Therefore, there is no official interpretation of the passage you cite. So I would only offer my own.

I think St. Matthew is saying that as great as John the Baptist was, anyone born into the Kingdom of Christ through Baptism is even greater than he. Why? Because through that sacrament, a person is born again through water and the Holy Spirit, freed from original sin, incorporated into Christ's paschal mystery, and equally made a member of His Church, His Body, which participates in the Kingdom in a unique manner. The verse, then, seems to be a statement more about the dignity of a Christian than about John the Baptist himself.

4. MORALITY

Anti-Christian music

Q. *I serve as a disc jockey at our high-school dances. Sometimes I'm asked to play music which I think is anti-Christian. How should I handle the situation?*

A. If that's your impression and you think it's justified, then you should take the appropriate action, which I would see as the following: Refuse to play such music, and then explain to your classmates your rationale. Surely you don't have to be nasty, judgmental, or abrasive; however, witnessing to the meaning of the Gospel in your life is both your right and obligation. Perhaps your honest and strong stand will lead at least some of your peers to consider what life in Christ is all about. Good luck!

Sunday obligation

Q. *Does watching Mass on television fulfill one's Sunday obligation? Is actual physical presence necessary?*

A. If someone is seriously ill and housebound, that person has no obligation to attend Sunday Mass. The television Mass, then, does not fulfill the obligation because there is none.

Without the excusing situation of sickness, all Catholics are bound under pain of serious sin to participate in Sunday Mass. Yes, that means physical presence; if a person cannot get into the church building (because of a large crowd, for instance), then one must be able at least to hear the prayers of the Mass and respond.

Couple receives bad advice

Q. *My niece is contemplating marriage in the near future. This would be her first marriage; her intended husband was married before. Neither was baptized.*

They have been advised by two priests to go ahead with the civil marriage and not wait for the Church annulment, which might take some time.

Is this permitted by the Church? Isn't this a serious sin?

A. I can't imagine a priest counseling people to live in sin. Furthermore, how does anyone know whether or not a decree of nullity will be forthcoming? Suppose no grounds are found, and the previous marriage bond remains intact? The advice your niece has received is imprudent at best and immoral at worst.

All priests must pray the Office

Q. Are priests still obliged to pray the Divine Office? I never see them with their breviaries anymore.

A. Yes, all priests and transitional deacons are bound to recite the Divine Office or Liturgy of the Hours each day. A very fine memorandum drafted by a canonist in the Diocese of Boise has come to my attention. Therein is outlined the importance of this obligation, from both a moral and canonical point of view, relying on documents like Vatican II's *Sacrosanctum Concilium*, the General Instruction of the Liturgy of the Hours, and the Code of Canon Law.

I would summarize the obligation thus: Morning and Evening Prayer (Lauds and Vespers) maintain the same degree of seriousness for a cleric as does the Sunday Mass obligation for all the faithful. The Office of Readings should be recited "faithfully" (secondary importance). Daytime and Night Prayer are to be "treasured" and are of tertiary significance.

It is unfortunate that people remark that they no longer see their priests praying in this way since, as a boy, I always found it both a source of edification and an impetus to personal prayer. I cannot think of a prayer form (except for the Mass) which could hold greater meaning for any Christian, clerical or lay. A truly commendable trend in some parishes is the communal celebration of Morning and/or Evening Prayer, making the Liturgy of the Hours once more available to the whole People of God. But one cannot underestimate the importance of the priest and deacon fulfilling their roles as the intercessors of and for the Church, by virtue of their sacramental ordination and their intimate connection with the sacred liturgy, which is the primary source of all intercession before Almighty God.

Boy Scouts arrange religious services

Q. My oldest son has joined the Boy Scouts, and he is very anxious to go on camp-outs on the weekends. But that would cause him to miss Sunday Mass. What should I do?

A. Unless the Boy Scouts have changed either their attitude or policy since I was a seminarian working for them, the troop leader should be making arrangements for them to participate in Sunday worship. Given the stated philosophy of the organization, everything should be done to foster a life of faith in the boys. I think you should have a talk with the scoutmaster. After all, there is no need to have a boy choose between God and a good time.

Daddy doesn't go to church

Q. My husband was raised Catholic but feels agnostic is a better description of his "faith." What should I say to our three- and five-year-old boys when they ask why daddy doesn't go to church?

A. When you think the boys are old enough to understand the situation, present it frankly and charitably. They should not be made to think less of their father, but certainly should be urged to pray for him to receive the gift of faith, with the reminder that since faith is a gift for all people, we are all in danger of losing it. Therefore, we need to be grateful and vigilant in guarding it.

Sunday obligation is not optional

Q. Can one make an arbitrary choice of a day other than Sunday to fulfill one's Mass obligation. I don't mean because of sickness or work, but simply so that the family can go on a trip, for example. A friend says a Franciscan nun told her this was perfectly acceptable.

A. No, it is not. Sunday is the Lord's Day and no other. When personal convenience takes precedence over the observance of God's commandments, then something is seriously amiss in one's living of the Christian life.

If a person cannot make Sunday Mass because of illness or necessary work, that person has no Sunday Mass obligation. Therefore, it is not correct to say that the obligation is shifted to another day. Out of personal devotion or a desire to worship the Lord through the celebration of the Eucharist at least once a week, one may decide to attend Mass on some other day, but not due to an obligation.

Racism still exists in our culture

Q. Will the Church marry a black/white couple?

A. Surely. The Church has no problem with interracial marriages. The only consideration that is important, it seems to me, is for the couple to reflect seriously on the difficulties facing them and any children, due to the racist sentiments still so strong in our culture. My own experience with children of such marriages is that they generally suffer from nonacceptance by both sides of the family. Very sad, but nonetheless true. Needless to say, all of this puts an additional strain on the marital relationship, requiring extraordinary strength on the part of both spouses.

Ecology: a Christian concern

Q. Recently, my son, who attends a Catholic school, brought home a flyer about selling trees as a part of "Greening the Garden State." The newsletter explains the ecological value of planting the trees. It seems to me we should be more involved in saving people, instead of saving the earth. Does this program seem rather "New Age"?

A. I have read the materials over and see no problems. When God gave the earth into the care of man, it was to be the custodian of this planet. Hence, ecology is a genuine Christian concern.

Now, I grant you, some people take this to an extreme and some quite illogically are more interested in saving seals from being made into coats than saving babies from abortionists. Intelligent and committed Christians, however, do not view this as an either/or situation. Starting with the Holy Father himself, they regard it as the obligation and privilege of Catholics to be actively involved in making the earth a better place for all God's creatures, but especially for man, the pinnacle of His creation.

OK to use new drug?

Q. What is the moral teaching of the Church regarding certain new drugs used in the treatment of impotence? The one in question is self-injected into the male organ and produces a prolonged erection. Is it morally permissible to use this drug?

A. I would see no difficulty in what you describe since it is simply designed to remedy a natural defect. Not being familiar with the drug, I would not be able to say anything more. Perhaps a physician-reader could advise me of any possible medical or moral problems that I have not detected.

Sorrow for past sins

Q. When I was a young girl, I committed some grave sins — fornication and procuring two abortions. I was not a Catholic at the time. Once in my thirties, I married the man involved, and we have been blessed with two beautiful children. I am overcome with sorrow for my past sins. My husband was raised a Catholic, and after prayerful consideration I decided to convert.

Before my Confirmation and First Holy Communion, the priest told me to make my first confession. I asked him if I was to confess everything I had done in my life until this time. He said I should only confess what I had done from the time I began my process of converting to the Church. Was this correct? Is there any way that I can make some kind of restitution for my past sinfulness? With such a past, do I even deserve to be a member of the Catholic Church? Finally, am I correct in praying for the souls of my (two aborted) babies?

A. I presume you had been baptized in some Protestant denomination, which is why you do not mention a Catholic baptism. If you had not been baptized earlier, you would have been baptized, and all sin (both original and actual) would have been removed at that time, enabling you to start with a clean slate. Why the priest told you to confess only those sins committed since a certain point in time, I cannot understand.

The simplest thing to do now is to go to confession, tell the priest the situation, indicating your spirit of repentance and your desire to perform some act of penance for those sins. I am sure a local priest would be very helpful and set your conscience at ease. Incidentally, no one is worthy of the grace of being a member of Christ's Church, so just thank God most humbly for the grace.

And, yes, by all means do pray for your aborted babies. Perhaps you should even pray *to* them, especially for the elimination of abortion throughout the world.

A critical distinction

Q. Is it acceptable (or even consistent) to be in favor of capital punishment in certain situations and at the same time admit to no circumstances that would make abortion morally licit?

A. Christian theology has always distinguished between innocent human life (which must always be protected from unjust aggression) and non-innocent human life (whose right to life can be forfeited for the common good). Therefore, the distinction is critical and primary. Once that difference is observed, however, the Church — especially in recent decades and beginning with Pope John Paul II himself — has expressed an uneasiness with capital punishment for several reasons: It has never been proven that it is a true deterrent; even one wrongful execution is too much and irremediable; the penalty seems to fall most often on those with little money or influence; in our contemporary climate of violence and revenge, capital punishment fans those already hateful flames.

And so, while I argue that the state has a general right to use capital punishment, I also argue against its use, preferring lifelong imprisonment (in real jails, not country clubs), always holding out for the hope of rehabilitation.

Operation Rescue

Q. We often see on television news footage of protesters being arrested for blocking access to abortion clinics. I agree that Catholics should openly express their opposition to abortion, but I have a problem with those who decide to break the law to make their feelings known. How far should we go in showing that we abhor the crime of abortion?

A. Let's deal with the moral issue first. The entire Christian Tradition of morality teaches us that an immoral law is not binding on the consciences of believers, and that it should be resisted in the most effective ways possible. Hence, if we do not think that women "have a right to choose" in reference to the killing of their unborn children, then we certainly do not believe that people have a right to run abortion clinics, either. And so, the question of interfering with a legitimate business is a bogus issue. In other words, according to an informed Catholic conscience, people have no more right to abort their babies or to operate clinics for that purpose than did Hitler have the right to set up death camps for the extermination of Jews and other innocent victims. With that understanding in place, we can now move on to the second phase of the question, namely, the matter of prudence or effectiveness.

Once people agree, for instance, that individuals trapped inside a burning house should be rescued, they need to decide on the most appropriate course of action. Even skilled fire fighters will disagree among themselves at times, but the goal is clear and absolute. In many ways, that is how committed pro-lifers face the enormous task of removing the scourge of abortion from our land.

The project is massive and needs to be mounted on a variety of fronts: legal, political, social, psychological, public relations. Therefore, not every person can or should be involved in every aspect of pro-life work. In fact, one could make a good case for having experts in various fields develop their competencies by restricting themselves to a particular sphere of action.

So, should all Catholics support Operation Rescue? Surely, no Catholic can say that what they are doing is immoral, even though one may say that OR's approach is not for him or, in one's personal judgment, may be counterproductive. But no Catholic need be directly active in such a movement.

Let me go on to be more personal. While I thoroughly endorse all efforts to save unborn lives, I am not called to participate in all of them. I pray each day for the reversal of *Roe vs. Wade* (the 1973 Supreme Court decision legalizing abortion), and I make sure to include petitions in the Prayer of the Faithful for that intention. I preach about the immorality of abortion and of the necessity for Catholics to be pro-life in their private judgments and public conduct, including the use of their vote. I give public witness to my position by marching and by speaking out on the topic whenever given the forum. I do not, however, participate in the blocking of clinics — even while applauding others who do.

A good book on Operation Rescue has just been published by Our Sunday Visitor: Philip Lawler's *Operation Rescue: A Challenge to the Nation's Conscience* (200 Noll Plaza, Huntington, IN 46750, $5.95, plus $3.95 for shipping and handling). I recommend it most highly, not only to understand the goals of the movement but also to come to grips with the fierce bigotry and hypocrisy of so many of OR's opponents, who are usually also the enemies of the Catholic Church.

Money and conscience

Q. Is it sinful to invest in a mutual fund whose holdings include pharmaceutical companies which make contraceptives and abortifacients? I have such investments and never thought about that possibility until recently when I examined a list of the drug companies the fund invested in. Does such an investment cause me to cooperate in the evils of contraception and abortion? Please give some advice.
A. I think your developed conscience has already answered the question for you. Obviously, we cannot distance ourselves from our money, allowing it to work for our good, all the while engaged in evil. That would be no different from a priest accepting money from a syndicate boss, alleging that he doesn't really know how the man got

all his money and not being honest enough to say that he doesn't really want to know, lest he be put in the embarrassing situation of accepting tainted money.

Determining morality of an act

Q. All my life I have been taught that sin is always committed in the will. The primary determinant of morality must be the motive, not the act itself (cf. Mt 5:28). Why is every sin committed in the will, except birth control? A married couple can agree to practice birth control, but it only becomes a sin in the act — artificial instead of natural contraception. I know I'm missing something. Can you please clarify this teaching?

A. Surely, the will is critically important in determining the morality or immorality of an act, but it is not the sole determinant. Undoubtedly, you remember the three criteria learned in grammar school in this regard: serious matter, full knowlege, full consent. Let's take a look at each one.

First, certain acts are, by their very nature, immoral because they completely distort the plan of God as revealed in nature. Murder, for example, is the unjust taking of innocent human life; no exception to this norm is possible. Artificial birth control falls under a similar prohibition. Why? Because the very act of marital intercourse is structured so as to fulfill a twofold goal: procreation and expression of love; for the act to be moral (that is, in keeping with the divine plan), neirher goal can be deliberately excluded (which is where the will comes in, by the way). Thus, some acts are immoral right from the start.

Second, one must be fully aware of God's law forbidding a particular action. Sometimes people do not know because they have never been taught, or a teaching has not been fully or properly explained to them. In those circumstances, they are invincibly ignorant: that is, their lack of knowledge is not their own fault. At other moments, people do not know about an act's immoralitiy because they have refused to become informed or have not had sufficent interest to do so; their ignorance is culpable.

Third, one must hive full consent to the evil act, knowing that it is seriously wrong and still consciously choosing to perform it. Responding to undue pressure takes away guilt very often. For instance, robbing a bank because a pistol is pointed to your head is not a free act and, hence, not sinful.

Some acts have their morality changed by circumstances, while others do not. Eating apple pie is a morally neutral act. For a diabetic to eat apple pie, knowing the serious consequences of the action, would be sinful. For a person to eat a whole pie by himself would be the sin of gluttony, while eating to the point of vomiting would be gluttony plus responsibility for harming one's health in a concrete way.

Therefore, all three conditions must be met for an act to be gravely, or mortally, sinful; while this is not easy to occur, it is possible. In regard to your specific concerns about artificial contraception and why it would be always and under all circumstances gravely wrong, I would refer you to earlier TCA columns that have dealt with that topic in some depth, as well as the distinction between natural family planning and artificial birth control.

Original sin and nudity

Q. Does the shame regarding nudity come to us as a result of the sin of Adam and Eve? I feel that attitudes toward modesty and nudity are learned cultural behavior.

A. Although there is no clear and absolute teaching of the Church on this issue, there is a rather constant position that shame is indeed a result of the original sin. In some sense, shame is a divine gift because it can keep us from following our now disordered human appetites into serious sin. I do not deny, however, that some aspects of modesty or approaches to it are cultural.

Temptation is not sinning

Q. In [a recent] issue of The Catholic Answer, the statement was made that "the Church does not teach that a sexual orientation is evil; instead, the question to be raised is what is done with one's sexuality." I thought the Church and Scripture teach that you can commit a mortal sin by thinking or desiring anything against the law of God. How could a homosexual ever be a priest when he knows in his heart that he would want to make love with his own sex?

A. Several areas of confusion seem to be present in your question.

First, we must not confuse temptation with either lusting or coveting. For example, even our sinless Lord was tempted. Lusting or coveting, on the other hand, is a deliberate or conscious craving after what is forbidden by the Law of God, involving the active cultivation of temptation by placing oneself in potentially sinful surroundings or by refusing to banish evil thoughts.

Second, you presume that all people with a homosexual orientation desire to have illicit sexual relations, which is not at all true. If you were correct, we would have to make the same basic statement about persons who are heterosexually oriented, too. No evidence, psychological or otherwise, exists to show that homosexuality makes an individual more inclined to act out his orientation than anyone else.

Third, a priest (because he is a human being) has sex drives like everyone else; whether they are directed toward the opposite or same sex, they must be kept within the bounds of chastity for all. A priest, then, as one who is unmarried, may not engage in any sexual/genital activity, which would violate the Sixth and Ninth Commandments, not just because he is a priest but because that is the Law of God binding on all people. In other words, an unmarried priest and an unmarried layman are held to the same observance of chastity because they are unmarried. Granted, a priest who sins against chastity commits an additional sin because he also goes against a solemn and public promise and, should his sin become known to others, would also result in the sin of scandal.

Annulments and legitimacy
Q. If a person gets an annulment, does that make the child a bastard?
A. No, it does not make children born of the union illegitimate because they are the fruit of what is legally (both civilly and canonically) known as a "putative marriage," that is, one that was entered in good faith and had all the appearances of a real marriage.

Man-made laws and mortal sin
Q. Years ago it was a serious sin for a Catholic to eat meat on Fridays. As a man-made law, it was changeable, and that happened. What happened, however, to all those souls who might have gone to hell for having committed what used to be a mortal sin but no longer is?
A. Let us presume that a Catholic from forty years ago had indeed fulfilled all three requirements for having committed a mortal sin (serious matter, sufficient reflection, full consent) by eating meat on Fridays. Why should one imagine that, for some reason or other, he should be released from hell because the law is now different? Let's examine this carefully.

In civil law, if someone were to run a stop sign and be penalized with a fine and with points on his driving record, but the stop sign were removed the following year, would one expect the fine to be returned and the points removed? I don't think so. Why? Because the person, knowing full well what the penalty was, still committed the crime, implicitly accepting the consequences of his action. Similarly, if someone knew how seriously the Church regarded the Friday abstinence law and yet deliberately violated it, he was saying (in essence) that he did not care whether or not God was offended by his action and would not worry about the results. Remember: Sins are not committed simply at the objective level; that is, the sinner must consciously choose to perform an action which he knows to be contrary to God's will. In that sense, the attitude behind the action is every bit as determinative as the deed itself.

One final comment on Friday abstinence: Church law still maintains Friday as a day of penance. If a person chooses not to abstain from meat, he or she must perform an alternative penance. As I have said before, this seems to be noted in the breach more than in the observance, to the detriment of all concerned. Without a spirit of penance, no one is able to progress in the living of the Christian life.

The Catholic view of homosexuality

Q. "Dear Abby" recently dealt with the topic of homosexuality. Like so many other people, she seems to believe that gays are born that way, and so it is "OK" and good. Even my good Catholic friends saw nothing wrong with Abby's answer. What is the Catholic answer?

A. The scientific data on homosexuality is rather inconclusive. Some experts maintain that it is caused by situations in early childhood or adolescence, while others argue that it has genetic roots. Most psychologists would agree that few people with a homosexual orientation have consciously chosen to be homosexual, any more than most individuals with a heterosexual orientation have consciously opted for that. Surely, then, we are dealing with a very complex question.

If a person has not freely chosen to be something, then that person cannot be treated as though he or she has done so. If, in fact, one is born in a particular way (with diabetes, for example), it is wrong to say that it is the person's fault. This understanding, however, is a far cry from declaring that it is "OK" to be diabetic and yet continue to eat sweets.

Being a diabetic is morally neutral, but it does create a set of circumstances which are problematic, so that what would cause most people no difficulty would indeed be very dangerous for the diabetic. Similarly, one who finds himself possessed of a homosexual orientation surely should not engage in self-hatred or self-denial but needs to avail himself of all the helps and supports possible to live a chaste life in accord with God's will and law, making for spiritual, psychological, and physical well-being.

A journal of medical ethics

Q. I am a young Catholic physician interested in publications that reflect the Church's positions on matters that I shall be confronting (e.g., abortion, birth control, sterilization). Is anything like this available?

A. Your interest in being faithful to Catholic principles in your medical profession is to be commended. So often we find professionals who try to divorce their "job" from their Catholic faith, to the detriment of both in the end. The Second Vatican Council talked about the apostolate of the laity, and what you are interested in is exactly what the Fathers had in mind.

Now to answer your specific question. A very fine journal, *The Linacre Quarterly*, is published by the National Federation of Catholic Physicians Guild. Information may be obtained by contacting them at 850 Elm Grove Road, Elm Grove, WI 53122; telephone: (414) 784-3435.

Sterilization is 'objectively evil'

Q. My sister, a fallen-away Catholic, went to a nearby Catholic hospital and obtained a tubal ligation. She says she was told this procedure was approved by the hospital's Medical Ethics Committee. Who are they? Are they entitled to make such judgments? I thought no Catholic institution could cooperate in such surgery.

A. In no way may any Catholic health facility participate in or counsel sterilization. Nor is the individual hospital's ethics committee competent to deviate from official Church teaching. This very topic was addressed by the Sacred Congregation for the Doctrine of the Faith in 1975. The relevant passage follows: "For the official approval of direct sterilization and, all the more so, its administration and execution according to hospital regulations is something of its nature — that is, intrinsically — objectively evil. Nothing can justify a Catholic hospital cooperating in it.

Any such cooperation would accord ill with the mission confided to such an institution and would be contrary to the essential proclamation and defense of the moral order."

Contraception and conscience

Q. My wife is a physician assistant in the field of obstetrics and gynecology. We are faithful to Pope Paul's teaching in Humanae Vitae, and she agonizes over the fact that she is expected to provide patients with the full range of contraceptive information, including the Pill and condoms. Where does my wife's responsibility end as a committed Catholic and that of the patient begin? Can she give out such information in good conscience?

A. In the past few months, a number of inquiries have come in from physicians, pharmacists, nurses, and legal personnel — all expressing concern about the conflicts they are experiencing over maintaining fidelity to their Catholic Faith and various life issues threatened by the performance of expected duties in their professional lives.

I can only say to you and your wife what I have said to others: We are living in a time when the choices between Christ's Gospel and the values of the world are becoming starker; that reality will require many of us to choose up sides in a manner not known to Christians of the West since the legalization of Christianity by Constantine. Whatever compromises the truth of the Gospel must be forsaken, regardless of the consequences.

The only promise I can make, however, is to repeat the promise of Christ that those who are faithful to Him in this faithless age will receive the reward of their fidelity (cf. Luke 9:23-27).

The same rules apply to everyone

Q. In a biography of Jacqueline Kennedy, it is alleged that Cardinal Cushing approved of her marriage to Aristotle Onassis, even though the Vatican did not approve of it, since she was a widow with two children. I do not understand.

A. Biographies of late have been characterized by so much muckraking that it is almost impossible to distinguish truth from fiction. Inasmuch as Cardinal Cushing is dead and cannot speak for himself, we are left with the author's word and that of Mrs. Kennedy, who will not discuss the matter in all likelihood. Having said that, I would simply note the following:

1. Cardinal Cushing could never justifiably counsel Mrs. Kennedy to enter into an invalid marriage. The law of the Church applies to all her sons and daughters, great and small alike.

2. The suggestion that being a widow with children could justify the action makes no sense on a number of scores. First of all, Mrs. Kennedy was hardly down-and-out when she became involved with Mr. Onassis. Second, her children were not babes in arms in need of a father or father-figure.

3. It is incorrect to say that "the Vatican" did not approve of her marriage to Onassis since the Holy See had no reason to have anything more to say about her invalid marriage than it would about your neighbor's. The only legitimate question was whether or not the marriage could be celebrated, and the answer was "no" because of Mr. Onassis' previous marriage bond. Therefore, the Church's ban on divorce and remarriage, following the clear teaching of Christ in the Gospels, is what was being applied. Mrs. Kennedy did not need a determination from the Holy See on this; her local parish priest could have told her as much — if she ever needed that information, to begin with.

Civil divorce and the marriage bond

Q. During your latest appearance on the Larry King Show, you said something, probably in the heat of debate, that I don't think you meant. You gave the impression that the Church teaches that an abused spouse must remain married to the offender. Could you state your position on this clearly now, so that I can share it with my non-Catholic friends who were somewhat confused by your comments.

A. You are right.

I was trying to say that suffering is a part of all human life and can be transformed for the Christian who unites it to the suffering of Christ. Surely a spouse should offer up difficulties encountered in marriage for a variety of intentions, not the least of which might be the reform of the offending spouse. When those difficulties become absolutely unbearable and graver problems come about as a result, it may well be time to seek a separation for the benefit of all concerned. The believing Christian, however, is always open to receive back a spouse who has erred, just as God does with us after we sin and repent. Divorce is wrong because, among other things, it states in the starkest of terms that one is not truly open to reconciliation. The Church tolerates divorce only as a means of settling financial matters, like division of property, child support, etc. The parties involved, however, should never imagine that the civil divorce has any real effect on the marriage bond, which lasts until death.

When does human life begin?

Q. On Respect Life Sunday, our pastor obeyed the bishop's directive and preached on the topic but informed us that the Catholic Church has never officially addressed the question of when human life begins. In fact, he said, St. Thomas Aquinas taught that life begins at about three months. What's the story here?

A. People like the ex-priest Daniel Maguire have made a great deal of St. Thomas' position; frankly, I wish they took the rest of his teachings as seriously.

Your priest is correct in asserting that the Church has not declared the moment when human life begins for a very simple reason: That is not her prerogative, since it is a scientific question and not a theological one. But the science of genetics has shown quite conclusively that from the moment when the egg and sperm unite, a human life has begun. Since the Church accepts the findings of science, she has declared that human life must be reverenced from the first moment of conception. In other words, the Church's theological position is grounded in a scientific fact.

Aquinas always taught that abortion at any stage of development was a grave sin (since human life is a continuum); however, he held for gradations of seriousness, based on fetal development. Working with the medical information available to him at that time and basing his concepts on the theories of Aristotle, he espoused a position now known as "delayed hominization," which means that an immortal soul is not infused into a body until it reaches a recognizable human form. That position has been totally discredited since it was rooted in a faulty biology; we now know that the entire person is present in the very first cell which is formed at the moment of conception. And so, the Church's traditional opposition to abortion — from the very beginning of the Christian era — is actually strengthened by the findings of modern science.

Preaching against artificial contraception

Q. I am ordained five years and take seriously my obligation to teach the Catholic Faith in its entirety, including the Church's stand on artificial contraception. Almost no one confesses it as a sin, and yet I know that most of my parishioners of child-bearing age are practicing birth control. When I have preached about it, I have noticed no appreciable upswing in confessions of that sin. Any suggestions?

A. More and more young priests are becoming alarmed at this phenomenon. Do not be discouraged, however, and keep bringing up the topic — gently but firmly — in your teaching and preaching. I don't think we need entire homilies devoted to the topic every week or month, but I do believe that a casual remark in homilies on materialism, hedonism, the Lordship of Christ, sin, repentance, and the like can be very effective in showing how aberrant this practice is.

Of course, the more basic problem is getting people to have a renewed sense of sin and to realize how devastating a desire for personal autonomy is in one who would be a follower of Jesus Christ. It is against that background that I discuss this matter.

St. Paul's views on marriage

Q. Could you please explain the meaning of Chapter 7 of St. Paul's First Letter to the Corinthians?

A. The entire chapter is devoted to a consideration of marriage and virginity. Apparently many questions had surfaced among the Corinthians (remember, they were not particularly known for chastity as a group and seemingly continued to have serious sexual problems in their community, even after conversion to Christianity), and Paul had to deal with them.

St. Paul begins by staking out his overriding principle, namely, that in his judgment, it is better to remain celibate for the sake of the Kingdom than to marry. He notes, however, that this is not a divine command but his own preference for all believers, based on his own experience.

Regarding the married, he repeats the Lord's teaching on the unacceptability of divorce and remarriage. Paul encourages Christian spouses to be faithful to their non-Christian spouses and especially to serve as examples of holiness to them, so that they might be the vehicles for the salvation of their unbelieving partners. He then enunciates what has come to be known as the Pauline Privilege: That a Christian spouse may divorce his or her non-Christian partner if that person refuses to live in peace with the Christian or if the non-Christian has, in fact, already abandoned the Christian; in that instance, the Christian party is free to marry another Christian.

Finally, Paul outlines a rather carefully worked-out theology of virginity or celibacy which is as valid today as it was then. He sees in consecrated virginity a source of great spiritual freedom, providing a unique ability to demonstrate one's love for God and neighbor in the most concrete ways. It should be added that Paul never devalues Christian marriage; he simply teaches that celibacy frees an individual to relate constantly to the things of God. In fact, his regard for marriage is such that he would hold that the demands of full-time Christian witness (e.g., in the ministry) would detract from the duties of being a spouse and parent, and vice versa.

Mass obligations when traveling

Q. On a trip this summer we stopped on a Sunday at a convent for breakfast. The superior, who holds a degree from The Catholic University of America in Washington, insisted that because we were traveling, we had no obligation to attend Sunday Mass, nor was there any need to observe the eucharistic fast. What's the Church's position on all this?

A. If someone is traveling, there is no Sunday Mass obligation — if there is no church within a reasonable distance. Certainly on a trip from Virginia to Pennsylvania one would find dozens of churches (some are even clearly visible from the interstate highway) where Sunday Mass was being celebrated.

Regarding the eucharistic fast, Church law still calls for it, and it is a serious responsibility that one observe it as part of a full and proper preparation for the reception of Holy Communion. In both instances, the nun in question reveals herself to be a minimalist, which is really another kind of legalist. When a man is in love with his wife, he doesn't ask her how little he can do to express that love; he does all that he can. Similarly, in our relationship with Almighty God, we should never seek to "get away with" as much as possible (a rather childish approach to both human and Christian living); on the contrary, we should endeavor to demonstrate our love for Christ in as many concrete ways as possible.

Spouse refuses sexual relations

Q. According to Catholic teaching, is a spouse permitted to refuse the other spouse sexual relations? I do not mean periodic abstinence, to

avoid pregnancy, or in times of illness; however, my wife seems to use
sex as a tool to assert her rights, to reward and punish me, etc. Is this
sinful?

A. The act of sexual intercourse has been designed by Almighty God as a means for spouses to express, in the deepest way possible, their love for one another. God made the act pleasurable, so that people would want to engage in this act, especially so that the propagation of the race would not rely on an odious procedure.

We know that some people seem to have greater sexual needs than others. When those needs are not evenly matched in marriage, it is necessary for spouses to communicate about the differences and to work toward a mutually agreeable solution. What that probably means in the concrete living situation is that one spouse may decide to engage in intercourse for the sake of the other, or that one will not press for relations if the other is not ready for it.

All of this presupposes, of course, that there is no physical reason why sexual intercourse should be avoided. It is unfortunately too common, however, for a spouse to use sex as a tool for gaining his or her specific objectives or for making statements about personal autonomy or rights. All of this is out of place in a Christian union. St. Paul also puts a practical angle on the whole question when he advises couples: "Do not deprive each other, except perhaps by mutual consent for a time, to be free for prayer, so that Satan may not tempt you through lack of self-control" (1 Corinthians 7:5).

Sex education

Q. Is it correct for a Catholic high school to teach about the use of
condoms in a required freshman course on human sexuality, as long as
they tell the students that the Church does not recommend their use?

A. It all depends on what you mean by "teaching about the use of condoms." I don't see how topics like AIDS and other sexually related matters can be discussed today without reference to condoms, inasmuch as the media have made so much mention of them. Even if the teacher does not mention them, surely one of the students will. Hence, it seems to me that the approach to be used is threefold: to challenge our students to live chastely; to note the rather high failure rate of condoms; and to offer a convincing discussion of the Church's position.

If all that is done, a student will be even better prepared to do the right thing — and know the reasons why, which is what good Catholic education should always do.

Pharmacists for Life

Q. In [a recent] issue of TCA, [a reader] sought counsel on the moral dilemmas of a Catholic pharmacist. Perhaps he and other interested people would like to contact: Pharmacists for Life, Larry Frieders, The Medicine Shop, 575 W. Illinois St., Aurora, IL 60506.
A. Thank you.

Information for pharmacists

Q. For more information for Catholic pharmacists, I suggest the following organization, which provides direction on all issues: The National Catholic Pharmacists Guild, 1012 Surrey Hills Drive, St. Louis, MO 63117.
A. Thank you.

'Humanae Vitae'

Q. My husband and I embrace the doctrine of Humanae Vitae wholeheartedly, but we know many married couples who do not because, they say, it is not infallible teaching. Can you clarify this?
A. They have been sold an unfortunate bill of goods by ecclesiastical minimalists. We do not believe things simply because they are infallibly taught; as a matter of fact, doctrines are infallibly taught because they have been consistently taught and believed by the Church.

Some theologians assert that the doctrine of *Humanae Vitae* is infallible because it is the only position the Church has ever held on the question of birth control. In other words, never has there been a magisterial statement in two millennia which countenanced the use of artificial means of birth control. And for that very reason, the Church can never teach otherwise than Pope Paul VI did in that encyclical.

But even if *Humanae Vitae* and/or its teaching were not infallible, listen to the words of the Fathers of the Second Vatican Council: "This loyal submission of the will and intellect must be given, in a special way, to the authentic teaching authority of the Roman Pontiff, even when he does not speak *ex cathedra* in such wise, indeed, that his supreme teaching authority be acknowledged with respect, and that one sincerely adhere to decisions made by him, conformably with his manifest mind and intention, which is made known principally either by the character of the documents in question, or by the frequency with which a certain doctrine is proposed, or by the manner in which the doctrine is formulated" (*Lumen Gentium*, n. 25).

The very fact that Pope John Paul II rarely misses an opportunity to reinforce this teaching should give one pause to reflect on how seriously he regards this doctrine and, therefore, how seriously committed believers ought to follow it.

The cost of an annulment

Q. I had an acquaintance say to me recently that a friend of hers paid $4,000 for a marriage annulment. If a couple is not married, why don't they have a right to know without cost? What is that much money used for?

A. I doubt very much that any diocese charges that much. In most instances, it is closer to $400. The costs for a decree of nullity are quite heavy because they involve psychiatrists, counselors, canon lawyers, secretaries, etc. Whom would you expect to bear the burden of the process, if not the person directly affected and benefiting from it? That having been said, true-hardship cases are never denied the possibility of a judicial procedure for want of finances.

Will marital status inhibit conversion?

Q. I am a non-Catholic mother of four, married to a Catholic man for fourteen years. Our marriage was performed in a Methodist church. I was married once before, also in the Methodist Church. Can I convert to the Catholic Church since I have been divorced? What can my husband and I do to get our marriage blessed by the Church?

A. Your Methodist marriage is valid in the eyes of the Church. You may submit a case to your local diocesan marriage tribunal for a judgment on its validity, in the hope of receiving a decree of nullity (not knowing any background, I could not say whether you would be successful there or not, but it's surely worth a try). You should also check with your parish priest about a possible "privilege of the faith" ("the dissolution of a marriage between a baptized person and an unbaptized person by the Holy Father") since you wish to become a Catholic. These are not easy to come by, however.

If the marriage is not straightened out, you could not be received into the Church because the previous marriage bond and the current marital arrangement, objectively speaking, make for an ongoing adulterous relationship. This is said not to be unkind or judgmental, but simply to help you comprehend what is involved here. My advice would be to check out the annulment route first.

To love God with our whole being

Q. I have become disturbed by Jesus' statement that we must love God with our "whole" heart, soul and mind. Is this to be taken literally? Does love for another detract from love for God? What about personal pleasure? Another New Testament passage that concerns me is St. Paul's command to "pray always." How is that possible?

A. The Hebrew language is given to what we Westerners would consider hyperbole; therefore, it is necessary to analyze very carefully passages like the ones you cite. That does not mean to analyze them away or to take away the sting, if there is one; it does mean understanding them as Our Lord's or St. Paul's audience would have done so.

To speak of loving God with one's whole being is simply saying that God must be put first in one's life, and that anything or anyone who leads a person astray from single-hearted commitment to the Lord has become an idol. Does pleasure fall into that category? Not if it is a good pleasure, which enables us to praise God for His goodness in giving us joy in living. Can another person be an idol? Jesus obviously does not envision that as a normal trap, since in the second of these two great commandments He demands love for neighbor as a concrete sign of one's love for God. A person can become the source of difficulty for an individual's wholehearted love for God when the love directed to him or her is disordered, that is, when it mistakes the creature for the Creator.

As far as praying always is concerned, it seems to me that St. Paul is speaking of being possessed of an attitude of prayer, such that a Christian spends his or her day in the presence of God. Furthermore, the Church has always suggested that we can best fulfill Paul's precept by making what is traditionally known as the Morning Offering — the prayer which dedicates one's whole day and every activity of that day to Almighty God.

What makes a sin mortal?

Q. When does a sin become mortal? The old Baltimore Catechism said serious matter, sufficient reflection, and full consent were all needed. But what is sufficient reflection, or full consent?

A. One of the weaknesses of some moral theology in "the old days" was creating the impression that mortal sin lurked around every corner. The problem today comes from the opposite extreme, as some people argue that mortal sin is well-nigh impossible to commit, except under the most unusual circumstances. The truth lies in the middle, I think.

As one very old and wise priest told me years ago, "Human beings are not as free as some moralists claim, nor as conditioned as some psychologists declare." Understanding this insight provides the key to determining the moral culpability of a person. When we talk about "sufficient reflection" and "full consent," we are referring not to the objective goodness or evil of an act, but to the human player in the drama. Therefore, critical questions to ask might be: Did I truly understand the inherent evil of this act? Did I think about the implications of performing it, especially in terms of my relationship to Christ and His Church? Did I know what the Church teaches about this matter, and did I understand it? Was I pressured into this action by outside forces which might have limited my freedom? Has bad habit so taken over that my freedom of action is effectively limited or even nearly eliminated?

Now, of course, people can rationalize their behavior and blame everybody in the universe for their unwillingness to lead a good and holy life, but we're not concerned with that type of person here. We're speaking about a true, committed believer who sincerely wants to do God's will in his or her daily life. So, is mortal sin possible? Yes, indeed. Is it inevitable? By no means, because, as St. Paul knew from personal experience, Christ's grace is sufficient to meet any challenge and to carry any cross.

Advertisements fall into simony

Q. Please comment on ads appearing in Catholic papers and magazines which advertise blessed rosaries, medals, or papal blessing scrolls for a certain amount of money. Isn't that simony?

A. Yes, it is, and Catholics should realize that and not become involved in such schemes. Furthermore, Catholic periodicals should not accept advertising from companies like that. Papal blessing scrolls are a slightly different story; the payment is for the scroll and not for the blessing; the payment is given to the company as a just remuneration for the materials and services provided. Beyond that, anybody can get a papal blessing just by watching the Holy Father offer it on television.

119

What is the 'Matthean exception'?

Q. In St. Matthew's Gospel, Jesus makes the statement: "And I say to you, that whoever puts away his wife, except for immorality, and marries another, commits adultery." What does the "except for immorality" mean as it relates to the present position of the Church on divorce and remarriage? What is the definition of "immorality" as used in this passage?

A. This is frequently referred to as the "Matthean exception," and much ink has been spilled on it over the centuries. Exegetes are divided on its precise meaning, with some holding that it must have been unique to the Jewish community to which Matthew wrote, since the parallel passages in Mark 5:32 and Luke 16:18 contain no such exception. Perhaps it had to do with a marriage that was illicit from its inception because it took place within an unlawful degree of kinship. No matter how one interprets the exception, however, it is clear that the constant practice of the Church (testified to even in pagan Greek and Roman literature) was to understand Our Lord as having prohibited divorce and remarriage under any and all circumstances.

Raising children

Q. I am dating a non-Catholic who is interested in the Church, but I don't know if he will convert. If he doesn't, is the non-Catholic still required to sign papers agreeing to the upbringing of children as Catholics?

A. The non-Catholic party must be apprised by the priest that the Catholic partner must do all in his or her power to see to it that any children of that union are baptized and raised Catholic. The non-Catholic need not agree to that, but must state that he knows that to be the intention of the Catholic.

Friday as a day of penance

Q. Is it correct that Pope Paul VI said that meat could be eaten on Friday, provided one abstained from meat on some other day of the week?

A. No. In *Paenitemini*, Pope Paul VI's apostolic constitution on penance, issued in 1966, he reminded all that the penitential character of Friday was to be retained, symbolized particularly by abstinence from meat. The Fridays of Lent had to remain meatless. Episcopal conferences could petition the Holy See, however, for a substitution to be made for their people for Fridays during the year. Thus if one does not abstain from meat on Friday, he or she is obliged to perform some other penance or work of charity in its place. Somehow or other, that has gotten lost in the shuffle, and most Catholics in this country think that Friday abstinence was abolished, period. Better catechesis in the classroom and better preaching from the pulpit on the nature of penance and the need for it in the life of a believer would go a long way to remedy the * situation.

Deacons, divorce, and remarriage

Q. Can a deacon still function as such if he gets a divorce?
A. If he is merely divorced, I see no reason for his status changing in terms of his diaconal ministry. If he has attempted remarriage, there is a twofold problem: First, without an annulment of his first marriage, his second union would be invalid; second, deacons are not permitted to remarry, even if that should be possible as a result of being widowed. The basic principle operative in the Church (for both East and West) is that while married men can be ordained, ordained men may never marry. That is why, for example, Anglican clergy who come to us with their families are able to retain their family life and obligations, but should their wives die, they could not remarry. The same applies to permanent deacons.

TCA reader joins Church

Q. I like TCA so much! I bet you get lots of angry letters from people, and I've been meaning to send you an appreciative one.

When I started getting TCA, I wasn't Catholic. I had the idea that the Catholic Church was legalistic and unreasonable about things like divorce and remarriage. But articles and answers in TCA helped me to see that the Church is trying to uphold God's standards of love for Him and His people. I think God used your magazine to give me the confidence to look further. I finally signed up for RCIA and was received into the Church.

I hope you enjoy editing TCA as much as I enjoy reading it!
A. I do; thank you for your kind remarks and for letting us know that God used this vehicle to bring you into the fullness of His life and love in the Catholic Church. Welcome!

Infertility and God's Law

Q. A friend of mine had testicular cancer, with the result that his reproductive system does not function. He is extremely anxious to have a child within his bloodline, and has suggested that mixing some of his semen with that of another relative might give them the child he and his wife so strongly desire. This sounds very wrong to me, but I am told that I am out of date on this issue.

A. For an in-depth response, I would refer you to *Donum Vitae*, the instruction on such matters issued by the Congregation for the Doctrine of the Faith. Let me make but a few points.

Your basic instinct is, of course, on target. Just listen to the problematic language, to start with: "He is extremely anxious to have a child within his bloodline." Does this sound like viewing a child as an inestimable, unrepeatable gift of God? Or does it sound like regarding a child as a means to an end, namely, to keep alive the family name or some other such concern? That kind of preoccupation caused King Henry VIII to break with the Catholic Church, so obsessed was he with having a male heir to take his place upon the throne of England.

In my experience, most couples are not so crass or materialistic; they simply want to have a baby, sometimes very desperately — a completely human, legitimate desire. But they must go about it in a moral manner. Separating love from life in the marital act is wrong whether it's done to bring about a birth or to prevent one. What do I mean? In artificial contraception, a couple endeavors to make the marital act signify merely love-making, without permitting it to be life-giving; in artificial conception, a person wants to bring about a new life, without its being the fruit of an act of love. Only by maintaining the necessary connection between life and love are spouses spared from becoming sex objects to one another and spared the sad situation of viewing a child simply as an object to be desired or shunned. In other words, God's Law safeguards human dignity.

In *Familiaris Consortio*, Pope John Paul II encourages infertile couples either to adopt (and there are thousands of unwanted babies, but usually not Caucasian) or to offer their gifts (time, talent, financial resources) to the community of the Church, so that they can share their love in other life-giving ways. We can surely ask why someone who does not want a child conceives while others dying to have a baby are left childless. The only answer is that God's ways are not ours, and we must accept crosses from Him as readily as we accept blessings.

Catholics cannot promote abortion

Q. A friend who is a registered nurse recently had to change jobs and is now working at a secular hospital. She works in the psychiatric department, where some teenagers come and are found to be pregnant. No abortions are performed there, but it is her job to arrange the abortions for these girls. She is against abortion and has expressed her feelings to coworkers. She is advised that if she goes to a "higher authority," she will be fired. She loves working with these troubled girls, but is against arranging abortions for them. What advice can you give her?

A. A committed Catholic must always operate from an informed Catholic conscience, which can never admit of compromise, especially on so basic an issue as the sanctity of human life. Furthermore, what kind of help is someone to a person in trouble when simply compounding difficulties by adding murder to the list of personal offenses? All public officials have a right to freedom of conscience, and no one should be blackmailed into waiving those rights.

Godparents must be good Catholics

Q. What are the requirements of the Church for someone to be a godparent? Can such a person be married outside the Church?

A. Anyone who wishes to be a sponsor for Baptism or Confirmation must have been baptized and confirmed and must be a practicing Catholic, that is, regular in Mass attendance, faithful to all his or her obligations as a Catholic, and eligible to receive the sacraments. Someone who is married outside the Church has failed in his obligation to observe the Church's laws concerning marriage and is thus unable to receive either the Sacrament of Penance or Holy Communion until he has resolved to regularize the marital situation.

While we are on the topic, it should be noted that non-Catholics may not be sponsors; they may be what are called "Christian witnesses." At least one practicing Catholic is required.

Voting for pro-life candidates

Q. You have said that voting according to an informed Catholic conscience means never voting for a politician who favors abortion in any form. If no candidate in a particular election is pro-life, may I in good conscience vote for the candidate who is the least extreme in his support for legal abortion, or is there some other course of action that I should take?

A. When no candidate fully reflects the pro-life view, the Catholic voter may engage in one of three approaches. First, he or she may simply abstain from voting in that particular election. Second, one may go the route of a write-in, if that is an option. Third, he may vote for the person who appears to offer the least damage to the effort to secure justice for the unborn.

Changing the words of the Commandments

Q. Our three children attend a Catholic school, and recently our youngest child brought home the enclosed listing of the Ten Commandments. They are not written the way I learned them, and when I questioned my child's teacher. I was told it was easier for children to learn them this way. Is this correct?

A. Rewording the Commandments for little ones is not a bad idea, as long as the substance of the original is left intact. "Thou shalt not take the name of the Lord thy God in vain" could be properly rendered as "Respect and honor God's name." As children get older, they should be introduced to the standard formulations of these and other traditional materials, in keeping with their age and maturity and always with an eye on bringing about their full incorporation into the whole Church.

Reconciling after a vasectomy

Q. My husband and I are both Catholic. He recently had a vasectomy to spare me from further danger during pregnancy. He found nothing wrong with having this surgery performed, but ever since, I have felt nothing but guilt. I no longer feel that our union is God-centered, and the thought of sex now repulses me. What can I do to become reconciled with myself, my husband and with God?

A. To the extent that you encouraged your husband and actively participated in the process. you incurred sin along with him. Therefore, I would suggest that you avail yourself of the Sacrament of Penance as soon as possible, and that you urge your husband to do the same. As I have said before in the context of this discussion, I think persons in your situation can demonstrate their true repentance and good will by relating to their spouses by way of natural family planning, that is, acting as if the surgery had not taken place (presuming that the procedure is irreversible, which question ought to be checked out first).

Your sentiments as you express them now give evidence of real contrition, which should be capitalized on, so as to achieve the reconciliation you so desire.

Contraceptive use is never justified

Q. Several issues ago you stated that a person who has been sterilized and has repented could "relate sexually" thereafter by practicing natural family planning (NFP). I assume that meant the couple should only have intercourse on "safe days." If this is acceptable, is it also possible to use contraceptives in combination with NFP on safe days only?

A. The use of contraceptives is always intrinsically and objectively wrong; therefore, their use can never be justified.

Catholicism and communism

Q. I have family in South America and frequently hear that the Catholic Church there has helped support communism. How can that be? Please help me so that I can answer them intelligently.

A. Undoubtedly, there have been serious problems in many Third World countries as some clergy, religious and theologians have been rather sympathetic to communist ideology. That the Church should be involved in social action to better the lot of the poor goes without saying, but that should never move into direct, partisan political action. Furthermore, that communism is diametrically opposed to Catholicism is clear from the historical record. Sometimes this dalliance between some members of the Church and Marxism goes under the name of "liberation theology."

This problem was responsible for two formal instructions from the Roman Congregation for the Doctrine of the Faith on acceptable and unacceptable elements of liberation theology. Pope John Paul II has repeatedly warned clergy and religious about the proper limits of political involvement for the Church in general and for them in particular. Very often the extremes of liberation theology have surfaced not from native sources as much as from North American and western European missionaries.

Canon Law and Mass attendance

Q. Is there still a Church law binding us under serious sin to attend Mass on Sundays and holy days?

A. Yes, there is. Here's what the Code of Canon Law has to say on this matter: "On Sundays and other holy days of obligation the faithful are bound to participate in the Mass; they are also to abstain from those labors and business concerns which impede the worship to be rendered to God, the joy which is proper to the Lord's Day, or the proper relaxation of mind and body" (Canon 1247). It is important to note that Canon Law is not a textbook in moral theology; therefore, the stipulation of the penalty of sin is not part of the language. Standard works of moral theology, however, do attach the penalty of sin to this omission, which violates the Third Commandment. It should also be observed that the Code repeats the traditional prohibition against what used to be called "servile work."

Adultery, mortal and venial sin

Q. When is adultery committed: when you're thinking about it, or when you do it? Also, what is the definition of mortal sin? Do we still believe in mortal and venial sin?

A. Our Lord makes quite a point in the Sermon on the Mount of discussing the sinfulness of sinful intentions and not merely sinful actions. One needs to distinguish between the temptation to perform an immoral act (not sinful in itself) and harboring the desire and even plotting its execution (truly sinful). So, let us say a man and woman are planning to commit adultery (arranging the time, renting the hotel room, making all the necessary excuses to cover their absence, etc.), but one of them gets into an accident and never appears at the site. Has adultery been committed? Certainly "adultery in the heart" has occurred.

Christianity is a way of life which concentrates not on the minimum but on the maximum; by that I mean that we do not seek to avoid only the worst sins but, due to our intense love of Almighty God and a firm desire to do His holy will, we endeavor to please Him always, even in the smallest details. Surely that would be the case in this discussion of adultery, and it applies equally to your question about mortal and venial sin. Is there a difference between the two? Of course. But should we be content or even proud that we commit "only" venial sins? Any offense against the all-loving God is too great to countenance, and thus all sin must be avoided, if one is both psychologically and spiritually mature.

Visiting a divorced and remarried child

Q. My daughter has divorced her husband and was remarried by a justice of the peace. Her father and I have consistently shown our disapproval of this act. We would like to visit her, but since she has moved to another state, this would necessitate staying overnight. Would this be right, or would she interpret this as a tacit approval of her living in mortal sin?

A. Parents are in the unenviable position of having to walk a tightrope in circumstances like these. Your standing for the truth is essential, and if your daughter could admit it, she expects you to do this and respects you for it, in all likelihood. At the same time, if your daughter is ever to make a return to Christ and the Church, it will probably be due to your influence in her life. And so, there is a need to keep the lines of communication open. St. Paul talks about "doing the truth in love," which is often easier said than done.

If you have made known your position consistently and refused to stay overnight in her home when she was nearby, maybe you can now make an exception in this way. Tell her how much you love her and wish her well, especially her salvation. Remind her that her present lifestyle offends Almighty God and that is why it offends you. Go on to indicate that you certainly want to see her and spend time with her, made difficult by her living further away. Therefore, you are going to visit and, yes, stay overnight (rather than going to a nearby hotel), so as not to insult or embarrass either her or her civilly acknowledged spouse — on condition that both she and he realize that you still believe the relationship is sinful and that you hope they will make a sincere effort to rectify the situation.

Sin works for the good

Q. Is it true that St. Augustine said that when St. Paul said that all things work together unto good, even sin is included? And if so, what does that mean?

A. I am not familiar with such a line from St. Augustine, but I can understand what it might mean for him, especially at a personal level. As you know, St. Augustine's road to God was a long and winding one. He engaged in nearly every kind of debauchery, and it seems that only when he hit "rock bottom" was he able to appreciate both the evil he had done and the greatness of the loving God Who kept pursuing him. Many priests will tell you that the Augustinian pattern is repeated to this day as the greatest sinners come to the finest experiences of conversion. It is in that sense that one can see how even sin "works unto the good."

Intent to abort causes problems

Q. Thirteen years ago, as a teenager, I went to a doctor for an abortion, which he did. Some time later, I learned that he had been arrested for performing "abortions" on girls who weren't even pregnant. I don't know whether or not I really had an abortion; however, I certainly intended to do so. Now I am back to Church, but this still haunts me. Could you help me with some questions:

a) If I confess in the traditional confessional, will I be excommunicated? b) Can only the bishop pardon my sin? Can he excommunicate me? c) Can my sin be absolved through the General Absolution service held in our church once a month? d) If I go to confession, I'm afraid because it's been so long that I truly forget how to go through the process. Please help me. I don't want to burn in hell for my sin, nor do I want to be excommunicated.

A. Your letter reflects a great deal of confusion, some of which is surely caused by your own attempts to come to grips with this tragedy and some by general misinformation. So let's try to sort this all out.

You seem to think that confessing the sin of abortion can cause an excommunication. That penalty comes about when the abortion is committed (presuming the girl or woman knows that is the penalty and still does it), not when it's confessed. In point of fact, the confession of the sin removes the excommunication. In many dioceses before the new Code of Canon Law (1983), abortion was classified as a "reserved sin," which meant that anyone seeking absolution from it had to confess directly to the bishop. That is no longer the case in most dioceses (in truth, I don't know of anywhere that it is still a reserved sin).

Whether or not you really had an abortion, you clearly intended to have one if you were truly pregnant. What you need to do is go to confession and lay out the whole sad story to the priest, express your sorrow, and hear Christ's consoling words of forgiveness. Then get this all behind you.

Finally, your parish has no right to be scheduling General Absolution services; such services are strictly forbidden, except under the most extreme circumstances.

Upcoming wedding causes pain

Q. My daughter is going to be married in a secular ceremony, in a Mormon temple. I cannot explain the pain she is causing not only myself, but our entire family, because she has chosen to leave the Church. Can you help?

A. Your question leaves me with a couple of questions. First, if she is marrying in a Mormon ceremony, that is not secular (albeit invalid). Second, nothing in your letter indicates that she "has chosen to leave the Church"; certainly she has chosen not to abide by the law of the Church by contracting such a marriage, but that is very different from leaving the Church. If she has formally left the Church, then she is not bound by the Catholic form of marriage at all. I am not trying to minimize the pain and tragedy involved here, and your sorrow is testimony to the vibrancy of your own Catholic commitment. But we do need to be careful in how we state things and clear in the implications, especially if we wish to be of assistance to the parties concerned.

For many years, Catholics in the United States lived in a kind of fool's paradise since so many of the problems connected with living the Catholic Faith had not hit us as they did our co-religionists in Europe. For the past twenty-five years, however, we know personally what Our Lord meant when He said that He had come to bring division and not peace, with the members of a household in opposition to one another because of Him (cf. Mt 10:34-6).

What concrete advice can I offer? First, state your own convictions firmly but lovingly, and give solid reasons for the positions you hold. Second, do not attend either the ceremony or the reception, explaining to your daughter how this would do violence to your Catholic conscience. Third, pray for her daily, and let her know you are doing so. Fourth, treat her and her new family with Christian charity, making sure to keep open the lines of communication. Fifth, every so often, broach the topic of the possibility of the validation of her marriage in the Catholic Church. Please note that all of the above assumes she has not really left the Church; if she has, then add her return to the true Faith to your intentions, and try to bring up that issue once in a while in a discreet manner.

Homosexuality and seminarians

Q. What can be done to weed out the large number of homosexually oriented seminarians?

A. I would like to know where you get the data to support your statement that there is a "large number of homosexually oriented seminarians."

Absent any proof one way or the other, prudence and charity would suggest that allegations should not be made.

Are there homosexually oriented seminarians? I'm sure there are, and always have been, and many of them have or will become priests. As I have noted on numerous occasions, the Church does not teach that a sexual orientation is evil; instead, the question to be raised is what is done with one's sexuality. For people with a homosexual orientation, the constant teaching of the Church is that such people are called to live in chastity. Beyond that, priests and future priests (whether homosexually or heterosexually oriented) are required by Church law to be celibate and by God's law to be chaste. Hence, the issue you address should be a nonissue, if everyone heeds Catholic teaching.

Is tattooing a sinful practice?

Q. Is it a sin to get a tattoo?

A. Unless it can be demonstrated that tattoos endanger one's health, I could not find any other grounds on which to declare the procedure sinful. I guess one could argue that such an "adornment" is a waste of money, and to that extent sinful, but that can be said about any number of things people commonly do (for example, hairstyling, manicures and the like) and should not be restricted to tattoos.

An invitation, not a rejection

Q. My daughter and her fiancé are both Catholic and have been engaged for two years. Our pastor insisted that he could not proceed with any marriage preparation until they are no longer living together. My daughter is angry and intends to be married by a justice of the peace instead. I do not approve of my daughter's living situation, but isn't this priest driving my daughter away from the Church?

A. More and more priests are coming to the conclusion of your pastor, and I think I would count myself among their number now too. Some priests estimate that fifty percent of the couples that come to them for weddings these days are already "playing house." Add to that the reality that most of them do not go near a church for months on end, and one has to ask why they want a church wedding and what the Church can truly do for them if they have no real intention of conversion or reform of life. When priests ask that such couples live apart for a set period of time before an ecclesiastical wedding, they are looking for signs of goodwill and an acknowledgement that fornication or cohabitation is wrong and sinful; without these indicators, many could indeed question the validity of a marriage between people who really do not accept Catholic teaching on the meaning of the marriage bond.

Therefore, I don't agree that your pastor is "driving (your) daughter away from the Church." In point of fact, she has been living outside of grace for a prolonged period of time, and your priest is inviting her to return to an honest and faithful living of the Gospel. Will living apart ensure that they are not having sexual relations? Of course not. But it will certainly make such relations more difficult and, most importantly, will be a powerful admission that the previous arrangement was morally illicit and displeasing in the sight of God.

Church praises all charitable work

Q. What is the position of the Catholic Church about giving money to interdenominational charitable groups that provide assistance to both Catholics and Protestants?

A. The Church applauds all charitable efforts. When Mother Teresa and her Sisters carry the dying off city streets, they do not ask if the person is Catholic or is interested in becoming a Catholic. Certainly, they use the moment of exercising Christian charity also to evangelize, but the human need of the person must be addressed first. The pagan Roman poet Terence once remarked that he considered nothing human to be foreign to him; the Catholic Church has always had exactly the same attitude.

When may NFP be used?

Q. Under what conditions is it moral for a married couple to make use of natural family planning to avoid pregnancy?

A. The norm for Christian married couples is absolute openness to new life; if couples have a healthy expression of love, that will presumably mean large Catholic families. From the beginning of the general availability of artificial means of birth control during the pontificate of

Pope Pius XII to the present Holy Father, the Church has taught this truth. Pius XII made it clear, as does Pope John Paul II, that natural family planning (NFP) is not to be used as a "Catholic" form of birth control. By that I mean that if the same attitudes possess Catholics on NFP as do those on, say, "the pill," then the quality of the moral action is not substantially different. Serious health or financial difficulties might recommend the use of NFP for certain designated periods of time, but surely not as a normal part of marital life.

In a talk to a group of Italian instructors in NFP, the Pope said that contraception "deforms" marital love and signals "moral degradation," adding that the Church's approach is a combination of self-control and natural methods when good reasons exist to limit family size. But notice once more that imitation of family size is not the norm but the exception. He went on to say that NFP should not be viewed simply as a technical solution but as a complete outlook on the nature and purpose of married love.

Don't tolerate Catholic-bashing

Q. The intermediate-level Spanish textbook "Conversación y Repaso" [published by Holt, Rinehart and Winston] contains an anti-Catholic dialogue which achieves no positive purpose. What might be done to have that type of Catholic-bashing removed from a textbook?
A. I was astonished at the virulent anti-Catholicism of the passage in question. For the sake of readers, let me summarize the content: A Hispanic mother questions her son's missing of Sunday Mass. The boy responds by pointing out the hypocrisy and superstition of Catholicism in general and the clergy in particular. When the mother registers her shock and disappointment, the son declares: "Values are changing. I am changing. Religion doesn't run life as much as it did before."

After receiving this piece, I contacted the publisher. After consultation with editors and other interested parties, it was agreed to delete the offensive material in future editions of the text.

All too often, Catholics take this kind of bashing on the chin, chalking it up to the need to "turn the other cheek." While turning the other cheek can be personally meritorious, it is either weakness or a lack of Christian conviction to allow our holy Faith to be held up to ridicule, especially since something like a textbook influences thousands of young minds and poisons them against the truth of Jesus Christ.

I commend our reader who brought this to my attention, and I encourage others who find similarly offensive material to do the same. Let's try to work together to eliminate the bigotry of anti-Catholicism.

A correct assessment

Q. My daughter has been divorced for the past eight years, has missed Sunday Masses and dated a divorced man for five years. I told her she cannot go to Communion since she has not been to confession in eight years and has missed all those Masses, as well as having committed adultery for that whole time. On Christmas Eve, she went ahead and still received Communion. Did she not commit an even greater sin of sacrilege?

A. You were absolutely correct in the evaluation of your daughter's situation. Now, of course, the task is to convince her of the truth of it all in as honest and loving a way as possible, so that she can make a good confession and return to a life of grace.

The importance of avoiding scandal

Q. My brother is planning a Catholic wedding. Due to various circumstances, he has decided to move in with his fiancée. He says that they will be living chastely and that I should not be concerned. Can I, in good conscience, still attend the wedding?

A. Whether or not they are living chastely is almost immaterial at this point. First of all, your brother and his fiancée are placing themselves in a proximate occasion of sin. Secondly, and just as importantly, they are giving public scandal. In this day and age, who would ever believe, rightly or wrongly, that a man and woman could be living together in a chaste manner? Our Lord was very sensitive to the matter of scandal and asserted that one who caused scandal would be better off dropped into the sea with a millstone around his neck (cf. Mk 9:42). St. Paul likewise indicated that he would refrain from doing even legitimate things if such actions would cause people to wonder or stumble (cf. Rom 14:21).

A genuine love for others and a concern for their salvation should move one always to act with the effects of one's deeds clearly in view. As an old seminary professor used to say, "Your actions must not only *be* good; they must *look* good."

I don't see how this situation, however, would influence a decision to attend or not attend the wedding, inasmuch as it will be a valid marriage.

Women Religious and abortion

Q. If a nun happens to be raped and gets pregnant, is it appropriate for her to have an abortion? Please explain the Church's position on this.
A. Human life is human life, regardless of how inconvenient the situation may be for anyone. Under no circumstances may a directly intended abortion be performed.

Your question may be the result of having heard that in the Belgian Congo some nuns were administered birth control pills since there was a danger of their being raped during the revolution. That is very different and rather complex. In the shortest form possible, let me explain the morality of it thus: Rape is the act of an unjust aggressor. The victim is just that, and in no way intends to make the act one of true human intercourse: as a matter of fact, she wishes to do everything possible to stave off the assault.

To protect oneself against the potential result of a rape is not immoral; it is not at all akin to the practice of artificial contraception by those interested in making love but avoiding the consequent birth of a child. In this instance, no act of love occurs, and hence the legitimacy of such preventative action. I should note that this has nothing to do with the fact that these women were nuns; the principle applies across the board.

When the incident mentioned took place, no one knew of the abortifacient possibilities of the pill. Were they known, the practice would not have been recommended by Catholic theologians, on the principle that one can never perform an evil act to bring about good.

Contraception and priestly compassion

Q. I thought the Church's position on birth control forbade artificial contraception, no matter how grave. My husband spoke to our pastor, and he said that because we already have six children and NFP doesn't work for us (three children have been born this way) and because the doctor told me not to have any more children and because of hardship, it would be all right for us to use artificial means of birth control. This has me confused.
A. The one who's confused is your pastor! I have never read anywhere in Scripture or Tradition that the law of God loses its binding effect after the sixth child or because of "hardship." Holding fast to the law of God is hard for all people; for some, the point of difficulty is avarice; for

others, it is anger or sloth. But that does not change the will of God for us. He expects us to conform our wills to His, and not the other way around.

I do not want to come off as harsh or unfeeling because that is not true, but it is necessary to state objective moral truth in a clear and objective manner; anything less does a tremendous disservice to all concerned.

Some priests have a mistaken notion of compassion, which leads them to water down the moral law out of pity. What a priest needs to do is understand and accept the teaching himself and then explain it with conviction and enthusiasm, encouraging people to respond with heroism and love and reminding them to rely on the grace of God, which alone can carry us through arduous responsibilities. Simply caving in to the depravity and self-centeredness of our secular culture is not the answer, as your own disquietude demonstrates. Your pastor gave you the answer he thought you wanted to hear, but that has not satisfied you because you know that God calls you to greatness and holiness of life — which can occur only when sacrifice is a part of the total picture.

Compassion comes from the Latin for "suffering with" another. A priest who does not share the whole truth of the Gospel with one of his flock and/or fails to accompany that person on the journey of faith does not "suffer with" the person and so really does not exhibit true compassion.

NFP: Available and effective

Q. Your answer on contraception and (false) priestly compassion was excellent. But as a certified NFP teacher and mother of six, I think that people with problems in this area need practical support in living with this teaching. The writer said NFP doesn't work for them (they had three children that way). Please allow me to address this.

If a couple has a surprise pregnancy using NFP, they should take their charts and go back to their teacher. NFP has been shown to be 99 percent effective. There are surprise pregnancies when the rules are followed accurately (just as there are with contraceptives), but most surprise pregnancies come from an inaccurate or inadequate knowledge of the method, taking chances or using contraceptives during the fertile time.

If we had three serious car accidents, would we give up driving or

go back and take more driving lessons? Please urge [the woman] and her husband to contact one of the major NFP providers for a refresher course in NFP. The Couple to Couple League, which teaches the sympto-thermal method, has certified teachers all over the country and also has a home-study course.
A. Thank you very much, not only for your intelligent and articulate response but also for your commitment to this important family-life apostolate.

Supporting pro-life activists in prison
Q. It's gratifying to see your consistent support of the pro-life cause in TCA. May I offer one more suggestion for those interested in being of further assistance?

At any given time, there are usually fifty to one hundred prisoners serving time for pro-life activities. Cards and letters are great morale-boosters and also a powerful witness of Christian solidarity to other prisoners, guards and the legal system. One organization that publicizes the names and addresses of such prisoners is: Prisoners of Christ, 1033 Franklin Road, #297, Marietta, GA 30067.
A. Thanks for passing along the information.

Regular examination of conscience
Q. I attend daily Mass and go to confession monthly. The priest will not give me absolution because I cannot think of any sins (even venial) since my last confession. I know the Scriptures say that even the just man sins seven times a day. Can you help?
A. Every sacrament has matter (the necessary material) and form (the prayer or rite to be followed). In the Sacrament of Penance, the matter is sin; in other words, if there is no sin, there can be no forgiveness, which is just basic logic, anyway. If you truly have no sins, why would you want absolution? Absolution from what?

On the other hand, I find it hard to imagine anyone passing a month without sinning. I would suggest that you engage in a careful examination of conscience each night, using the commandments as a guide for determining your failures to live up to God's Law and the virtues as means of discovering the progress you are making or not making in living the Christian life. I think what you need to develop is a greater sensitivity to the nature of sin and a realization of how harmful sin (any sin — mortal or venial) is to one's relationship with the God Who calls each of us to the holiness and perfection of His own divine life.

Guide to natural family planning

Q. Are there any good medical guides for natural family planning?
A. I have just come across an excellent work, *Human Ecology: A Physician's Advice for Human Life*, by Robert Jackson, M.D., published by St. Bede's Publications (Box 545, Petersham, MA 01366). The author, a physician for over fifty years, integrates his wealth of knowledge and experience in the practice of medicine with the Church's teaching on artificial contraception, offering a solution to some of the problems facing contemporary society. He shows, from a scientific, medical viewpoint, the wisdom of the Church's encouragement of natural methods of birth control, including its effect on the health of the mother, the child and the family unit. This book is "must" reading for every priest, for people contemplating marriage, for married couples, and for anyone involved in preparing others for Christian marriage.

Is taping rock albums stealing?

Q. I used to tape rock albums for, and from, my friends. I now realize that this is stealing from the record stores, music groups and everyone in between. Should I go out and buy these albums?

P.S. Will you be the first "preacher" to tell someone to buy rock 'n' roll?
A. You are correct that pirating tapes is an act of theft since it cheats an artist and others out of the legitimate profit which should flow from their professional work.

Will I encourage you now to go out and buy the albums? No. I think you'll survive quite well without them — probably better. While I'm not the type of "preacher" who gets terribly upset with rock music, I do see the problems that it causes or at least exacerbates. I think it is simplistic to argue that if we did away with rock music our culture would return to normalcy. In my opinion, rock music is more a symptom of a sick society than the immediate cause of the sickness.

Participating in contraception

Q. Is it a sin to refuse sex because of birth control?
A. I am supposing that you mean the following: You are married and

your spouse does not accept the teaching of the Church on artificial contraception. May you morally engage in acts of contraceptive intercourse if that is the only way your spouse will do so and he/she insists on your obligation to participate?

If that is the correct statement of the dilemma, let me urge you to try as often as feasible to get your spouse to read, study, and come to understand the Church's teaching in all its liberating beauty. Unfortunately, we are living in a difficult age, in which Christian values are rather generally disregarded — not unlike life in the early Church during the last days of the pagan Roman Empire. If you are truly opposed to contraceptive intercourse and are not rationalizing in any way, and if you accede to your spouse's demands solely to preserve the marriage bond (especially if there are children) and to prevent the spouse from lapsing into adultery, then I think such action could be justified since you are not an active participant in the contraception (e.g., your wife takes the pill without your consent and perhaps even without your knowledge). It was in line with this logic that the old pre-Vatican II manuals of moral theology permitted Catholics to engage in contraceptive intercourse with their non-Catholic spouses who rejected Church teaching on birth control.

I would caution very strongly, however, about the need for absolute honesty with oneself, lest one become involved in a massive endeavor of self-deception.

Returning after excommunication

Q. I would like to know how someone gets back into the Church if excommunicated? For example, if someone had an abortion.
A. Generally speaking, the authority who leveled the excommunication is the one to remove the penalty. If the excommunication was what is technically known as *latae sententiae*, that is, automatic (in other words, no special administrative decree is needed for the excommunication to take effect), then a confessor in the context of the Sacrament of Penance can remit the penalty, along with the conferral of absolution. The follow-up would then require either the penitent or the confessor to inform the appropriate ecclesiastical authority of the reintegration of the individual into ecclesial communion.

Using abortion as the example, let's consider two alternatives. First possibility: A Catholic owner of an abortion clinic is warned by the local bishop to give up this sinful and scandalous business or else face excommunication. After all the requirements of the law are fulfilled and the person remains adamant in the practice, the bishop may excommunicate. That action jars the abortion-clinic owner sufficiently that he realizes the seriousness of the crime, gives up the clinic, and goes to confession to be reconciled with Christ and the Church. Since the actions of both clinic owner and bishop were public, the bishop must be directly and publicly involved in the lifting of the penalty. Second scenario: A woman procures an abortion for herself, knowing full well that the act is both a serious sin and an excommunicable offense. She later repents and avails herself of the Sacrament of Penance. Since her sin was private, the lifting of the excommunication is also done privately, in the context of sacramental reconciliation.

I should stress the fact that the primary purpose of a penalty like excommunication is to deter people from performing particularly heinous crimes. The Church's hope is that a person who has committed the sin anyway will come to his senses by making amends and returning to full communion with the Church. In other words, the goal is not punitive at root but medicinal.

Remarried teachers of religion

Q. I know of a divorced Catholic married to another Catholic, by a justice of the peace, and teaching religion to third- and fourth-graders. How can this be?

A. I have no idea. Your instincts are, of course, correct. How can someone teach the Faith to little ones when he or she fails to live it herself? Now some people may think this is a narrow or closed-minded view, but I think it simply corresponds to basic logic.

Let's consider some possible explanations: 1. Everyone knows that a Catholic teacher — let's call her Mrs. Smith — is living in an adulterous relationship as far as the law of Christ is concerned. How can she teach children respect for the law of God, especially the Sixth Commandment? 2. No one knows that Mrs. Smith is party to an invalid marriage. However, people wonder why she does not receive Holy Communion at Sunday Mass. Sooner or later, the question is going to be raised, causing no small degree of embarrassment to Mrs. Smith and perhaps a significant amount of disillusionment to impressionable children. 3. Mrs. Smith goes to Communion regularly: therefore, no one suspects anything. All such Communions are sacrilegious and fly in the face of authentic Christian morality.

Marriage is public or communal by its very nature, which is why the Church generally requires it to be celebrated as a public rite. Exercising various apostolates in the Church (e.g., teaching) also affects the whole community. Hence, there must be consistency between what one is and what one does. While no one should condemn another for failing to live up to the fullness of Christ's commands, neither should one who has fallen short expect the community to pretend that what has happened really hasn't. At the same time, people caught in unfortunate situations like divorce and remarriage (especially when there are children from the second union) need our prayers and love to endure what must be a very painful deprivation of sacramental grace.

NFP and sexual abstinence

Q. NFP calls for abstinence if a woman is in her fertile time. This is the time when a woman enjoys the sexual act most, sometimes the only time for both physical and psychological reasons. Could you comment?
A. The following of Christ involves the carrying of the cross in union with Him. I know this is not popular to assert today, but that is at the very heart of the Gospel message. Therefore, I can only refer you to other items on this topic.

I should say that I am pleased by the number of questions that come to TCA on the morality of artificial contraception. Believe it or not, I take it as a positive sign that we might be recapturing some sense of what Christ and His Church are calling for in the marital state. Frankly, I do not think this volume of questions would have surfaced on this topic even ten years ago. I suspect that means that the Holy Father's repeated message is getting through, and that a number of younger priests are beginning to preach and teach the whole truth about the married state with fidelity.

Guilty feelings after confession

Q. If a Catholic still has guilty feelings about past sins, what should he do?
A. The first conviction needed for a good confession is the awareness that God's mercy is greater and more powerful than our sinfulness. Therefore, once a sin is sincerely confessed and repented of, it is a thing

of the past. Surely, it may take time for God's forgiving love to sink in, and we do have to atone for past sins (some saints engaged in lifelong penances for the sins of their youth), but that is not the same thing as unresolved feelings of guilt.

Guilt can be good or bad. If I've just murdered someone and feel guilty, that is good — a sign that I'm still human. If a debilitating form of guilt remains years after a sin has been committed, repented, and confessed, something is wrong. That should be discussed with a priest, spiritual director, and/or psychologist.

One's conscience and peace

Q. I signed for my husband's vasectomy after our third child since he threatened to leave me if I didn't. We are now divorced; I am not remarried. May I receive the sacraments?

A. If you confess your part in your husband's sterilization and any other sins committed since your last worthy confession, you are free to return to the reception of Holy Communion.

I would like to take this occasion to note that violating one's conscience for the sake of peace rarely accomplishes that goal for long. The present writer demonstrates that effectively, after having suffered a great deal in the process.

Divorce rate and Catholic grace

Q. Statistics show that the divorce rate among Catholics is almost as high as that among non-Catholics in the United States. I find this hard to imagine for one basic reason: Since the Catholic Church is the only Church that can consecrate the Eucharist, our people have an unfathomable source of grace available to them, which is not so to others. How can the failure rate be the same then?

A. First of all, a correction: The Catholic Church is not alone among Christians with valid Orders and hence a valid Eucharist; Eastern Orthodox, Old Catholics, Polish Nationals, etc., all possess true sacraments.

To the point of your question, I would simply say that grace builds on nature. How many young people attend Sunday Mass regularly, for starters? Of those young married couples who do, how many practice artificial birth control and are thus in a state of objective mortal sin? When we determine those who do go to Mass every week, who do not practice birth control and who do receive Holy Communion worthily, how many are we talking about? Maybe those are the very ones who, because of their cooperation with the graces flowing from Baptism, Matrimony and the Eucharist, have been able to remain faithful unto death.

Gambling

Q. I love to play bingo and lotto, but I hear so many people say that all this gambling is wrong and the Church shouldn't be involved with it. Would you please give some straight answers on the morality of gambling in general and the Church's association with it in particular?

A. Gambling is no more inherently evil than is drinking. Circumstances dictate whether the behavior is problematic or not. For example, if you like an evening out with other people, enjoy the excitement of chance, and use money which is not needed for any other purpose, I see nothing wrong with bingo or other games of chance. When gambling becomes compulsive or causes a person to fail to live up to genuine commitments (financial and otherwise), then a moral difficulty exists.

Divorce and the sacraments

Q. I've often heard that Catholics may receive Holy Communion if they get divorced, so long as they don't remarry. Is that true?

A. Yes, it is. Remember: The divorce in and of itself does not constitute a moral or canonical problem for a Catholic. The difficulty surfaces when remarriage is involved because the second marriage is not recognized in the eyes of God and is, therefore, to be viewed as an ongoing state of adultery — and that is why the reception of Holy Communion is not possible.

Nor can the Sacrament of Penance be received, since one of the prerequisites for a worthy confession is the intention to avoid the sin in question in the future. Living as husband and wife in an invalid union and intending to continue doing so does not demonstrate a firm purpose of amendment.

Pro-choice Catholics

Q. I go to a Catholic high school. In religion class the teacher told us that if a boy helps to pay for his girlfriend's abortion, he is excommunicated along with her. That makes sense to me, but if that is true, then how come the governor of our state is not excommunicated?

After all, he is responsible for paying for thousands of abortions every year.

A. Touché!

It's exciting to see young people begin to think and make connections on their own.

First, I should note that the excommunication for someone who assists another in procuring an abortion is automatic; in other words, he needs no "special delivery" letter from the bishop informing him of the fact. Simply performing the action incurs the penalty, presuming he knew that was the penalty in advance.

In a recent meeting of the National Conference of Catholic Bishops, the hierarchy adopted a strong statement on abortion, which included the following words: "No Catholic can responsibly take a 'pro-choice' stand when the 'choice' in question involves the taking of innocent human life." In other words, a pro-abortion position is incompatible with the living of a devout Catholic life. We have also witnessed the banning from Holy Communion of a pro-abortion Catholic politician on the West Coast. What are we to make of these developments?

It seems to me that the bishops are becoming increasingly impatient with the patent dishonesty of Catholics who wish to lay aside their Catholic value system to curry political favor, all the while alleging to be Catholics in good standing. Certainly the Church forces no one to accept her teachings; however, personal integrity requires one to adhere to ecclesiastical policy if one wishes to remain within a particular ecclesial body. Unfortunately, there are many Protestant Christian denominations where a pro-abortion position is completely acceptable; why not join one of those bodies?

I am neither a canon lawyer nor a moral theologian, but the logic of your question (and the answer implied therein) surely offers ample food for thought. Some bishops are beginning to lead the way in this regard, and it will be important for committed Catholics to lend them their support and encouragement because they are going to suffer much from the secular media and others for taking such a courageous stand on behalf of the sanctity of human life.

Nun's activity is 'grossly imprudent'

Q. We have a nun living in our rectory. She belongs to the Sisters of Christian Community, a group I've never heard of. I understand they

*have no motherhouse and no superior. Do you think it appropriate that
she live with the priests?*

A. I think it's grossly imprudent. This just gives fuel to people
(including many bigots) who believe that priests and nuns have always
had affairs with each other.

As far as her community goes, it is a non-canonical community,
mostly comprised of women who left other congregations of Sisters. By
"non-canonical" I mean that there is no official recognition of this
community by the Church. In effect, they have no more ecclesiastical
standing than a sorority or social club.

5. LITURGY

Christ's presence in the Eucharist

Q. Please comment on the enclosed article from our parish bulletin, which talks about Christ's equal presence in the "presider," the community, the Word, and the Eucharist.

A. The most troubling line is the one which says that Christ is *"equally present"* (emphasis in the original) in each of these ways, and that "by kneeling during the Eucharist, it would seem to place additional emphasis on the eucharistic presence."

Some people have gotten this notion from a misreading of a conciliar quote: "The Church has always venerated the divine Scriptures as she venerated the Body of the Lord, in so far as she never ceases, particularly in the sacred liturgy, to partake of the bread of life and to offer it to the faithful from the one table of the Word of God and the Body of Christ" (*Dei Verbum*, n. 21).

Some commentators stretch the analogy too far because they fail to read far enough, that is, to the second clause which begins with "in so far as." In other words, the equation is made between the Church's reverence for the Word and her reverence for the Eucharist, in so far as she makes both available to the faithful and both come from the same loving God.

The presence of God in His Word is a true presence, of course, but qualitatively different from Christ's Presence in the Eucharist. And the Liturgy Constitution of Vatican II makes that clear by speaking of the various degrees of presence and the gradual unfolding of Christ's Presence in the celebration of the Mass, so that we find Him in the community gathered for worship, in the celebrant, in the Word proclaimed, in the gifts offered, in the gifts transformed, and in the gifts received — moving in symphonic style until we reach a crescendo in the Consecration and Communion (cf. *Sacrosanctum Concilium*, n. 7).

In previous eras, perhaps some Catholics did not have a sufficiently well-developed appreciation of the importance and power of God's Word; however, the budget is not balanced by negating the correct insight in regard to the unsurpassing and unsurpassed dignity of the Blessed Sacrament.

145

Preparing an adult for first confession

Q. My son and his non-Catholic wife were married in the Church. Subsequently, she became a Catholic, but the priest who received her never heard her confession. Three years later, she has still not received the Sacrament of Penance.

A. That such a thing could happen is a result of sheer carelessness at best. I would suggest that you speak to her very gently and let her know that she should be frequenting the Sacrament of Penance. Perhaps you might prod her by saying something like, "I'm going to confession this afternoon. Would you care to come with me?" Then help her prepare to receive the sacrament for the first time. It might also be a good idea to precede her into the confessional and let the priest know that the next penitent is making her first confession, so that he is prepared.

What about backyard weddings?

Q. Does the Church allow a couple to get married in their backyard?

A. The general norm is that the Sacrament of Matrimony is to be celebrated in a sacred place. Most dioceses have specific regulations prohibiting the very situation you describe. Why? If marriage is to be seen as a holy state of life in the Church, then it should begin in a holy environment. Very often people who want backyard weddings have that desire because they "can't relate to the church building." If that is the case, then they probably have trouble relating to the Church in general which, of course, raises the question as to why they want a Church ceremony, for starters.

The only occasions on which most dioceses permit marriages to occur outside a sacred place would be: (1) a Catholic marrying a non-Christian, whose family is hostile to the Church, resulting in their refusal to participate in the ceremony if it took place on "Catholic turf"; (2) a close relative (for example, a parent) of one of the spouses is housebound and desires most sincerely to attend the ceremony.

Future bride needs sacraments

Q. A friend of mine is being married next year. She is merely baptized, not having received either Eucharist or Confirmation. Shouldn't she receive those sacraments before her wedding?

A. Unless a grave cause exists, no one should be married in the Church without being confirmed, let alone not having made her First

Communion. I am sure that the parish priest will bring this to your friend's attention and initiate her instructions in preparation for Penance, Confirmation, and Eucharist.

Confirmation for infants?

Q. Maronite-Rite Catholics have the practice of administering Baptism and Confirmation at the same time. I don't understand this practice, since there can be no preparation for Confirmation (as in the Latin Rite). I have asked the local priest to explain it to me, but I have no confidence in the answer he gave me. Please comment.

A. Believe it or not, it is only the Roman/Latin Rite that administers Confirmation at a delayed date. All other Catholics, and indeed all Eastern Orthodox as well, baptize, chrismate (confirm), and communicate infants all in one fell swoop.

Why would any more preparation be needed for Confirmation than for Baptism (which is surely far more basic)? The Churches of the East are quite comfortable in allowing the sacraments to do their work primarily as signs of divine activity rather than human effort. Now, of course, we all know that grace operates in a dialogical manner — that is, divine initiative and human response — but the stress in the East is much more on the divine than the human, whereas the West has tended (especially in recent years) to emphasize human cooperation with divine grace.

I should mention that the Latin Rite has an additional problem, and that is the order of the sacraments of initiation, which should be Baptism, Confirmation, Eucharist, as it is in the East). It was that way in the West, even with the delay of Confirmation and Eucharist, until the time of Pope St. Pius X, who introduced Communion at the age of reason (age seven). Prior to that, infants were baptized, children were confirmed around the age of twelve or thirteen, and then made their First Holy Communion. When Communion was moved to an earlier age, Confirmation did not move, thus bringing about the anomaly of having unconfirmed children receive Holy Communion.

The 1983 Code of Canon Law, however, anticipates children's reception of Confirmation at the age of reason, unless the national hierarchy decrees otherwise. Our bishops are now in the consultation process to determine what the practice should be in the United States. My personal hope is that we will celebrate

147

Confirmation at the age of reason, with First Holy Communion thereafter.

Certain abuses do not affect sacraments

Q. Recently you stated that the omission of the Creed during Sunday Mass (except for Easter) was not permitted. Do I fulfill my Sunday obligation if the Mass I attend does not contain the Creed? What about other practices, such as women distributing Communion while the priest does not, etc.? What if these occurrences are not occasional but habitual in my parish?

A. The Church is very hesitant about declaring sacraments null and has some very minimal requirements (e.g., for Baptism, water, correct formula, anyone with a proper intention). Therefore, as egregious and reprehensible as some of these aberrations may be, generally they do not affect the validity of the Mass. That does not mean, however, that a priest can continue to inflict such things on the people, nor that the people should tolerate them. The Code of Canon Law makes it eminently clear that the faithful have a right to the celebration of the liturgy according to the approved rites of the Church (cf. Can. 214).

Nuns, deacons and anointing the sick

Q. Our parish recently had a special Mass for the anointing of the sick, the elderly, and the handicapped. Anointing these were the priest, a Sister and a deacon. My question is regarding the nun, whose action apparently was authorized by the priest. Should she have participated in the anointing, or was this a mockery of the sacrament of the anointing of the sick?

A. Neither the nun nor the deacon should have done any of the anointing. The Sacrament of the Sick can be validly administered only by a priest or bishop.

Preparing for a sick call

Q. What preparations should be made in the home before a priest is called to administer sacraments to the sick or dying?

A. If the sick person himself can make the preparations, or else a relative or friend, the following things should be taken care of: a table near the sickbed should be set up with a crucifix, two lighted candles, holy water — all placed on a white linen cloth.

The room should be free of any distractions (for example, radio, television, stereo). When possible, if the priest is bringing the Blessed Sacrament, he should be quietly and reverently greeted at the door and led to the room by someone carrying a lighted candle, and then announced to the sick person, so that he or she may become attentive.

When such preparations are not possible, then the best should be done to ensure that the infirm individual and the priest (along with any family or friends present) can have an environment in which prayer is possible. In recent years, many priests have marveled at the lack of respect shown to the Blessed Sacrament, as well as the insensitivity to a time of critical importance, often evidenced by people standing around talking and joking, with stereo blaring. These are indications of a total disregard for the sacred and of the rise of a form of neopaganism; frankly, even the pagan Romans would have accorded such a moment greater significance than some contemporary Catholics.

If the truth be told, not infrequently priests have aided in the secularization process by telling people not to make a fuss during a sick call or to be "natural." But there's quite a difference between being "natural" and being irreverent and disrespectful.

Strange liturgical practices

Q. We have some strange liturgical things going on in our parish: at least I think so. What is your opinion on the following: May a priest with laryngitis have a laywoman stand with him at the altar and read all the prayers of the Mass? Is it right for the celebrant to leave the altar during the Our Father to hold hands with the people? Are the extraordinary ministers of Communion and choir supposed to be given Communion before the priest receives, so that they can all receive together with him? Is socializing in church permitted? What is your thinking on the enclosed newspaper for extraordinary ministers of Holy Communion?

A. No, a lay person (male or female) cannot say the priest's prayers of the Mass for him, acting as his ventriloquist.

No, the celebrant is not supposed to leave the altar for any reason once the eucharistic prayer has begun — not for the Our Father nor for the sign of peace.

No, the priest is to receive Communion first, then the deacon, then any other liturgical ministers, then the congregation. The liturgy documents make it clear that the hierarchical nature of the Church is to be demonstrated in the reception of Holy Communion.

No, socializing in church, whether before, during or after the liturgy, reveals a lack of awareness of the presence of the eucharistic Christ and of the sacredness of the place of worship. Reverential silence should characterize a Christian house of worship. That does not mean that one cannot or should not respectfully greet one's neighbor upon entering the pew, but that act of Christian courtesy should not devolve into a social hour.

Regarding the paper, I guess I've seen everything now: a newspaper specifically geared to people whose ministry is intended to be *extraordinary* — that is, rare and unusual. The purpose of this journal seems to be to convince readers of the necessity of making the extraordinary ordinary. Once again, I say this approach to lay involvement in the Church is a direct slap at the nobility of the lay vocation, which is different from but complementary to the priestly vocation.

Group does the Church no good

Q. I have just received the enclosed pamphlet from the Coalition in Support of Ecclesia Dei. Are these people in union with Rome or not? It's hard to tell from their literature if they support [the late Archbishop Marcel] Lefebvre. I know you endorse having Latin Masses available, but this says they have only been allowed since 1984. What's the story here?

A. For the information of our readers. *Ecclesia Dei* was the decree of Pope John Paul II allowing once again, with the permission of the local bishop, the rite of the Mass which was celebrated from the time of the Council of Trent up until 1970. One of the conditions for availing oneself of this papal indult is the stipulation that the current, normative rite be acknowledged as valid (which many devotees of the so-called Tridentine Mass do not accept).

Like you, I found the brochure in question to be very problematic, especially since it suggests that Mass in Latin was forbidden after the Second Vatican Council and consistently uses the expression "traditional Mass" to refer to the rite codified at the Council of Trent (implicitly saying that the current rite is not "traditional"). I expressed these concerns to the Coalition in Support of Ecclesia Dei and received back a very nasty letter, which I followed up with a phone call, confirming all my suspicions about Lefebvrist tendencies, if not a strong position in that camp.

Traditionalism like that does the Church no good, especially since it ends up "more Catholic than the Pope."

Reader shocked by revelations

Q. A friend of mine says he just finished reading the memoirs of Archbishop Annibale Bugnini, the man who orchestrated some of the worst changes in the liturgy under Pope Paul VI, who finally saw through the man and eventually exiled him as the nuncio to Iran, where he died in ignominy. Is any of this true? I find it all rather shocking.
A. Believe it or not, I have just finished reading the work in question (*The Reform of the Liturgy, 1948-1975*, Collegeville, Minn.: Liturgical Press, 1990). A thousand pages long, it is not for the fainthearted or those who have only a passing interest in the liturgy. However, for those who want to know some (perhaps most) of the internal workings that produced the reform of the various rites of the Church after Vatican II, this is an indispensable guide.

Archbishop Bugnini kept detailed notes on every meeting of the Consilium (the group charged with the implementation of the conciliar document on the liturgy), for which he functioned as secretary for the entire fifteen years of its existence; for six of those years, he also served as secretary of the Congregation for Divine Worship. The text itself is rather straightforward and has valuable information on the whole process of development. It is in the footnotes that one discovers somewhat frequently the unsavory character of the man whose style comes across, unfortunately, as manipulative or Machiavellian. I say this in full knowledge of the Latin proverb "*De mortuis, nil nisi bonum*" ("Nothing but good should be spoken about the dead"), but the memoirs invite that as an inescapable conclusion.

Now I am sure that some extremists on the right will use all this to argue against the validity of the whole liturgical reform, even citing accusations of Archbishop Bugnini's alleged Masonic connections. The truth of the matter is that on numerous occasions (astonishing in frequency, really) one finds Pope Paul VI directly intervening in the process so as to forestall the production of rites of dubious orthodoxy or ones which would aid and abet the already accelerating pace of secularization and disobedience to liturgical law. A sad and consistent revelation is how often the Pope and the Curia were confronted by the adamant hostility of bishops from around the world and simply backed off in apparent fright.

Whether or not Archbishop Bugnini was "exiled" by Pope Paul or died in "ignominy" is not possible to say. What is clear, though, is that he seems to have died an unhappy and broken man, disappointed that much of his program for reform never gained the necessary papal or curial acceptance. He ends this massive volume with an apologia, written just before his departure for Iran:

"At a great moment in history, we tried to serve the Church. . . . Builders of the new 'sanctuary,' humble and trusting 'cultivators' of 'God's field,' at times 'unknown soldiers' in the good fight (even if not always victorious), we labored with generous dedication, freedom of spirit, loyal zeal, and prompt obedience for the liturgical renewal and the defense of the goals reached."

Nun may not give homily

Q. In our parish, the pastor allows a nun to give the homily at least once a month. Is this permissible?

A. It is not permissible. This topic was discussed and voted on by the National Conference of Catholic Bishops at their November 1991 meeting, with the result that the norm of law has been maintained, namely, that no unordained person may deliver the homily at Mass.

A brief address (unrelated to the liturgy or readings of the day) on a specific topic (such as the right to life, Marriage Encounter, and so on) may be given by someone either *after* the homily or after the Post-Communion Prayer, at the regular time for announcements.

Priests sharing in the sign of peace

Q. With regard to your answer about the sign of peace in [a recent] issue of TCA, I would like more information about the manner in which it should be performed. Is it proper for the celebrant (and concelebrants) to leave the vicinity of the altar and go to the pews, even down to the rear of the church? Is it proper for individuals to wander about to greet individuals? Perhaps you would allow the concelebrants on some occasions to go to the pews, for example, at a funeral service to greet the mourners or at a wedding to greet the relatives of the couple. At our concelebrations the main celebrant greets each of the concelebrants, no matter how many. Some of the concelebrants do the same. Please clarify this matter.

A. No one should leave the sanctuary during the celebration of the liturgy. Frankly, I find the desire of the priest to play a central role in the sharing of the peace to be a particularly offensive form of clericalism.

Marriage Mass is not Sunday Mass

Q. My family and I attended a wedding at 3:00 on a Saturday afternoon. Afterwards we were told that the pastor gave everyone a dispensation and no one had to attend Mass on Sunday because the wedding Mass counted (even though the liturgy was not Sunday's). Can a pastor declare such a dispensation?

A. No, he may not. Sunday does not begin until 4:00 p.m. on Saturday, with the possibility of the recitation of First Vespers of the Sunday. If three o'clock is acceptable, then why not two or one or noon? In this way we find ourselves reaching the point of the ridiculous. Besides all that, why can people not go to Mass again the next day, especially the newlyweds? Wouldn't that be a wonderful way to launch their first full day of married life, setting a pattern for every future Sunday morning in their new life together?

What is the 'Catholic form of marriage'?

Q. If one is not bound by the Catholic form of marriage, is that marriage considered valid by the Church? Can a Catholic attend a wedding where the party is not bound by the Catholic form of marriage?

A. Let me explain some terms of your question, for the benefit of readers who may not know the technicalities.

By "Catholic form of marriage," we mean a ceremony that takes place before a priest/deacon and two witnesses. All baptized Catholics are bound to the Catholic form of marriage.

Failure to observe the Catholic form or to obtain a dispensation from that form renders a marriage invalid. Non-Catholics are not bound to the Catholic form of marriage, and the Church recognizes unions of non-Catholics as fully valid. Certainly, then, there would be no reason not to attend such a wedding.

The question of non-Catholics and marriage sometimes becomes important when a previously married non-Catholic divorces and wishes to marry a Catholic, because the Church regards his first marriage as valid; hence, the Church considers him still bound to his first spouse. Very often Catholics have difficulty understanding this position. But as was stated earlier, the Church recognizes marriages of non-Catholics as completely valid.

Marriage and the unbaptized partner

Q. If one partner in a marriage ceremony isn't baptized, is the marriage both valid and a sacrament, or just valid?

A. The marriage is valid but not sacramental, which would require both partners to be baptized Christians (not necessarily both Catholics, however).

'Sanatio in radice': a 'healing at the root'

Q. A good number of years ago, I read in a Catholic publication that the Catholic party of a stable marriage which had not been contracted in the Church could take steps unilaterally to have the union regularized. Is this still possible?

A. What you are referring to is technically known as a *sanatio in radice* (literally, a "healing at the root"). If a Catholic is party to an invalid marriage, and there are no canonical obstacles to having the marriage regularized but the other party refuses to go through with the process, the union can be regularized as you suggest. This process is described in Canons 1161-1165. Such a sanction accords validity to the marriage all the way back to its beginning, hence "at the root."

'Assembly line' penance

Q. I was told that it is no longer important to tell the priest when you made your last confession. In our parish, we have had a service with a general examination of conscience, and then, with the priest standing at the altar, everyone would go individually and tell him the one thing bothering him the most. At the end, a general penance would be assigned, and then the people would be dismissed. Was this an authorized version of the Sacrament of Reconciliation?

A. Let's start at the back. The proper name is Sacrament of Penance, which is experienced in one of three different rites of reconciliation. The normal and most commonly used form is that of individual confession of sin with individual absolution.

The second is that of a communal penance service (often used in parishes during Advent and Lent), during which there is a Liturgy of the Word (with homily), a communal examination of conscience, private confession and individual absolution, followed by the dismissal of the congregation. If this option is used, an integral confession must still be made; that is, the penitent tells the priest how long it has been since the last confession (How else will the confessor know how to judge the situation? After all, missing Mass once in five years is very different from missing Mass since last week), all mortal sins (not just the *one* causing the most distress) and any other venial sins which the penitent may want to confess. That is followed by the counsel of the priest, who gives an individual penance that is tailored to the sins and needs of that particular penitent, and then absolution.

The third option is that of general absolution, which involves the conferral of absolution without private confession, to be used in emergency situations (most recently, for example, this was done with soldiers leaving the States to go to the Gulf War). The law of the Church requires that anyone who has received absolution in this manner must subsequently go to private confession as soon as possible thereafter and certainly before receiving general absolution a second time. The American bishops have decreed that general absolution cannot be granted here, except if the person would not have access to a priest for over one month, which, in effect, makes it practically impossible in this country. In other words, simply because a large crowd has materialized for a penance service and there is only a handful of priests, that does not give warranty to general absolution since there is no reason why everyone has to receive the Sacrament of Penance on that particular occasion — presumably, both they and the priest(s) will be available the next day and the day after, and so on, unlike a combat situation or a mission territory where the priest comes once or twice a year.

As you can see, the Church takes very seriously her ministry to sinners, so as to be of the greatest assistance to them in the process of repentance and return to holiness, as well as ongoing growth in sanctity. That cannot be done in assembly-line fashion. Christ comes to us personally — and not in an anonymous group — and the Church must reflect that same approach, particularly in so important a ministry as that of the reconciliation of people to their God.

Whom does the priest represent at Penance?

Q. In the Sacrament of Penance does the priest represent God or the "community" as stated in an article recently in U.S. Catholic, written by a priest?

A. First and foremost, the priest represents Christ in the administration of every sacrament; the priest as an *alter Christus* (another Christ) acts in *persona Christi* (in the person of Christ). This is eminently clear in the absolution formula for the Sacrament of Penance: "I absolve you *in the name of* the Father, and of the Son, and of the Holy Spirit." However, the priest surely represents the community of the Church as well, especially in welcoming a returning sinner back to the fold of the Church.

Confession and Confirmation

Q. If a person who makes a bad confession then makes the profession of faith and receives Confirmation, would he be truly "received" into the Church? Would such a Confirmation be valid and could the matter be rectified by making a good confession afterward?

A. A "bad confession" does not invalidate a sacrament, although it does render its reception sacrilegious and "blocks" the flow of graces normally coming from such sacramental encounters. So, yes, a person would be truly "received" into the Church if in a state of serious sin, but he or she should make a good confession as soon as possible, making sure to explain the previous difficulty.

Communion before the act of penance?

Q. Is it permissible to receive Holy Communion before performing the penance given in confession?

A. I would have no problem with that, particularly if the confessor had assigned the penitent a penance which would span several days (e.g., abstain from meat for a week or read a chapter of the Gospels every day for a month). It seems to me that the goodwill and positive intention to complete the penance enable a person to return to sacramental Communion.

Tampering with the baptismal rite

Q. Our fourth child was just baptized. The priest began the ceremony by saying that he wasn't going to say anything about sin or the Devil; that we need to feel good about ourselves; that we know that we all sin but must be positive; that God loves these babies and Baptism won't change the amount; that Baptism is mainly for parents, godparents, etc., to reaffirm their own Baptism. There was no mention of a sacrament or original sin, and anything referring to Satan or sin was skipped.

When the baby was baptized, the priest anointed his head but not his chest and then baptized him with holy water, which he said we should all bless together (since anyone can do that and not just a priest).

I guess I'm writing to say that I am concerned about whether or not my baby was truly baptized.

A. The only essential element of the Sacrament of Baptism is the pouring of water over the forehead, while saying, "I baptize you in the name of the Father, and of the Son, and of the Holy Spirit." Thus if that was done, your child is validly baptized.

That having been said, if the priest said and did (or did not do) all that you suggest, the man has a serious problem of faith which needs to be brought to the attention of the local bishop. Belief in original sin and a personal, real Devil, and the special character conferred in sacramental ordination is not optional in Catholicism; they are defined dogmas. And, of course, playing footloose with the liturgy is always problematic. The very reason the Church composes particular prayers for her various rites is precisely so that certain key doctrines can be taught and reaffirmed at critical moments in the life of the Church. His elimination of such items betrays a spirit of disobedience but also a refusal to accept what the Church teaches; as even the most dispassionate observer could see, this kind of dissent cannot be tolerated. After all, the Code of Canon Law guarantees to the faithful as a primary right the presentation of the Catholic Faith in all its fullness and the celebration of the rites according to the liturgical norms; the priest in question violated both aspects of your right in this regard.

Valid baptism and confirmation

Q. *In a recent issue you informed a questioner wishing to convert that his "baptism as an Anglican is certainly valid and could never be repeated. You would be required to go to confession, make a profession of faith, and be confirmed. . . ." Since the Church says that Anglican Orders are invalid, doesn't that make his Baptism invalid? And why does he need to be reconfirmed but not rebaptized?*

A. You will undoubtedly recall upon second thought the traditional Catholic teaching which holds that anyone may baptize in an emergency; it is that principle which makes us consider non-Catholic baptisms (done with water in the Name of the Trinity and with the correct intention) valid. The "reconfirmation" is necessary because, as you note, the Church does not accept the validity of Anglican Orders and a validly ordained minister is needed for the valid conferral of Confirmation. In reality, this is not a "reconfirmation," since Confirmation can be received only once, like Baptism and Holy Orders.

Priest's delay was wrong

Q. Is it right for a priest to refuse a baby's baptism? Our grandson was four months old and due for surgery the next day. The priest said that since the mother had not yet finished the classes, he could not baptize the child. As a result, the baby's other grandmother baptized him. Was that a valid baptism?

A. Stories about refusals of infant baptisms get stranger all the time. I cannot imagine a priest denying baptism to a child in danger of death and for the reason, of all reasons, that the mother had not yet finished pre-baptismal instructional classes. Talk about legalism run amok!

I can understand telling parents that a baptism would be postponed until certain conditions were met (such as the parents' return to the sacraments, their completion of classes, and so on), but never in an emergency situation.

The grandmother did the correct thing, and it was most certainly a valid sacrament she administered, assuming it was done in the prescribed manner.

One more thing: Contact the diocesan office and let them know of this terrible abuse of power and lack of sensitivity.

Valid baptisms?

Q. Sometimes priests insist that parents be married in the Church before agreeing to baptize their babies. Suppose the parents lied to the priest, just to get the children baptized. Would the baptisms be valid?

A. Yes, they would. Unlike questions asked in a prenuptial interview, such a question does not bear on the validity of the sacrament. If a priest asked a couple contemplating marriage if either was previously married, and one was but lied, clearly the lie would stand in the way of a valid union, were it to go undetected. Rather than lie, the parents would do better to tell the priest the truth and seek to have the situation straightened out. In fact, that is one of the special graces and side effects associated with baptisms, weddings, and funerals: Very often several people end up being brought closer to the Church because of the first instance, thus forming a genuine "web of grace."

Limiting Communion-in-the-hand

Q. In watching the Christmas Midnight Mass broadcast from St. Patrick's Cathedral in New York, I noticed that Cardinal O'Connor only gave Communion on the tongue. Can he decide to do this? Can any priest do the same?

A. I checked with the New York Archdiocesan Communications Office on this and was told that it was purely coincidental that everyone received on the tongue. That having been said, let me note that any bishop has the authority to limit or totally restrict the practice of Communion-in-the-hand. For example, I know of one diocese in this country where one must be over the age of eighteen to receive in that manner. Furthermore, in situations where desecration of the Eucharist is a viable possibility (like St. Patrick's, where it has already happened), any bishop (or priest) must take action to preserve the Blessed Sacrament from profanation.

Communion on the tongue still valid

Q. *Our Religious Education Director is teaching children who are about to receive their First Communion that they shouldn't receive Communion on the tongue. Is this information correct?*

A. That person is denying children the right to receive Holy Communion in the traditional manner — a right guaranteed all people in the Church, including children just beginning to receive. Communion on the tongue is not to be retained only for past generations too stubborn to change; it is the normative manner of receiving the Eucharist, and when the option of Communion in the hand is explained, it should never be presented as the preferred or new way, so as to suggest that the traditional method is obsolete.

When the celebrant receives the chalice

Q. *Can the celebrant of the Mass receive the Precious Blood after all communicants have received? For example, at Mass the celebrant gives the Precious Blood to a concelebrant who distributes the Blood. The celebrant distributes the Host. After all have received, the celebrant then receives the Precious Blood from the concelebrant. Is this practice correct?*

A. The normal procedure for the reception of Holy Communion is in hierarchical order, the only exception being the deacon, who may correctly receive from the chalice when everyone else has done so. The only legitimate circumstances for what you describe might be that the celebrant realizes that he has a cold and thus would not want to endanger the health of those who would receive from the same chalice after him. As a regular practice, however, it is wrong.

Should priests greet communicants?

Q. It is my understanding that some priests and extraordinary ministers of Holy Communion use the name of the communicant before saying "The Body of Christ." What is the official stand on this? Also, I have seen priests carry on conversations with people in the Communion line and even get down on the floor to shake hands with children and fool around with them while holding the Communion dish in the other hand. Any comment on that one?

A. Regarding the use of the communicant's name, I would note that the rubrics do not tell the minister to do that; therefore, it should not be done. In the Byzantine Rite, on the other hand, the priest may use the communicant's name in saying: "John, the servant of God, receives the Body and Blood. . ." But their ritual is not ours. There is also a practical issue here, namely, in most of our large parishes, it is nearly impossible for the priest to know everyone by name; to call some by name and others not would cause hurt and resentment, just what we don't need at Communion time.

As for the other matter, the priest should not confuse various moments. The time for greeting people (children included) is after Mass at the door of the church. Many priests (myself as well) do, however, give little children too young to receive Holy Communion a special blessing, particularly when they are carried up by their parents. A blessing, however, is a liturgical act, not a social one, and that difference is critical to observe.

One last word: The name for the "Communion dish" is either "paten" or "ciborium" (a larger receptacle for more hosts).

Disposing of a soiled Host

Q. Our extraordinary ministers of Holy Communion have been told that if a Host is soiled by a sick person. It should be taken home and buried in a flower bed. Is this the correct procedure?

A. That is truly bizarre counsel. The correct procedure would be to return the Host to the church and place It in the ablution cup (located next to the tabernacle) until It dissolves, at which time the contents of the cup should be poured down the sacrarium (the special sink in the sacristy, whose pipe goes directly into the ground, rather than the city sewer). The difference is that the Sacred Host not be disposed of when It is still recognizable as such.

Dirty hands at Communion

Q. Why must the ushers pass the collection plate at the same time the priest holds up the Host? Also, why must the shaking of hands come before Communion, as I cannot receive Communion in the hand after shaking hands with people with sticky and sweaty hands?

A. Your first question has me confused. Do you mean that a collection is taken up during the Consecration and Elevation of the Mass? Or are you referring to the offering of the bread and wine during the Presentation of the Gifts or Offertory? If the former is the case, a grave violation is being practiced and should be stopped immediately. If the latter, you need to realize that the rite in question is really a private preparatory ceremony, usually done in silence by the priest while the congregation sings an appropriate hymn.

Regarding your second question, let me note the following: 1. Many people have asked the Holy See to consider transferring the Sign of Peace to the beginning of the Liturgy of the Eucharist (ideally when the gifts are brought to the altar in procession) because they view the rite as too disruptive in its present location. 2. No one has to shake hands with anyone else; one could, for instance, very courteously bow and smile to one's neighbor, wishing him or her the peace of Christ. 3. No one should receive Holy Communion into dirty hands, and no one should place It there if that is the case.

When the priest breaks the Host

Q. In the Communion Rite, the priest breaks the Host over the paten and then puts a small particle in the chalice. What is the significance of this?

A. Many liturgical actions have a whole history behind them, and some are lost in history. This one, however, is quite lovely. As you know, in each celebration of the Eucharistic Sacrifice, we commemorate and renew the Lord's passion, death, and resurrection. At the Consecration, the priest prays over the separate elements of bread and wine, with the result that the Body and Blood of the Lord are separate, signifying His death. In Holy Communion, however, we receive not the dead Christ but the Risen Lord; therefore, the priest mingles a particle of the Lord's Body with His Blood, symbolizing the reuniting of the Body and Blood, so that we in truth receive the Risen One.

Eucharist under only one form

Q. Altar breads are made of pure wheat flour. Our grandson, who will be ready for his First Holy Communion soon, is highly allergic to wheat, and the doctor says the allergy is probably permanent. What can be done for him?

A. The simplest solution would seem to be to ask the priest if your grandson can receive Holy Communion only under the form of wine — a completely legitimate request and an option often used for the sick who are unable to consume solid food.

Communion while kneeling

Q. What can I do when my priest refuses to give me Communion kneeling? I always wait until the end, so that I won't disrupt the flow of communicants, and he just passes me by. I have written to my bishop and have never gotten an answer. The pastor has told me to leave the parish, so I drive a hundred miles once a month to a place where the priest will allow me to kneel.

A. I cannot understand how or why priests would behave in that manner. Certainly the moment of eucharistic Communion should not be a time for polarization. While you surely have a right to receive kneeling if you so choose, I hope you do not think that kneeling is the only proper way to receive Holy Communion, since the Church of the East has had a tradition of standing for centuries.

If the priest in question refuses to discuss this matter with you and resolve it satisfactorily, speak to the dean of the area or the vicar general of the diocese. If none of that works, then contact the apostolic pronuncio in Washington, the Pope's personal representative in the United States.

I must say, however, that I find it nearly incredible that you must drive a hundred miles to find a priest who allows you to kneel for Holy Communion. In the ten-block radius of my parish, you could find every single priest in eight parishes who would permit it, with no questions asked.

Private Masses

Q. We do not have Mass in our parish on the priest's day off. He says a private Mass that day. I don't understand why he does this since the Church does not encourage private Masses and about a dozen people would happily attend. How can we educate our priests on the great value of the Mass for the people?

A. The only reason I can come up with for what your pastor does is that he does not want to be tied into a particular time for Mass on his day off. You are surely correct in noting that private Masses are not encouraged by the Church and should be rather exceptional. I know from personal experience, having been in a situation for almost five years which obviated a public daily Mass for me, that this is a less than ideal approach to the liturgy; the Church permits this only reluctantly and for serious cause.

Facing the people at Mass

Q. As a priest, am I obligated to the prevailing "custom" of facing the people at Mass?

A. As I have noted several times before, the rubrics of the Mass presume that the priest does not face the people, but East (that is, both priest and people face the altar together). I happen to believe that both methods of celebration have assets and liabilities and that perhaps the best way to handle the situation is to utilize both.

The so-called Tridentine Mass also envisioned the priest facing East, but notable exceptions have always existed (for example, St. Peter's Basilica in Rome). Beyond that, throughout Europe decades before the Second Vatican Council, many places had "Mass facing the people." I think a free-standing altar offers the ideal opportunity for both forms of celebration to coexist and to be used interchangeably.

However, many people on both extremes of the liturgical spectrum have turned the issue into one of intense ideology, so that one's acceptability is determined by the direction one faces to offer the Eucharist (I should note that this is an almost uniquely American "hang-up").

Do you have the "right" to celebrate facing East, according to your own preference? Yes. If, however, a strong contrary policy exists, should you withstand it? I'm not so sure that would be a prudent course of action, especially if we say that both postures have had a long and venerable tradition in the Church.

Priest as celebrant of the Mass

Q. At a recent workshop for lectors in our parish, we were told that the priest who says the Mass should not be called the celebrant but the presider, because he does not celebrate the Mass but presides over the assembly. Could you explain what "preside over the assembly" means, as opposed to "celebrate Mass"?

A. There is a sense in which it is quite acceptable to use the terms "celebrant" and "president of the assembly" as interchangeable. Most people who make a big point of doing this, however, have a theological problem with the idea that the priest "celebrates" the liturgy in a way unique to him. They argue that the whole community "celebrates" the liturgy. Let me explain.

While it is certainly true that the priest does not preside at the liturgy in isolation from the rest of the Church, it is also true that his role is indispensable because of his having been configured to Christ through the Sacrament of Orders. In other words, thousands of people could theoretically gather for the liturgy and if there were no ordained priest among them, they could not offer the Eucharistic Sacrifice; just as, theoretically, one could say that if a Mass were scheduled and no one but the priest appeared, he could validly celebrate the liturgy alone (even though the Church does not encourage private Masses).

It is that point which some find offensive about the use of the word "celebrant." A "presider" could be anyone, in reality, not necessarily an ordained minister, whereas "celebrant" emphasizes the fact that his particular presider does so in *persona Christi*. All of this obviously goes back to the relationship between the priesthood of Christ, the priesthood of the faithful, and the ministerial priesthood, dealt with so carefully by the Second Vatican Council in *Lumen Gentium*.

Questions on concelebration

Q. I've found your "Catholic Answer" columns very informative. I've especially liked and followed carefully your "Rubrics of the Sacred Liturgy" articles.

There are a couple of things that I've wondered about when I act as a concelebrant: 1. Do I answer the responses with the people or just keep silent when the principal celebrant makes invocations to the people? 2. Do I, as a concelebrant, stretch out my hands at the Lord's Prayer along with the principal celebrant or do I keep my hands joined? 3. Do I kiss the altar with the principal celebrant when I am standing next to him at the altar just before leaving for the sacristy?

A. The questions you raise are good ones, Father.

1. When serving as a concelebrant of the Mass, the priest should respond to the prayers as a member of the congregation, except for those parts which are properly his own as a concelebrant. For example, he should answer "Amen" to the Opening Prayer; he should not, however, do so at the conclusion of the eucharistic prayer because he sang (or recited) the concluding doxology with the principal celebrant and, therefore, should not answer himself!

2. Hands extended or joined are both legitimate options. I have observed that in Europe, priest-concelebrants generally tend to extend their hands for the Lord's Prayer, while we frequently do not in the States. Whichever option is chosen, it should be uniform for that particular service.

3. Reverencing the altar at the end of Mass is optional for concelebrants. Again, a decision on this ought to be made before Mass begins so that all are doing the same thing.

Who may preach at Mass?

Q. At daily Mass our priest preaches and then asks if anyone in the congregation has anything to add. Often people get up and give their own opinions on Church matters. Is this correct?

A. Such a procedure is completely at odds with good liturgy and Canon Law. Regardless of what we call it, this amounts to having lay people preach at Mass, and only bishops, priests and deacons may lawfully exercise that ministry in the context of a Mass, with no exceptions.

Misinformation on diaconal role

Q. I am a permanent deacon and am somewhat confused by conflicting rubrical information. In this diocese, deacons are trained to lead the congregation into the memorial acclamation by saying, "Let us proclaim the mystery of faith." However, the Roman Missal says this is done by

the *"celebrant alone." Can such a change be made at the diocesan level?*
A. No, it can't, but the practice you cite is nearly universal in the United States. In my judgment, this is due to a faulty English translation, which leads people to conclude that the text you mention is indeed a diaconal one. Let me explain.

The Latin text says, *"Mysterium fidei,"* which is best translated as "the mystery of faith." It is a simple statement of fact. The English version we have takes the statement and turns it into an invitation to prayer or a directive, which is, of course, a diaconal function in the liturgy (e.g., "Let us offer each other the sign of peace," "Bow your heads and pray for God's blessing," "The Mass is ended, go in peace."). In point of fact, however, the particular line in question is part of the consecratory formula, where it was before the revision of the liturgy, and that is obviously a priestly prayer.

I do not posit ill-will of people who argue for it as a diaconal part; they are simply misinformed. But a careful reading of the Roman Missal (such as you have done) will reveal the proper proclaimer of that line.

Deacons and the celebration of Mass

Q. If deacons, both transitional and permanent, cannot celebrate Mass, why are they permitted to concelebrate so many of the parts? Why are they allowed to self-communicate?

A. Deacons, transitional or permanent, are not "concelebrants" of the Mass; they do, however, perform those parts which are theirs. In the liturgy, there is a diversity of roles and ministries: The lector proclaims the first two readings; the cantor leads the people in sacred songs; the altar boys serve the priest. Similarly, the deacon plays his part by leading the invocations of the Penitential Rite and the General Intercessions; by proclaiming the Gospel and preaching (if permitted to do so); by preparing the altar; by assisting with the distribution of Holy Communion. What makes someone a concelebrant is reciting the words of institution along with the principal celebrant. One also needs to avoid the appearance of concelebration; sometimes other ministers (deacons included) stand next to the celebrant at the altar, and that is incorrect; the deacon should stand behind and to the side of the celebrant, so that the wrong impression is not given. Furthermore, the deacon should kneel from the epiclesis (the invocation of the Holy Spirit) to the end of the consecration. No other ministers should be anywhere near the altar during the eucharistic prayer; rather, they should be positioned at kneelers.

Chasubles during the summer

Q. The priests in our parish discontinue wearing chasubles during the summer months for both daily and Sunday Masses. Our church is air-conditioned. Is this permissible?

A. Whether or not a church is air conditioned is immaterial. The General Instruction of the Roman Missal requires the principal celebrant of the Mass to wear a chasuble and encourages all concelebrants to do so as well (although they may wear only an alb and stole, if necessary). The only time the principal celebrant may be excused from using the chasuble is if he is offering Mass outside a sacred place (e.g., outdoors), and then only if necessary.

'Chasu-alb' is no alternative

Q. In lieu of wearing the chasuble over the alb and stole when celebrating Mass, my parish priest wears a white robe and stole only. When questioned, he cited the enclosed article. Could you please comment?

A. The so-called "chasu-alb" was permitted by a decree of the Congregation for Divine Worship on May 1, 1971, under the following circumstances: concelebration (but not for the principal celebrant) or for Masses celebrated outside a sacred place. That is all; in fact, the document makes the point that "the traditional liturgical vestments are to continue in use: the amice [when needed to cover the neck completely], the alb, the stole, and the chasuble. . . ."

Therefore, there is no justification for the argument presented, suggesting that a chasu-alb is simply a legitimate alternative to the traditional vestments; it is not.

The stole

Q. Our pastor does not wear a stole when he hears confessions; he says it's no longer required. Is that true? Are the confessions he hears valid?

A. A stole must be worn by a priest (or deacon) for each and every celebration of a sacrament, and for preaching as well. In other words, any time a priest exercises his priestly office, he should wear a stole as the outward sign of the authority to do what he is doing. However, failure to wear a stole in no way invalidates a sacrament; for invalidity, either the matter or the form of a sacrament must be tampered with, and the stole does not touch on either.

The color of Mass vestments

Q. At a Sunday Mass recently the priest wore a blue vestment. When may blue vestments be worn? What about gold vestments?

A. Since your letter came during May, I suspect your priest may have been wearing a vestment with a Marian motif; I likewise suspect that the vestment was not really blue but white with much blue banding and other decorations. Blue is not a liturgical color in the Latin Rite. Some liturgists have pressed for the use of blue for Advent, to distinguish that season from the more somber violet or purple of Lent, but no such change has been approved. In the ancient Sarum (English) Rite, blue was used for Advent, but that rite has been defunct for centuries. Spain also had an indult for blue vestments for Marian feasts, but that certainly does not apply to this country.

Gold vestments are used for solemn occasions — an alternative to white.

Wearing a biretta during Mass

Q. We have an old priest who helps out in our parish. He wears the biretta coming and going from the rectory to keep his hair from blowing around. The older people in the parish would like him to wear it at Mass, but he says that he does not know when to put it on and off at the Mass anymore since the changes of Vatican II. I remember years ago my pastor wore it when he sat at the sedilia for the readings, and for the Gloria and the Creed. He took it off at the "et incarnatus est." He also wore it when he left the altar. There seems to be nothing about the biretta in the new documents. Would you be able to clarify when the biretta is and is not to be worn during Mass?

A. Since the directives do not call for the use of the biretta, it should not be worn during the liturgy. Presumably, it is now to be regarded as part of the regular and/or academic garb of a cleric. I must say, however, that I have noticed that the canons of St. Peter's Basilica in Rome use the biretta for Sunday Vespers.

How should lay ministers dress?

Q. In [a recent] Catholic Answer, your guideline article on the sacred liturgy touched on the dress or garb of the reader. In our parish for the past twenty years, all lay men and women who served as commentators, eucharistic ministers, altar boys, and choir members wore vestments — robes, cassocks or surplices. It never occurred to us that we had mini-clerics taking part in the services. We feel that wearing the vestments raises these positions a little above "street level" (they are a part of the services). Have we been wrong all these years? Are your guidelines a MUST by Church authority, or do they fall under traditions, customs, etc.?

A. What I said was not by way of law but simply a reflection of the general consensus of liturgists. Surely a case can be made for providing people with some kind of uniform for liturgical functions, especially when one sees all too often the bad taste exhibited by some people. My only point was that, as a norm, lay people performing roles proper to laity should look like laity; the one notable exception to that is the situation with altar boys, who have always imitated the garb of clergy since they really serve as substitute seminarians, as it were.

The origin of the sign of peace

Q. I would like to know how the sign of peace came about. Also, does it have to be at a certain point during the Mass?

A. The scriptural origin of the sign of peace may be found in Matthew 5:24, wherein Our Lord reminds His listeners of the need to be reconciled with one another before offering one's gift at the altar. The rite was incorporated into the liturgy at a very early date, being located in different places at different times and even having slightly different meanings. When the sign of peace occurred before the Offertory of the Mass, it signified the desire to make peace with one another in the family of God; when it was transferred to its present location, it became much more a declaration of love and unity. Initially, it was exchanged by the entire congregation and then restricted to those in the sanctuary. In the postconciliar liturgical reform, the rite was restored to all present.

The rite is always optional, that is, up to the discretion of the celebrant. In my parish, for instance, we refrain from the sign of peace during Advent and Lent, so as to make its meaning shine out more clearly at the great feasts of Christmas and Easter, and also to remind everyone that one cannot have peace with one's fellowman if he is not at peace with his God and himself first. In the Anglican liturgy, the rite of peace takes place at the Offertory.

In the Latin Rite of the Catholic Church, the Neo-Catechumenate Movement has an indult from the Holy See to follow the same usage. It seems to me that many people object not to the sign of peace itself but to its location, as it can be disruptive at one of the peak moments of intimacy with the Lord. I know that some liturgists have been asking the Holy See to consider such a change in the placement of the rite, and I would favor that move. However, until such a change is adopted (and there is no evidence to suggest that it will be), the exchange of peace is to take place only after the fraction of the Host or else omitted.

Omitting the sign of the cross at Mass

Q. I've noticed that for certain rituals of the Roman Rite, such as the Funeral Mass, the celebration of the Sacrament of Baptism, the Masses of Palm Sunday, and the Presentation of the Lord, the Sign of the Cross is omitted in the ritual books for the beginning of the Rite. Is this omission in the ritual books because it is assumed that celebrants will automatically include the sign of the cross in these rites, or is the sign of the cross to be omitted in these cases?

A. At times, the Missal notes that the celebrant "begins Mass in the usual manner." That means, of course, with the sign of the cross and the greeting. If that is not said, then one does not include them. It is important to recall that the Roman Missal gives complete directives, and one should not attempt to supply items which do not appear, either from one's private judgment as to what should be there or from one's experience and/or knowledge of prior rites.

Sign of the cross before the Gospel

Q. Can you please explain the significance of making the sign of the cross on the forehead, lips and heart before the reading of the Gospel at Mass?

A. The action empresses a desire that the Lord would be in our minds, on our lips, and in our hearts as we hear the Gospel and then proclaim it by the lives we lead in the world.

The sign of the cross

Q. Should there be a sign of the cross at the conclusion of the Penitential Rite? I have been told that the new rubrics call for one only at the beginning and end of the Mass. However, I cannot find any such directive in the Sacramentary. And if that is true, then does it also apply to the sign of the cross during the Roman Canon at the words, "Let us be filled with every grace and blessing"?

A. Ritual gestures used in the Mass are indicated at the appropriate moments in the text. If a gesture is not mentioned, it is not to be employed. Sometimes people try to reintroduce gestures used in earlier rites and justify the practice by saying that the revised rites do not forbid their use, but that is to misunderstand the nature of liturgical directives — which tell a celebrant what *should* be done, not what should *not* be done.

Now on to your specific question. The rubrics do not call for a sign of the cross at the conclusion of the Penitential Rite. Some priests and people recall that in the old Mass the rite did end that way; however, it was for a different prayer.

The *Misereatur* (which is retained) was followed by the *Indulgentiam* (which was dropped), and that was the prayer that had the sign of the cross. And, yes, the prayer to which you allude in the Roman Canon does call for a sign of the cross.

January 1

Q. When I returned to the practice of the Faith some years ago, I discovered that the Feast of the Circumcision (January 1) had been changed to the Solemnity of Mary, Mother of God. Why the change, especially since I remember being taught that the old feast was so important because it was the day Jesus first shed His blood. Please comment.

A. I cannot think of another day which has had more name changes than January 1. Obviously, the Church has an instinctive desire to observe the day in some way. As you correctly note, the feast once commemorated Our Lord's circumcision, which was also the occasion for His naming. However, the celebration in honor of Mary's maternity is perhaps the most ancient Marian feast in the liturgical calendar. Then, of course, we have the secular observance of New Year's Day, along with Pope Paul VI's addition of the notion of January 1's being a "World Day of Prayer for Peace." Needless to say, any one of these themes would provide a homilist with much fodder for preaching; with amazing good effect, some priests actually tie all the themes together in a very coherent and sensible manner.

As far as the importance of the day being linked to Jesus' first shedding of His blood, I think that notion would be much more in line with older approaches which tried to find hints or clues about Jesus' later life and ministry hidden away in His infancy or early manhood. If that kind of piety is meaningful to you, by all means feel free to avail yourself of it, but it is no more than one way among many to relate to the celebration in question.

First Communion on Easter only?

Q. Why is it "liturgically correct" to have First Communion on Easter Sunday only?
A. It's not. The solemn reception of First Communion can take place at any time after the candidates are properly catechized and have made their first confession.

For adult converts to Catholicism, the ideal time for reception into the Church is the Easter Vigil, receiving the "sacraments of initiation" in the sequence of Baptism, Confirmation, Eucharist. For those converts coming into full communion with the Catholic Church from another Christian body, Confirmation and First Communion can take place at any time; however, the Easter Vigil is also appropriate for them — unless that time would unduly delay their coming into Catholic unity.

The Feast of the Incarnation

Q. When is the Feast of the Incarnation? March 25 is traditionally celebrated as the Feast of the Annunciation and, of course, December 25, the Nativity of Jesus. As I read Webster's Dictionary, to make "incarnate" is to give bodily form and substance, and it defines the Incarnation as "the union of divinity with humanity in Jesus Christ." If the Church recognizes the Nativity as the Feast of the Incarnation, isn't it a contradiction to teach that life begins at conception? On the other hand, if the Feast is on March 25, why is it not a major feast — a holy day of obligation? Certainly the "annunciation" of the Incarnation wouldn't take precedence over the Incarnation itself when they both occurred on the same day, or would it?

A. The liturgical commemoration of the Incarnation is March 25, when Our Lord began His human existence in the womb of the Blessed Virgin Mary. Christmas itself is a late-comer to the liturgical calendar; the much more important feast was that of the Epiphany, when the Lord was manifested to the Gentiles. March 25 is a solemnity, equal in rank to Christmas. Remember: Not all solemnities are holy days of obligation, for we have only six in the United States.

Instrumental music during Lent

Q. *I understand that the organ should not be played during Lent. Is that correct?*

A. The directives indicate that no instrumental music should be played during Lent (or Advent) and that instruments should be used most sparingly even to accompany the singing; where possible, they should not be used at all during Advent and Lent. Given the situation in most parishes, however, *a capella* singing would result in musical disasters.

Congregational refrains at Mass

Q. *Cardinal Jean-Marie Lustiger expressed disapproval of the use of (congregational) refrains in the singing of the Gloria. He seemed to believe that the succinctness of the prayer was intentional and repetition diluted the liturgical effect. Is there a just cause for his objection?*

A. I tend to concur with the Cardinal's judgment on this. One of the first efforts of the liturgical movement (way back at the time of Pope St. Pius X) was to eliminate wanton repetition. Many older Catholics will recall a Gloria or Sanctus which was interminable because of lines being repeated *ad nauseam* (e.g., "*et in terra pax, pax hominibus, hominibus bonae voluntatis, bonae voluntatis. . .*"). The Roman liturgy has always been known for its simple, straightforward style, which is very often compromised by refrains. Furthermore, a refrain has a way of establishing a theme, and at times the refrain chosen is not in fact the theme of the prayer. The one exception which quickly comes to mind is the Gloria for the "Mass of the Bells," in which "Glory to God in the highest" or "Glory to God" is the congregational refrain. Not only is that the theme, but it enables the people to participate with a very simple line in an otherwise intricate and lovely composition.

The Church does not have a hard and fast rule in this area, relying instead on the professional expertise of good liturgical musicians.

173

Which liturgical music is best?

Q. Which is more important for the liturgy: Gregorian chant or contemporary hymns? Please explain.

A. I do not like to deal in dichotomies unnecessarily. By that I mean that most things in life are not either/or situations, and where it is possible to combine rather than divide, I favor that option because it is more inclusive and more "catholic," in the sense of "all-encompassing."

As most TCA readers know, I have a high regard for Gregorian chant; this is not a personal idiosyncrasy but a conviction that Gregorian unites people with believers of past ages and with diverse cultures today. I think those considerations, plus the very nature of the origins of Gregorian music specifically designed for worship in the Roman Rite, moved the Fathers of the Second Vatican Council to declare that "other things being equal, [Gregorian Chant] should be given pride of place in liturgical services" (*Sacrosanctum Concilium*, n. 116). It is also eminently "singable," even by the young and untrained voices.

The question comes in when we ask what "other things being equal" means. In the American context, it is often related to a plastic or disposable mentality, which is very shallow, holding that everything must be new at every turn and catering to an immature disposition that gets bored with things all too quickly. When we talk about "contemporary hymns," the repertoire often consists of compositions that are superficial, both musically and theologically. The best professional assessment of the situation appears in Thomas Day's *Why Catholics Can't Sing*. To be perfectly honest, the issue is not that Catholics *can't* sing, but that they don't *want* to do so, most often because of bad music and even worse musicians and leaders of song. Given the present state of liturgy in the United States, the average parish could probably do best by using a healthy combination of Gregorian chant for the Ordinary of the Mass and some of the truly inspiring works that come from Anglican and Lutheran hymnody.

The role of a cantor in the liturgy

Q. What is the role of a cantor in the liturgy? Are there any restrictions in terms of age, sex, etc.? May a cantor do a solo at any point during the Mass (e.g., as a post-Communion meditation)?

A. A cantor is essentially a leader of song — that is, one who leads the congregation in making the appropriate sung responses and in singing those parts of the Mass which pertain to them. Aside from faith and right living, the only other qualification is that the person be possessed of musical ability which enables him or her to perform the assigned task. Over the years, I have found that people accustomed to doing solos generally make poor cantors, since their style of singing does not usually inspire people to join in with them but rather to listen to them.

As far as the cantor performing a solo, I would think it inappropriate since it would tend to confuse two distinct musical roles. Therefore, solos should be done by solo artists and congregational leading by cantors.

Offering both species at Mass

Q. In our parish, wine is served quite often at daily and Sunday Mass. Also, many people take the Host and dip it in the wine. Are these practices allowed?

A. Once more, let me begin by cautioning a more careful use of language: Wine is not served at Mass; Holy Communion offered from the chalice or under both species is the way you should express the practice. Where permission of the bishop has been granted and there are sufficient ministers for the chalice(s), offering both species is permitted. It is never allowed, however, for people to self-communicate by dipping the Host in the chalice.

Communion and self-communication

Q. I read in another question-and answer column that a communicant cannot take the consecrated Host from the priest and then dip into the chalice himself. What's the difference, if a person is allowed to touch the Host to begin with?

A. It's not a question of touching the Host, but of ministering It. When a person takes the Host, dips It into the chalice and then consumes It, that person is self-communicating. There are two correct ways to offer communicants the option of both species: first, the priest dips the Host into the chalice and then places It on the communicant's tongue; second, the priest presents the communicant with the Sacred Host, and then the communicant proceeds to a station where the chalice is available, at which point the communicant is presented with the chalice, from which he or she drinks.

The Church is very concerned that it never appear that a person is "helping himself" to Holy Communion; we do not take Communion; we receive Communion. The difference in verbs is crucial, since it underscores the fact that the life of grace is initiated by Christ and not by ourselves.

Conditions for intercommunion

Q. As an Episcopalian, when traveling in countries where there are no (or few) Anglican churches, I attend Roman Catholic Mass. Since our branches of the Church are not in communion with each other, I refrain from receiving Holy Communion. However, a friend of mine says that there is a provision in Roman Catholic law which permits Anglicans, in certain circumstances, to receive. I am almost certain that this is not the case, but I would appreciate a clarification.

Q. Some time ago I went to a Lutheran wedding. At Communion time, the pastor said that anyone who believed that this was the Body and Blood of Christ could come forward to receive. I was surprised to see some Catholics do so because I thought we couldn't.

A. The general law of the Church permits only Catholics in the state of grace to receive Holy Communion. Non-Catholics may do so under the most restricted conditions: The Christian in question must not have access to his or her own minister for a prolonged period of time and should be in a situation of grave spiritual need (e.g., a time of religious persecution); that same person must profess the same eucharistic faith as the Catholic Church; and he or she must request Communion on his or her own initiative. As should be obvious, these conditions would be rather hard to verify in most places, but especially in the United States.

Under similar conditions, Catholics can receive from non-Catholic clergy only if that minister were validly ordained; otherwise, he would be unable to confect (consecrate) the Eucharist: No valid priesthood, no valid Eucharist. For the most part, that would mean that Catholic reception of Communion could only occur through the ministrations of Eastern Orthodox priests. I should note, however, that the Orthodox are even stricter on the question of intercommunion than we are, so that even if our law permitted it, theirs would not, at least in general practice.

Self-communication is only for celebrants

Q. I sent a copy of your answer on intinction, self-communion, and self-intinction (The Catholic Answer Book, pages 100, 101) to our pastor. The two latter situations occur in our parish. He responded to self-communion for extraordinary ministers (I am also one) by sending me a copy of the Rite for Commissioning a Minister of Holy Communion, which I'm sure he received from the archdiocese.

The paragraph he checked and underlined is as follows: "Our brother (sister) N., has been entrusted with the important duty of distributing Holy Communion to himself (herself) and to his/her fellow Christians and of bringing communion and viaticum to the sick and to those in danger of death."

Since your article, I have become very uncomfortable self-communicating when scheduled as an extraordinary minister at Sunday Mass but would ache if I were not to receive. Please help!

A. The only time an extraordinary minister of Holy Communion is to function as such is when an ordinary minister is unavailable, right? Therefore, ipso facto an extraordinary minister cannot give himself Communion when a priest is present. The clause your pastor cited refers to Communion services in the absence of a priest. No one (bishop, priest or deacon — all included) may ever self-communicate, the only exception being when a priest celebrates or concelebrates Mass (because in that moment he is functioning most clearly *in persona Christi*). And so I stand by my original statement.

The Orthodox and Communion

Q. Can a Russian Orthodox man married to a Catholic woman rightly receive Communion weekly in the Catholic church in which they were married?

A. No, he may not. His own Orthodox Church does not permit it, nor do we (except in cases of extreme emergency).

It also surprises me to read that he and his wife were married in a Catholic rather than an Orthodox church, because our general procedure is to urge such mixed marriages to be celebrated in the Orthodox Church. Why? Because the Orthodox Church regards the priest as the minister of the Sacrament of Matrimony, while we speak of the couple themselves as the ministers, with the priest or deacon serving as the official witness of the Church. Since our priests and deacons do not have the intention to administer the sacrament, Orthodox theology reasons, no sacrament is actually confected (that is, an invalid marriage). On the other hand, the Catholic Church has no difficulty in simply granting a dispensation from the Catholic form of marriage, thus allowing the ceremony to take place in the Orthodox Church, where it is held to be valid by both communities.

Is bigger better?

Q. Is it better to use one large host, which is broken into many pieces for the Communion of the faithful, than individual ones? I was told the fraction of the host is to remind us that Jesus allowed Himself to be broken in order to save us.

A. The purpose of having one large host, which is then broken into smaller particles, is intended to symbolize the oneness of the loaf that is the Body of Christ and its being shared by the many members who form one Body as Christ's Church. Thus, the eucharistic Body of Christ and the ecclesial Body of Christ are intimately related to each other. What you were told might be pious speculation, but that is not the Church's primary understanding of the rite in question.

Breaking the host

Q. At the beginning of Lent, our parish began using an extra-large host at Mass. At Communion time, the extraordinary ministers of the Eucharist, standing alongside the priest at the altar, take half of the large host and break it into smaller pieces for distribution to the faithful. It seems to me this confuses the role of the extraordinary minister with that of the ordained priest. Our pastor said it was just for practical reasons. Please comment.

A. Only the priest (or deacon) may perform the fraction (the technical name for the action you describe). "Practicality" is not a legitimate criterion for liturgical practice, particularly when it introduces confusion about the distinct roles of the ordained and non-ordained.

Communion: More than once?

Q. How many times may we go to Holy Communion in a day?

A. The norm for reception of Holy Communion is once a day. However, if one attends a second Mass, he may receive a second time, provided he has attended the whole Mass. No one may receive more than that, even if fulfilling a liturgical role (e.g., cantor, lector, and so on) at several Masses on one day. A priest celebrating more than two Masses is obviously exempt from that norm since his reception of Holy

Communion is essential to the offering of the Mass, but a priest should not unnecessarily concelebrate, if that would make his third or fourth Mass for the day; in that instance, he should simply assist at Mass like any other member of the faithful.

The Blood of Christ

Q. I am a fourteen-year-old boy and serve Mass every Tuesday. Our pastor said that we may receive the Eucharist under both species. When some young people (my age) went to the extraordinary minister of the Eucharist to receive the Precious Blood, she said they weren't allowed. Am I permitted to receive the Blood as well as the Body?

A. To answer your question simply, yes, you are permitted to receive Holy Communion under both forms, regardless of your age. That having been said, let me note that my own experience with this practice for elementary- and secondary-school students has been less than edifying. While there are notable exceptions, most children and adolescents tend to react to reception from the chalice in a silly or giddy fashion.

Of course, proper catechesis should precede the practice. But human nature being what it is at that age, I'm not too sure if we're not looking for trouble. The easiest way to handle it all, however, is to distribute Holy Communion by intinction, which offers both species without either the connotations conjured up by drinking from the chalice or the health hazards. By the way, why has the extraordinary minister overruled the pastor?

Intinction: who may do it?

Q. You have written about intinction on a number of occasions, but my question is, who may do that? Must it be a priest, or may an extraordinary minister of Holy Communion distribute Communion that way?

A. Intinction is one of three normal ways to distribute Holy Communion in the Western Church (the other two being the Sacred Host alone and consuming the Host, and drinking from the chalice). As such, it is an option left to the discretion of the distributor of Holy Communion, whether that be a priest, deacon, or extraordinary minister. If one is not the celebrant, I think it would be a good idea to consult with him before deciding on the particular procedure to be followed.

Recipe for Communion hosts

Q. Are there any rules regarding what Communion hosts are to be made of? If so, would you please furnish an approved recipe?

A. Altar breads for the Western Church are to be made of pure wheat flour and water, with no additives (e.g., honey, sugar, salt, etc.).

Holy Communion at funerals

Q. We had a funeral at our church some time back at which the priest did not distribute Communion to anyone except the altar boys — at the family's request. Was he within his rights to do that?

A. Not knowing all the details, I could only guess that perhaps the family advised the priest that many family members were in irregular situations as far as the Church was concerned or that many were non-Catholics and, hence, ineligible to receive Holy Communion. To avoid embarrassment, they may have asked the priest not to offer Holy Communion to anyone in the congregation.

While this would have been motivated by a desire to safeguard the integrity of the sacrament and to respond in a sensitive manner to a ticklish problem, it would still be an incorrect way to go about it. If you look in the missalettes used in parishes, you will find a statement prominently displayed that indicates regulations on the reception of Holy Communion, which include the eucharistic fast and other necessary conditions (having full membership in the Catholic Church and being in a state of grace).

Since the priest usually needs to guide the congregation through a funeral liturgy (either because there are many non-Catholics present or because many Catholics there do not go to Mass regularly), I find it very easy and not at all awkward at Communion time to say something like this: "We are now approaching the time for Holy Communion. I invite all baptized Catholics in the state of grace to come forward to receive Holy Communion. If you are not a Catholic, may I suggest that you use this time to pray for the unity of Christ's Church, so that one day we will be able to share in full eucharistic Communion. If you are a Catholic who, for whatever reason, are unable to receive Holy Communion, I would urge you to resolve now to regularize your situation with Christ's Church as soon as possible, so that you may be able to share fully in the Lord's Eucharistic Sacrifice by receiving His Body and Blood."

The paten is still useful

Q. When I was an altar boy in the mid-'70s, we used to hold the paten under each communicant's chin, to catch any particles that might fall between the priest's fingers and the person's tongue. Since Communion-in-the-hand has become fashionable, I don't see that done anymore. Aren't we concerned with crumbs now, since some will certainly be dropped from many people's hands?

A. I agree with you. In fact, one of the arguments against Communion-in-the-hand is that the eucharistic particles are apt to be lost. Interestingly, when Anglicans practice Communion-in-the-hand, they do not pick up the Host from their hand and then place It in the mouth; they bring their hand to the mouth and consume It directly, to avoid the very situation you mention.

No liturgical document has ever indicated that the paten should not be used, and you will notice that at papal Masses, the master of ceremonies does hold a paten beneath the chin of each communicant — even though everyone is receiving Holy Communion on the tongue, where there is far less danger of lost particles than on the hand.

History serves as basis for statement

Q. In a past issue of TCA, you stated that "altar boys . . . serve as substitute seminarians, as it were." I can't find any basis for that anywhere.

A. The history of altar servers demonstrates my statement. Originally, those who served at the altar were young men en route to the priesthood, usually ordained to the ministry of acolyte. Gradually, as candidates for the priesthood were trained in seminaries and lost contact with parishes, service at the altar was supplied by young boys, often enough those interested in pursuing a priestly vocation. And that connection is as strong today as it ever was. Most priests will tell you that it was the combination of serving Mass and a Catholic-school education which brought them to discern and develop their call to the priesthood.

General absolution and altar girls

Q. I am enclosing two of our parish bulletins which deal with general absolution and altar girls, both of which you say are forbidden by Church law. Here we are told, however, that Canon 87 of the revised Code of Canon Law gives the Bishop of Rochester the freedom to "disperse [sic] from both universal and particular disciplinary laws established for his territory or for his subjects by the supreme authority of the Church." Is this true?

A. Your parish bulletin does a great disservice by quoting only part of the canon in question. First of all, the verb is "dispense," not "disperse." The fact that the word is consistently misspelled in your bulletin suggests that the person responsible is less than familiar with canonical language, and that this is not just a typographical error.

The canon cited goes on to say that a diocesan bishop "cannot dispense, however, . . . from those laws whose dispensation is especially reserved to the Apostolic See or to another authority." Among such matters "reserved to the Apostolic See" are those concerning the sacred liturgy. Therefore, no local bishop may dispense from the universal law so as to allow for either altar girls or general absolution (in the latter case, when the universal norms are not followed, that is, prolonged impossibility of receiving the Sacrament of Penance).

Beyond that, Canon 392 reminds us that "since [the bishop] must protect the unity of the universal Church, the bishop is bound to promote the common discipline of the whole Church and therefore to urge observance of all ecclesiastical laws. He is to be watchful lest abuses creep into ecclesiastical discipline, *especially* concerning the ministry of the Word, the celebration of the sacraments and sacramentals, the worship of God, and devotion to the saints, and also the administration of property" (emphasis added).

Requirements for altar servers

Q. I know that females are not permitted to serve Mass, but must male servers be single? Is there a particular age limit?

A. If you are simply referring to those who serve at the altar in an unofficial capacity, without formal institution into the permanent ministry of acolyte, there are no requirements regarding age or marital status. In the United States it is unusual to find older men serving, but in other countries that is not necessarily the case.

OK to have female servers?

Q. I am a new subscriber to TCA and am writing about the use of female altar servers, a practice widespread in my diocese. I wrote of my concerns

to the auxiliary bishop for our region and received the reply which I enclose.
His reply refers to the 1917 Code of Canon Law (813, no. 2), which
prohibited female servers at the altar. He further states that the same
prohibition was not retained in the 1983 Code. From this, he draws the
conclusion that the General Instruction of the Roman Missal of 1969 or
the instruction Inaestimabile Donum (on dealing with eucharistic
abuses) of April 3, 1980, should be interpreted in view of the new Code
of Canon Law which abrogated Canon 813 (no.2) and came into effect
in 1983.

He related a conversation at the Congregation for the Sacraments
and Divine Worship with then-Archbishop Virgilio Noé, who said the
"question of service of females in the sanctuary is an issue best left to
the judgment of local diocesan bishops in accord with the customs of
local time and place." The bishop referred me to an article in The Jurist
(48, 1988, pp. 692-708) for further explanation.

I am not trying to cause trouble. Was I wrong in assuming that
women should not be serving at the altar? I realize you may have
addressed this topic before. Should I "back off" on this issue?

A. Yes, I have dealt with the issue on numerous occasions, and, no, you
shouldn't back off for several reasons. To be frank. I am answering your
letter because I am shocked by the dishonesty of the reply you received
from the bishop.

As our regular readers know, I am not a "bishop-basher"; if
anything, I generally try to make as rational a defense of bishops'
positions as I can. But the answer you got is beyond the pale.

Any bishop should know that the Code of Canon Law, by its own
statements, makes clear that it does not deal with liturgical matters as a basic
principle, and only when that is absolutely necessary — usually for
questions of validity, liceity, and so on. Therefore, when the 1983 code did
not repeat the prohibition of the 1917 code on altar girls, that was not a
unique or revelatory act; it was merely "cleaning up" the code and getting
rid of things that really have no place in it. The code also notes that any law
not specifically abrogated by the new law remains in force. Therefore, with
no contrary statements from the Holy See permitting altar girls and dozens
of replies from the Congregation for the Sacraments and Divine Worship
reinforcing the prohibition, as well as letters from our own nuncios (both
Cardinal Pio Laghi and Archbishop Agostino Cacciavillan), what more
evidence could anyone want on this matter?

Furthermore, as I observed in an earlier question, if altar girls are permitted, why have various American bishops asked Rome for permission for the practice? And surely, why has the third draft of the women's pastoral letter raised this topic up for discussion; we don't discuss what is already licit, do we?

As for the alleged statement of now-Cardinal Noé, there are three points. First, we have no proof that he ever said any such thing, inasmuch as it is simply hearsay. Second, if he said it, that was no more than his private opinion, which is worth no more than yours or mine. Third, the archbishop would have known better than to say such a thing because he knows that liturgical law is not in the hands of the local bishop and must always reflect universal law, unless an indult has been obtained to deviate from the universal practice.

A blessing for prayer books?
Q. Can breviaries and other prayer books be blessed?
A. Yes, the ritual for blessing these items can be found in *The Book of Blessings*.

A crowing rooster
Q. Recently, while visiting a Midwestern monastery, I noticed that the cross atop the church steeple was replaced by a crowing cock. Upon inquiring, I was told that since Vatican II we celebrate the Resurrection, "which we all know is represented by a crowing rooster." Please comment.
A. I'm always cautious when told that "we all know" something, because it's usually not so, especially in this instance.

Is the respondent suggesting that prior to Vatican II we did not celebrate the Resurrection? Or that since the Council the Crucifixion has lost its centrality as the means of salvation? If so, he knows neither history nor theology. Good Friday and Easter Sunday are two sides of the same coin; you can't have one without the other.

As far as the crowing rooster being a symbol of the Resurrection, I always thought it was a reminder of Peter's denial of Christ!

Electric candles at the altar
Q. I read somewhere that electric candles should not be used during the Holy Sacrifice of the Mass. I have shared this concern with my previous

pastor, the present one, and the parish council — all of whom have chosen to ignore me. Who's right?

A. I presume you are referring to the candles used at the altar. If so, you are correct. A response from the Holy See on this matter puts it thus: "Candles intended for liturgical use should be made of material that can provide a living flame without being smoky or noxious and that does not stain the altar cloths or coverings. Electric bulbs are banned in the interest of safeguarding authenticity and the full symbolism of light."

Some people will undoubtedly ask, "Then what about electric vigil lights?" Although there has never been a pronouncement from the Holy See on this specific issue, I think the operative words given above ("living flame" and "authenticity") should offer reasonable guidance, such that one could conclude that electric candles would not be used, even for devotional purposes.

What qualifies as a crucifix?

Q. Does a cross bearing the figure of the risen Christ qualify as a crucifix?

A. I suppose you are referring to a risen Christ imposed onto a cross, and I imagine that it does — although I think it tends to merge two symbols in a not altogether felicitous manner. On the other hand, may a statue of the risen Christ replace a crucifix? No.

The use of the paschal candle

Q. Are there any specific rules or regulations regarding the paschal candle, and if so, what are they?

A. I'm not exactly sure what you mean, but let me try to answer anyway.

The paschal candle (or Easter candle) is to be blessed each year at the Easter Vigil Liturgy and should be a real candle. In other words, (1) it should not be used over and over again; (2) it should not be an artificial candle (a tube-like item, with a candle stuck in the top). Since it symbolizes the risen Christ in our midst, it is lighted for all liturgical events of the Easter season (i.e., up to and including Pentecost), and it should be located in a prominent spot for that period of time. After Pentecost Sunday, it should be returned to the baptistery. During the rest of the year, it is used during the celebration of baptisms and funerals, once again to highlight the connection between those events and the Lord's paschal mystery.

Statues enhance the Mass

Q. Is there any regulation against having images of Christ or the Blessed Virgin in the liturgy section of the church? Does the Church consider these to be distractions from the Mass?

A. No, there isn't. The only relevant text comes from the General Instruction of the Roman Missal, which says the following: "There should not be too many . . . images, lest they distract the people's attention from the ceremonies, and those which are there ought to conform to a correct order of prominence. There should not be more than one image of any particular saint" (n. 278).

Properly positioned, statues or other images can actually enhance the worship of the community. These sacramentals are visible signs of the communion of saints, with whom we offer the Eucharistic Sacrifice to the Father. However, statues can be a distraction when they are gaudy or too numerous. I once helped out in a parish church which had seven different representations of Our Lady in the sanctuary alone, not including various side shrines! So the Church is saying that there can indeed be too much of a good thing. But that is a far cry from a Puritan kind of iconoclasm which makes our sanctuaries and churches antiseptic chambers.

Location of the tabernacle

Q. Why is the tabernacle being removed from the center of the churches? I've seen no documents from Vatican II which state this must be done.

A. You've seen no conciliar documents on this because there are none. As I've noted on several previous occasions, the Code of Canon Law makes abundantly clear that "the tabernacle in which the Most Holy Eucharist is reserved should be placed in a part of the church that is prominent, conspicuous, beautifully decorated, and suitable for prayer" (c. 938.2).

Some liturgists argue that this is in conflict with earlier postconciliar legislation which called for separate chapels for eucharistic reservation. Some elucidations might be helpful here.

First, later legislation always supersedes earlier norms with which there is a conflict. Therefore, if there is a conflict, the newer regulation has the force of law.

Second, some people maintain that the document "Environment and

186

Art" of the bishops' Committee on the Liturgy strongly endorses a separate chapel for the Blessed Sacrament. While that is certainly true, that document has no legal status at all — and never did. At most, it offers guidelines for those who wish to follow them and has as much authority as the people who produced it. It should also be observed that the document in question was not even a statement of the entire hierarchy of the country.

Third, while at least one postconciliar (but pre-1983 code) Roman document does seem to encourage a separate eucharistic chapel. I think it would be fair to say that by the time the code was finalized many people had come to see rather negative effects emerging from isolating the Eucharist from the main body of the church (e.g., Who bothers going to that chapel to pray? What is behavior like in church before the liturgy, precisely because the Blessed Sacrament is absent?).

Fourth, a Blessed Sacrament chapel makes perfectly good sense for a cathedral or historic church which functions as much (if not more) as a tourist site as it does a house of worship, but that is certainly not so for the average parish church.

Fifth, when canon law speaks about the tabernacle's "prominent" position, that does not require "dead-center," in my opinion, but I think it would certainly imply visibility from the central axis of the church.

To the objection that the presence of the Eucharist in a central location "inhibits" celebration, what can one say? If God is a problem in liturgy, we're in serious trouble. If one wants to hold for the gradual unfolding of Christ's presence in the liturgy, the simplest solution is to situate the tabernacle in such a way that a grille or drape can be drawn before it whenever the Eucharistic Sacrifice is being offered, while leaving it open to view at other times.

Guidelines for church decor?

Q. I visited a "worship space" in another diocese recently. It had no crucifix, no statues or Stations of the Cross. It was bare of any symbol of faith. I wrote to the diocesan bishop, who replied that "it is not an empty building. It is filled up with marvelous prayerful people." Are there not specific authoritative guidelines which govern the building or renovation of churches? Is the bishop able to dispense from these requirements?
A. Universal liturgical norms are rather general in regard to the decoration of churches, if for no other reason than the fact that the

Church spans so many different cultures. What is considered gaudy in one place might be viewed as quite beautiful in another. Therefore, we find a requirement for a crucifix to be placed on or near the altar during the offering of the Eucharistic Sacrifice.

The Second Vatican Council called for statues to be retained but to be few in number and of high artistic quality. The rest is left to the good taste and goodwill of the locals. Unfortunately, both are often in short supply in some quarters today.

Corporal still used at the Mass

Q. Our new pastor will not allow a corporal to be placed on the altar for Mass. Two of our older priests are very uncomfortable with this but go along with him. The pastor claims Vatican II did away with this special cloth.

A. Paragraph 100 of the General Instruction of the Roman Missal says the following: "The servers place the *corporal*, purificator, chalice, and missal on the altar" (emphasis added). That says it rather clearly, I think.

The first Eucharist explained

Q. How could Jesus have consecrated the bread and wine at the Last Supper before He had experienced His death and resurrection?

A. Jesus' eucharistic actions at the Last Supper were unique, in that they were anticipatory — awaiting their consummation in His passion, death, and resurrection. That notion comes out clearly in His use of the future tense: The Body *will* be given up; the Blood *will* be shed. This should also help us realize that although the Mass has elements of a sacred meal about it, it is primarily a sacrifice, for that is what gives meaning to the meal — as you have suggested by your insightful question.

Graduation during Mass?

Q. Is it proper for a Catholic high school to confer diplomas during Mass (after the readings)? I am uncomfortable with all the clapping and commotion of commencement exercises during Mass.

A. If graduation ceremonies are held during Mass (and I would prefer that there be a separate baccalaureate Mass), the conferral of diplomas and the like should not occur after the readings since that position in the Liturgy of the Word is only for the administration of any sacrament (Baptism, Matrimony, and so on) that may take place during the Mass.

The appropriate spot for a graduation ceremony would be after the Post-Communion Prayer and before the final blessing and dismissal.

Like you, I would rather keep the church for absolutely sacred events and schedule the graduation proper for an auditorium. I do know, however, that very often a church is the only building large enough to accommodate such large gatherings. In that case, people should be asked to observe the proper decorum, especially if the Blessed Sacrament is kept in the church during the ceremony.

Committal rites at cemetery

Q. I am a seminarian who was recently asked to perform the committal rites at the cemetery. In using the new Order of Funerals, I was surprised to see that the celebrant is not directed to begin the ceremony with the sign of the cross, which I thought was to begin every act of official Christian prayer. Please comment.

A. The committal rite at the cemetery is simply the continuation of the Funeral Mass which, in turn, is the continuation of the wake service. The sign of the cross begins the first phase, but neither the Mass nor the graveside ceremony begins with that action because they are not self-contained rites.

Non-Catholics and the liturgy

Q. My wife teaches at a very fine Catholic school, but at a school Mass some time back non-Catholic children read the Scriptures and brought up the offertory gifts. Is this "kosher"?

A. As a general norm, non-Catholics may not perform liturgical functions, for obvious reasons. If, for example, a couple wants a non-Catholic to proclaim the readings at their wedding, in most dioceses permission for that must be obtained from the bishop. This discipline of the Church is not intended to be punitive, but is merely designed to guarantee the integrity of the Church's liturgical life. How can we speak of the liturgy as the worship of the one Church of Christ and then permit people not fully one with the Church to play significant roles in that worship?

When one brings the issue down to the level of little children, it is even more important to be clear, lest they get the impression that religious distinctions are just a matter of indifference. This would be most tragic, both for their life of faith as children and as adults, and for the potential to have a reunited Church in the future. Careless and sloppy ecumenism is always counterproductive.

Women in the sanctuary

Q. My Vatican II book states that women cannot be in the sanctuary, and that if they are readers, they must do so outside the sanctuary. How come, then, that is not followed? Or does the United States have special permission for women in the sanctuary? And just what should we consider the "sanctuary" to be, now that altar rails are gone from most churches?

A. The General Instruction of the Roman Missal does indeed say that women who proclaim the Scriptures at Mass must do so outside the sanctuary. However, before that was promulgated in the United States, the American hierarchy had obtained permission for any lay person, male or female, to proclaim the readings from the lectern within the sanctuary.

What is the sanctuary now considered? It is the area which immediately surrounds the altar, a distinction still quite possible in that even most renovated churches have maintained (as they should) an elevated area for the placement of the altar. Therefore, that space should be considered as limited to clergy and to those who serve them at the altar.

Role confusion

Q. In our parish we have been introduced to a new change. Now the people who bring up the offertory gifts are told to go up to the altar, where the priest is, face the congregation and raise the gifts slightly for all to see before placing them on the altar. Is this permissible? Seems like a confusion of roles between priest and people.

A. I've never heard of such a procedure, and surely the liturgical directives do not call for this.

Many liturgists over the past few years have expressed concern that we are making entirely too much of the Offertory Procession to begin with; after all, it is a fairly minor rite, whose principal purpose is simply to get the gifts to the altar. What you describe is somewhat akin to gilding the lily, and yes, I would concur that it smacks of role confusion.

Ways to increase liturgical devotion

Q. Do you have any suggestions for increasing reverence and devotion, especially at the liturgy?

A. Yes, I do. Try a few of these on for size!

1. A respectful silence when in church, in keeping with an attitude of awe and mystery in the presence of the Divine.

2. A better use of "body language" in worship. For example: genuflecting when passing before the Blessed Sacrament; striking one's breast at the *Confiteor*; bowing at the appropriate lines of the Creed; bowing one's head at the Name of Jesus; making the proper reverence before receiving Holy Communion.

3. Dressing for church in such a way that people might imagine that you truly believe you are going to encounter the Lord of the Universe.

How's that for starters? Anybody have any others?

Is there more here than meets the eye?

Q. Our parish priest has made three changes in our church that appear to be minor at first glance, but are really "chipping away" at the reverence for Christ's Eucharistic Sacrifice. First, we no longer have a "fixed cross" on the altar because of the alleged need for a processional cross. Second, our priest intends to stop the use of the altar bells at the Consecration because, he says, since God is present throughout the Mass, we "would have to ring bells constantly to be consistent." Third, there is a proposal to abolish kneelers in favor of using pillows!

Please comment on these proposals. Am I being paranoid about this subtle but consistent "chipping away" here, or is there more of a battle going on than meets the eye?

A. On the first point, there is no real difficulty, inasmuch as the only requirement is that a crucifix be present for the liturgy; ideally, that should be the processional cross.

Second, your pastor's treatment of the bells is silly at best and theologically confused at worst. While the rubrics do not mandate the use of bells any longer, they are surely permitted and even encouraged as means of alerting people to more central parts of the Mass. And certain parts are more critical than others, the Consecration being one of them. To say that God is present throughout the Mass is no different than saying that God is present throughout the universe; the truth of the matter is that God is more present in some places and at some times than others. That is what the ringing of bells highlights, and that is precisely what some priests and liturgists find offensive.

Third, I find no problem with substituting pillows for kneelers, just as long as people are given something on which to kneel at the appropriate moments of the liturgy. In fact, pillows might actually be more comfortable, surely a lot less noisy, and perhaps less nuisance in terms of maintenance. Many of our Anglican friends are familiar with pillows in their churches.

In sum, two out of three points go to your pastor. While it is good to be vigilant, one can become paranoid, and that is not helpful, either for the individual or for the good of the Church.

Proper reverence is needed

Q. What is the correct reverence to be given to the following: tabernacle, cross, altar. Some people bow to all three. Some, including priests, do nothing at all.

A. The proper reverence for cross or altar is a bow. One should always genuflect whenever passing before a tabernacle in which the Blessed Sacrament is reserved (and that includes during the liturgy). Some people argue that in the Eastern Church bowing is the proper gesture before the Eucharist, so why not for us in the Latin Rite? That begs the question. We are not the Church of the East, and they are not the Church of the West. However, very often those same questioners would not be happy if we adopted the lengthy and heavily penitential Lent of the East or their prohibition of Communion in the hand.

Consistency and honesty are important in genuine human communication. The truth is that many Latin-Rite Catholics fail to genuflect nowadays for one of three major reasons: (1) lack of proper catechesis and example from the clergy; (2) laziness; (3) loss of faith in the Real Presence of Christ in the Eucharist. All the more reason, therefore, for teachers and clergy to emphasize this sign of adoration and for faithful Catholics to perform the gesture with devotion and love.

Abuses are not the answer

Q. In the church where I attend Mass, most people do not genuflect, girls serve at the altar, and the entire congregation stands for all of the eucharistic prayer. When I complained to the local bishop, he said the Church had to do these things so that young people keep coming to church. Am I wrong to think these are abuses?

A. No. What you have listed are abuses. Who says young people want these things? Surely, my experience of more than two decades of teaching at the elementary, secondary, and college levels gives no indication of such interest. On the contrary, young people generally tell me that one of the principal reasons they do not go to Sunday Mass is the carnival atmosphere they are offered in all too many parishes. Disobedience to Church authority and a decreased sense of the sacred would hardly be worthy ways to bring anyone into the Church, even granting that it might be effective for the handful who desire such things.

The truth of the matter is that youths will return to a full and enthusiastic practice of the Catholic Faith when they are properly catechized, when the liturgy reflects the holiness of God, and when the lives of their elders (clergy, Religious, and laity alike) are models of Christian living. That is obviously a lot harder than making superficial (and unwarranted) liturgical changes. But I am convinced that no "quick fix" is going to do the job.

After Communion: Kneel or sit?

Q. Is there any indication in the rubrics whether one should kneel or sit after receiving Communion?

A. No, I do not believe there is. My own disposition would be to remain kneeling until the Sacred Species are returned to the tabernacle. If movement of people from the pews to receive Holy Communion makes this impractical or difficult, then sitting would be acceptable.

A 'ministry of movement'?

Q. Our parish has young girls come down the aisle twirling banners and refers to this as the "ministry of movement." Could you please explain the nature of this ministry? Is it legal or not?

A. Repeatedly, the Holy See has indicated that liturgical dance (that would include any "ministry of movement" done in the context of the Mass, the Liturgy of the Hours, or the administration of any sacraments) is an unacceptable practice. That norm has also been passed on by the U.S. Bishops' Committee on the Liturgy in Washington.

Now it seems that your parish has decided to call it something else, so as to evade the net of the legislation. This is pure and simple dishonesty. Over and above that, what could ever be the purpose or meaning of such a silly procedure?

'Sit-down' Masses

Q. In a recent issue of TCA you state that it is incorrect for anyone but the principal celebrant and concelebrating priests to stand at the altar. At a retreat for teachers at the Catholic high school where I teach, the cafeteria tables were placed in a circle and the priest invited anyone who wished to sit at his table. He then celebrated Mass while remaining seated the whole time, not even standing for the Gospel, nor making any of the prescribed gestures that could not be performed sitting. Are "sit-down" Masses an approved option?

A. "Sit-down" Masses are prohibited. If a priest is physically incapacitated, that is one thing, but for reasons of laziness or casualness, this cannot be justified.

Socializing in church before Mass

Q. At a recent liturgical workshop, we were told by the priest-instructor that at the "gathering together" for Mass everyone should walk into the church, greet one another, and chat. He further stated that persons who enter, genuflect, and go into a pew without speaking are "un-Christian" and exhibit a "God-and-me" mentality. Please comment.

A. Many postconciliar documents deal with the question of a "sacred silence," but let this one from *Musicam Sacram* (1967) stand as representative: "At the proper times a holy silence is also to be observed. That does not mean treating the faithful as outsiders or mute onlookers at the liturgical service; it means rather making use of their own sentiments to bring them closer to the mystery being celebrated" (n. 17).

Your instructor has a very one-dimensional view of reality, limited to the horizontal, but Christianity is both horizontal and vertical. In other words, the "God-me" relationship is basic and foundational; without that, nothing else makes sense. When that is in place, it necessarily overflows into one's relationships with others, especially within the community of the Church. If one is aware of the "mystery" (to quote the document already cited) present in the Eucharist, one becomes awed by the nearness of God and at the same time one's own natural unworthiness to approach the mystery. Silence is the appropriate response. The time before Mass should be dedicated to preparing oneself

194

to enter into the mystery, while the time immediately following should be for thanksgiving. I see nothing wrong with greeting the person occupying the seat next to you upon entering a pew, but a smile or quiet "hello" should suffice. Socializing is inappropriate in the body of the church; that is for the vestibule and parish hall. Perhaps a display of Christian charity in the parking lot would also be a positive development.

When the Christian life is reduced to the horizontal, it is diminished to the point of having nothing to offer. When the vertical is properly acknowledged, the horizontal automatically comes into play.

Women may be lectors at Mass

Q. Some issues back, you spoke against women lectors. Do you mean that women should not read at Mass when many men are present and able to do so, or do you mean that women should not read at all?

A. I have never spoken against women lectors. From the very beginning of the liturgical reform, women have served as readers and have done so with the complete approval of the Church. The only stipulation about female lectors is that they cannot receive the permanent ministry of reader, which is the liturgical rite formerly referred to as a minor order and then received exclusively by candidates for the priesthood.

Some bishops at the Extraordinary Synod of 1985 suggested that the Holy See take a closer look at the ministries of acolyte and lector, to determine if they should be restricted once more to seminarians (which could then justify female exclusion) or else to declare formally that there is no linkage between these ministries and the Sacrament of Holy Orders, thus potentially opening these up to women. The matter is currently under study in Rome.

Who may go to the tabernacle?

Q. During the celebration of Mass, who is authorized to go to the tabernacle, other than a priest or deacon?

A. First of all, the norm calls for the Hosts being distributed as Holy Communion to be consecrated at the Mass at which they will be received. Therefore, there should be no reason to go to the tabernacle before Communion. Of course, there will be times when an excess of Hosts exists and it is desirable to consume them before consecrating any additional ones. At times, more people are receiving than anticipated, thus necessitating Communion from the reserved Sacrament.

That having been said, if it is necessary to go to the tabernacle before Communion, it should be done by a priest or deacon and not an extraordinary minister of Holy Communion. Why? Because it is the celebrant who should present the extraordinary minister with the ciborium (to make clear that this is an act of delegation), and not the other way around.

Reverence for the Eucharist

Q. Inasmuch as you often speak about the need for reverence for the Eucharist. I thought you might appreciate the following exhortation written for priests by St. Francis of Assisi; it seems to be as valid now as it was eight centuries ago:

"We clerics cannot overlook the sinful neglect and ignorance some people are guilty of with regard to the holy Body and Blood of Our Lord Jesus Christ. They are careless, too, about His holy name and the writings which contain His words, the words that consecrate His Body. We know His Body is not present unless the bread is first consecrated by these words. Indeed, in this world there is nothing of the Most High Himself that we can possess and contemplate with our eyes except His Body and Blood, His name, and His words, by which we were created and by which we have been brought back from death to life.

"Those who are in charge of these sacred mysteries, and especially those who are careless about their task, should realize that the chalices, corporals and altar linens where the Body and Blood of Our Lord Jesus Christ are bred in sacrifice should be completely suitable. And besides, many clerics reserve the Blessed Sacrament in unsuitable places, or carry It about irreverently, or receive It unworthily, or give It to all comers without distinction. God's holy name, too, and His written words are sometimes trodden underfoot, because 'the sensual man does not perceive the things that are of the Spirit of God' (1 Cor 2:14).

"Surely we cannot be left unmoved by loving sorrow for all this; in His love, God gives Himself into our hands; we touch Him and receive Him daily into our mouths. Have we forgotten that we must fall into His hands?

"And so we must correct these and all other abuses. If the Body of Our Lord Jesus Christ has been left abandoned somewhere contrary to all the laws, It should be removed and put in a place that is prepared properly for It, where It can be kept safe. In the same way, God's name

and *His written words should be picked up, if they are found living in the dirt, and put in a suitable place. We all know that we are bound to do this, according to the law of God and the prescriptions of Mother Church. Anyone who refuses to obey should realize that he will have to account for it before Our Lord Jesus Christ on the day of judgment.*

"Anyone who has this writing copied, so that it may be obeyed more widely, can be sure that he has God's blessing."

A. Thank you for sharing this with our readers.

Priest's behavior vexes parishioner

Q. Our pastor sits with the laity in the pews during those daily Masses celebrated by other priests in our parish. When it is time for Communion, he joins the line with the laity and receives Communion from whoever is distributing on his aisle — half of the time, a layperson. We have had meetings with him on this, referring him to the Holy Father's reference to this type of behavior in Inaestimabile Donum (on dealing with eucharistic abuses) as "reprehensible," but to no avail.

He also refuses to genuflect before the Blessed Sacrament and merely bows. He says he sees no difference between the two. What can we do?

A. Vatican II's Constitution on the Sacred Liturgy declares that "in liturgical celebrations each one, minister or layperson, who has an office to perform, should do all of, but only, those parts which pertain to that office. . ." (n. 28). In other words, your pastor should be concelebrating the liturgy, if he is not required to be the principal celebrant, and certainly should be distributing Holy Communion.

The refusal to genuflect is particularly odd, especially since he says he sees no difference. If there is no issue, why make one of it?

Speak to the dean or vicar for your region about these problems. If you get no satisfaction there, write directly to the diocesan bishop.

Confusion of roles and ministries

Q. Our pastor has instituted a new change in the liturgy, wherein the extraordinary minister of Holy Communion pours the wine and water into the chalice at the Offertory, then hands it to the celebrant. I thought this function was only permitted for the ordained, that is, deacons or priests.

A. You are correct. An altar boy hands the cruets to the deacon or the celebrant (or a concelebrant who might be fulfilling diaconal functions in the absence of a deacon), who prays, "By the mystery of this water and wine, may we come to share in the divinity of Christ who humbled himself to share in our humanity." What you describe is rubrically incorrect and contributes to the confusion of roles and ministries in the Church.

Orderly procedure, but 'poor liturgy'

Q. Some time back, our parish council voted to have the ushers guide people to Communion three pews at a time, to make the whole procedure more orderly, and it worked very well. Then our archbishop visited the parish and said the practice had to stop because it was "poor liturgy." Do you know what he might have meant?

A. I could only second-guess your archbishop. My own reaction to the practice of pew-by-pew Communion is strongly negative for a very important reason: It almost forces people to go to Communion who might otherwise not do so because of being in the state of serious sin, being non-Catholic, etc. While the procedure is undoubtedly orderly, it creates genuine problems of conscience for more people than we might imagine at first consideration. Therefore, I would never permit the practice for that reason alone.

'Modernist experiment'?

Q. In our parish, during Lent, the holy-water fonts were emptied. A little leaflet explained that Lent is a time of penance and preparation for our renewal of baptism at Easter. "The dryness of these fonts is a symbol of our thirst for God." Is this practice of emptying the holy-water fonts for Lent permissible or is it another modernist experimentation?

A. I don't know whether or not I would go so far as to refer to the practice you cite as "another modernist experimentation," but it is surely incorrect, and silly, too.

The Church directs us to remove the water from our holy-water fonts for the duration of the Paschal Triduum, that is, from the Mass of the Lord's Supper on Holy Thursday until the Easter water is blessed at the Vigil on Holy Saturday. If people would stick with the Church's counsel on these matters, instead of trying to go one better, we'd all be better off.

Should Mass intentions be announced?

Q. When should the intention be inserted into the Mass? Should it not be included in the vocal prayers?

A. The intention of the Mass need never be stated aloud. It suffices for the priest to know it in advance and to make his intention for the Mass that of the donor of the stipend.

In many places, however, the intentions are printed in the parish bulletin. Sometimes they are announced at the beginning of the Mass. Yet again, the intention may properly be included in the General Intercessions.

When the Second or Third Eucharistic Prayer is used, the name of the deceased may be mentioned in the commemoration of the dead. I would caution, however, against doing this in daily Masses for the dead, restricting that practice to Funeral Masses instead.

Sunday Mass in a parish church

Q. I live in a priests' retirement home, and we obviously have a number of lay employees here. Can they fulfill their Sunday Mass obligation by attending a Mass offered here, or must they go to a parish church?

A. The Code of Canon Law of 1983 does not require the faithful to fulfill their Sunday Mass obligation in a parish church, as did the old Code.

Is proper intent needed for a valid Mass?

Q. In the traditional Latin Mass, the celebrant has to state his intention specifically to offer the sacrifice. In the Novus Ordo Missae, the celebrant's intention is known only to himself. If he does not intend to perform the transubstantiation, is the Mass valid?

A. I do not know what you refer to when you speak of the priest's having to "state his intention to offer the sacrifice" in the Tridentine Mass. Intentionality is required in both rites and, once again, only the minimum is essential, namely, that the priest not exclude from happening what the Church intends to occur.

Some readers might get nervous with such meager requirements for validity, but the Church's wisdom and experience over the centuries have led her to introduce as few possibilities for invalidity as she can. After all, we could find ourselves in the position of never knowing whether a valid sacrament had been administered: Were my sins truly forgiven? Were the bread and wine consecrated? Was I properly ordained? The Church tries to restrict questions of validity to very objective, observable realities, lest intense subjectivity cause graver problems and disquiet the consciences of the faithful.

With regard to the term *Novus Ordo Missae*, please see another item in this section (p. 205)

Conditions for a valid Mass
Q. Are correct form, correct matter, and proper intention still required for a valid mass?
A. Yes, they are.

Overuse of a eucharistic prayer
Q. Before the liturgical changes, we had only the Roman Canon, now the First Eucharistic Prayer. When the other three came out, the idea was that this would add greater variety, avoiding monotony. How is it that the Second Eucharistic Prayer has become a kind of new "Roman Canon," in that it is used almost as invariably as when we had only one eucharistic prayer?
A. If a priest uses Eucharistic Prayer II as much as he used the Roman Canon in the old days, something is wrong. First of all, the second anaphora (the technical name for a eucharistic prayer) should never be used on Sundays, except in the most dire situations. Prayers I or III should be used on Sundays; Prayer IV cannot be used whenever there is a proper preface, since it has its own. Priests who resort to the quickest way out are liturgical minimalists; they are usually the same breed as those who, before the Council, celebrated Requiem Masses every day, simply because they were the shortest. We are in no race when we worship Almighty God, or at least we shouldn't be.

A reverent celebration of Sunday Mass, with everything sung and a five-to seven-minute homily, with a congregation of six hundred and two or three priests distributing Holy Communion, can usually be accomplished within an hour — not too much for anyone, I hope.

Substitution of words at Mass
Q. My pastor habitually makes substitutions: "friends" for "disciples," "sinfulness" for "sins," "The Lord IS with you" for "The Lord BE with you." Are these minor, permissible changes or not? I think not.

A. Sometimes substitutions are motivated by goodwill but misinformation; other times by arrogance; and yet others by a clear theological agenda at odds with Catholic doctrine.

"Friends" is used for "disciples" in some eucharistic prayers approved by the Church (some Masses for Reconciliation or for Children). However, those Masses could not be used for a regular Sunday celebration. "Sinfulness" is a permanent state of humanity after the Fall; "sins" are actions or omissions of an individual, revealing his or her sinfulness in concrete ways; obviously, then, they are not the same. When the Church directs the celebrant to say "The Lord be with you," it is to convey a wish or prayer that the Lord would be with all; it is not a statement of fact. To be grammatical, we are utilizing the subjunctive mood, not the indicative. In other words, the Church is not declaring that the Lord is with an entire congregation because we have no way of knowing that, and, as a matter of fact, our personal sins (especially of a serious nature) keep God at bay. So the hope expressed is that the congregation would accept the grace of Christ being offered, so as to fulfill the prayer in their daily lives. To say "The Lord is with you" is a premature canonization decree.

Of course, the simplest and safest route for celebrants to take is to stick to the text, which I consistently urge.

Repetition of the Mass

Q. A few Saturdays ago there was no particular Mass for the day; the missalette we use said to use the previous Sunday's Mass, but the way the dates fell, we were unable to do so because that missalette had already been discarded. Could we have used the following Sunday's prayers?

A. On a day with no assigned text, the celebrant is free to use any Mass in the Missal, that is, a votive Mass, any of the Masses for particular intentions, or the propers from any of the Sundays throughout the year. During the summer months this situation arises rather frequently, and many priests (and sacristans) think they must just repeat Sunday's Mass over and over, which is not the case.

Singing the consecration

Q. In [a recent] issue of TCA, you responded that the consecration at Mass may be sung. In reviewing your series on the rubrics of the Mass,

*there was no mention of singing the consecration. A priest-friend of ours
told us very adamantly that the consecration may not be sung and that
we do not get the full benefit of graces when it is sung because Scripture
indicates that Jesus spoke the consecration at the Last Supper. Has it
always been liturgically correct for the celebrant to choose to sing the
consecration (even prior to Vatican II)? Or is it a choice given by the
American Catholic bishops to priests in this country?*

A. I did not mention singing the consecration in my rubrics brochure
simply because it is usually not done, due to both time constraints and
the rather meager musical abilities of most priests. Your priest-friend's
comments are very strange indeed. In the liturgy, we do not mimic Jesus,
for starters, but how do we know if He sang or recited the words of
institution, anyway? After all, the Passover was a ritual meal, filled with
singing.

As far as obtaining less grace for having a sung consecration, I can't
believe the assertion was seriously made. Is he saying that God would be
angered by singing? St. Augustine obviously didn't think so when he
declared that he who sings well prays twice!

The choice given to celebrants is not by the American bishops but
by the General Instruction of the Roman Missal, and all anyone need do
is look at the back of the definitive Latin text to find the musical settings
for the entire eucharistic prayer.

The option did not exist in the old rite since the whole canon was
recited in a quiet, inaudible tone.

Changes are distracting

*Q. One of the priests in our parish changes the words during the
consecration of the chalice from "Do this in memory of me" to "Do this
as often as you remember me." He says that this is a more accurate
interpretation of the Greek. Is this claim true or false? Is the change
acceptable or not? The change has been mentioned to the pastor, who
continues to allow it.*

*Is there any reason one should prefer to refer to Our Lord as "the
Master" instead of "Jesus" during a homily? I don't mind admitting
being intimidated by his educational background, but nevertheless I find
such changes distracting during Mass.*

A. First of all, the institution narrative of the Mass is not a verbatim
citation from Sacred Scripture. So, which passage is he claiming to

translate more accurately? It seems rather pompous to suggest that one's own translation is not only better than the Church's but also to be used, without any authorization to do so. At any rate, the official Latin text is normative — and not something in the Greek New Testament — and that text says this: "*Hoc facite in meam commemorationem*," which is quite simply rendered as, "Do this in memory of me."

I have said on many occasions that the committee which made the English translation of the Mass did a horrendous job in many ways, but I would never dare to change the texts to suit myself. The Latin formulas, however, are extremely careful workings of ancient texts, including good translations of the Greek, when that is applicable.

As far as calling Jesus "the Master," it does seem to have been the term of choice by His disciples and is surely quite respectful, even humble and reverential. It properly emphasizes His role as teacher and ours as students. My own preference in both preaching and teaching is to use a variety of names and titles for the Second Person of the Blessed Trinity, inasmuch as the mystery of His Person is so great that no one name or title is sufficient or exhaustive.

A lack of reverence?

Q. It seems so many things are diminishing the reverence owed to the Blessed Sacrament, especially in language. Doesn't the term "eucharistic prayer" lessen the fact that the Mass is the unbloody Sacrifice of the Cross? Is it proper to refer to "taking" Communion? And should we not speak of Holy Communion, instead of just Communion?

A. I have made several of your points before. Namely, we certainly have had a serious problem with eucharistic faith and devotion over the past twenty years, due in large measure to defective catechesis and preaching, as well as liturgical aberrations and irreverence during the liturgy. A recent Gallup Poll revealed that only thirty percent of American Catholics who regularly receive Holy Communion regularly truly believe that the Eucharist is the Body and Blood, soul and divinity of Our Lord Jesus Christ. Ironically, more Lutherans accept that statement than do Catholics! How did this happen?

First, many catechists and priests have failed to communicate the full truth about the Eucharist and have reduced it to a "community meal" or to an event that takes its significance from the faith of the people in attendance rather than the other way around, whereby Christ present in the eucharistic elements strengthens His people. But even where the true faith in the Eucharist is shared, our liturgical practices have often been flawed, so that they do not buttress — at a visible, or sign, level — what we teach and say we believe.

So, do we really treat the eucharistic Species as though we believe that God Incarnate is in our midst? Many of you readers will recall a quote from a Protestant minister cited in a TCA article, in which he said that if he believed what the Church teaches about the Eucharist, he would have to crawl up the center aisle on his belly to receive!

You see, so many of our recent liturgical practices (for example, extraordinary ministers of Holy Communion, Communion-in-the-hand, mitigated fast), while certainly not heretical, have the effect of undermining faith in the Church's traditional eucharistic doctrine. Faith comes not only from hearing but also from seeing; therefore, when we see something that suggests that the Eucharist is no different from ordinary bread, how long can we continue to believe that It is indeed incomparably different?

Now, for your specific points. No, I don't think the expression "eucharistic prayer" is problematic. At any rate, that is the name for only a part of the Mass and not the totality.

Certainly, "Mass" in and of itself does not connote "sacrifice." My own preference is to speak of the "Eucharistic Sacrifice."

Catholics do not "take" Communion; they "receive" It. We are fed by another, who represents The Other in a very real way. Now if the truth be told, that humble act of reception (rather than an arrogant self-assertion of a right to access) is more apparent when one is clearly fed the Sacred Host by an ordained minister who places It on one's tongue, a truth hit upon by Pope Paul VI in *Memoriale Domini*, his document on Communion-in-the-hand. And yes, I think we need to surround our sacral activity with sacral language, and so we should say "Holy Communion," "Blessed Sacrament," and so on.

The Nicene Creed

Q. What is the reason that we so seldom hear the Nicene Creed recited at Mass any longer?

A. I couldn't answer that because it is required for every Sunday and solemnity of the year. The only possible exception is at Masses when the majority of the congregation is composed of children, in which case the Apostles' Creed may be substituted.

Which doxology may the laity recite?

Q. [In a recent] issue of TCA, you stated that "the priest should recite neither the Great Amen nor the doxology for the embolism because they are responses to his prayers." I agree with you about the Great Amen, but not the doxology recitation. Several years ago, a special rescript from the Holy See stated that only the priest and not the laity should recite the doxology, because of an abuse such as you mentioned (laity saying prayers assigned to the priest). Surely, you couldn't have meant what you wrote.

A. The doxology to which I was referring was not the "through Him, with Him, in Him" doxology, but the "For the kingdom, the power, and the glory" doxology (at the embolism). Thanks for helping me to clarify the point.

No such thing as a 'novus ordo Missae'

Q. Even though Pope Paul VI had the legal right to promulgate the Novus Ordo Missae, does that justify the moral right, considering all the liturgical aberrations we have witnessed?

A. I consistently remind people that there is no such thing as a "*novus ordo Missae.*" There is only an "ordo Missae," one from the Council of Trent and one from Vatican II. It was a mischievous attempt on the part of some reactionaries to tag the adjective "novus" (new) onto the title of the liturgy, in an effort to discredit it as a modernistic invention.

While I am no strong devotee of the so-called Tridentine Mass, neither am I a basher of it. As I have written on numerous occasions, when it was celebrated well, it provided marvelous access to the divine; on the other hand, when poorly or irreverently done (and that happened with sad regularity), it was no more edifying than today's aberrations. The solution to our liturgical problems is not in recapturing a former rite but in responding to the call to worship God in spirit and truth, with obedience, love, and faith. Those sentiments are needed, regardless of the rite we use.

Questions about the Offertory

Q. In our parish, after the presentation of the gifts, the celebrant approaches the altar, makes a profound bow, and proceeds at once to the Lavabo. Is it permissible to omit the Offertory prayers? Is it still necessary to be present for the Offertory to fulfill the obligation of attending Mass?

A. Your first question requires an absolute "no." Once more, we remind everyone that no priest can tinker with the liturgy at will. What's really strange in this scenario is why the priest would bother washing his hands if he dropped out the rest of the rite. If the truth were told, most priests who play around with this part of the Mass do the prayers for the bread and wine but omit the Lavabo.

Your second point obviously reflects a recollection from the preconciliar law of the Church, which mandated attendance at the Offertory, Consecration, and Communion of the Mass to fulfill one's obligation. All liturgists and moralists I know would say that one must participate in the Liturgy of the Word and the Liturgy of the Eucharist. In other words, the law is stricter today than in the recent past because of a clearer understanding of the centrality of the Word and its role of preparing one for the Eucharist, as well as the inherent unity of the two parts.

Group promotes use of Latin

Q. Is there any association for lovers of Latin that hasn't been overtaken by "Tridentinites"? I am so depressed over the almost automatic connection made between those who have an appreciation for Latin and those who resist any kind of liturgical development or change.

A. While I would never disparage those who have an affinity for the so-called Tridentine Mass and who do accept the validity and normative nature of the Mass of Pope Paul VI, I have also become concerned about the linkage you noted and what that might mean for the future of Latin in the mainstream of the Church. For that very reason, at the end of September 1989, I began the St. Gregory Foundation for Latin Liturgy, which is committed to the preservation of Gregorian Chant and the availability of the Mass of Paul VI in Latin on a regular basis.

The foundation produces a newsletter with important information on matters of concern to the membership; it sponsors seminars and workshops for priests, seminarians, musicians and other pastoral workers. In this second regard, I should mention a special two-week summer institute for seminarians interested in obtaining a better grasp of Latin for both liturgical and theological reasons.

Anyone interested in information on the foundation or on the seminarians' workshop should write to: St. Gregory Foundation for Latin Liturgy, 207 Adams St., Newark, N.J. 07105; or call (201) 344-6847.

No right to alter official language

Q. I have told my parish priest that your column always says that priests have no right to make arbitrary changes in the prayers of the Mass, which he always does in regard to so-called "inclusive language." He handed me the enclosed statement from the International Commission on English in the Liturgy, which calls for just about everything he does. It also says that this was all approved by the U.S. Bishops' Committee on the Liturgy.

Q. One of our lectors consistently changes words in the readings to reflect inclusive language. He says he was told to do this in a diocesan lectors' training program. Can this be so? Most members of the congregation find this annoying and distracting.

A. Neither the International Commission on English in the Liturgy nor the Bishops' Committee on the Liturgy, and surely not a diocesan liturgical commission, has any competence whatsoever to make liturgical changes. Their role is to *propose* any such changes, which must then be voted upon by the entire body of bishops. Should their vote be affirmative, their action then must be approved by the Holy See. Only then are the changes permissible.

Needless to say, neither a priest nor a lector has authorization to amend officially approved texts.

OK to stand at the Great Amen?

Q. The missalette used in our parish instructs the congregation to stand after the Amen of the eucharistic prayer and before the Lord's Prayer. I stand at the Amen, as a way of giving greater affirmation to my Amen. Who's right?

A. The missalette. While your motivation is noble, it does not correspond to the rubrics. The congregation remains kneeling during the Great Amen because that word is the last word of the eucharistic prayer, for which the congregation is to kneel. On the other hand, all rise to recite the Lord's Prayer. Therefore, the directive in the missalette is correct.

Just one last point: For one person to engage in an action not in keeping with the rest of the congregation can be quite distracting and even disruptive of unity. I am referring, naturally, to an action which is wrong. For instance, I know of parishes where priests tell the people to stand for the eucharistic prayer, but some do what the Roman Missal requires; in that instance, the disrupter of unity is not the individual but the priest who has exceeded his authority to begin with.

Eucharistic prayer: May it be silent?

Q. In the Mass of Pius V, the Canon was silent. Is there any time when the eucharistic prayer may be silent in the revised liturgy?

A. Your question took me off guard since I have always presumed that one of the clearest changes made in the liturgy was the recitation of the eucharistic prayer out loud. Nevertheless I thought I should still go back to the Roman Missal, just to be sure. And it's a good thing that I did!

Here's what I discovered in the Order of Mass, just before the beginning of the Preface dialogue: "In all Masses the priest MAY say the eucharistic prayer in an audible voice" (emphasis mine). In other words, the Sacramentary gives permission to say the words aloud but does not mandate it. I must confess, however, I would be hard-pressed to suggest why the words should be inaudible.

Mass in Latin

Q. It seems that many dioceses are now scheduling Latin Masses of both the old rite and the new, but I was shocked to hear recently from some friends that in other dioceses bishops have actually forbidden the celebration of Mass in Latin according to either rite. Is this possible?

A. It is happening, I know, but when a bishop prohibits the celebration of Mass in Latin according to the revised rites, he is acting beyond his authority. Why do I say that? Because the Code of Canon Law says the following: "The eucharistic celebration is to be carried out *either in the Latin language* or in another language, provided the liturgical texts have been lawfully approved" (canon 928, emphasis added). In other words, no permission is ever needed to offer Mass in Latin; permission is needed to use the vernacular, however. Of course, this canon merely reflects very accurately the position adopted by the Fathers of Vatican II in their Constitution on the Liturgy.

Seasonal response for psalms

Q. In our parish we sing the same response to the psalm for five or six weeks, ignoring the refrain that's given in the missalette. Is this correct?
A. Yes, it is. There is such a thing as a seasonal response (e.g., for the seasons of the year like Advent, Lent, etc.). This enables the congregation to get to know a few refrains well, rather than making them learn a new one each week.

Kneeling at the Consecration

Q. Why do people stand during the Consecration? In my day, I was taught that this part of the Mass was very special.
A. No one is supposed to stand during the Consecration. I have discussed this in previous issues of TCA but will restate the correct discipline now: From the end of the Sanctus until the conclusion of the Great Amen of the eucharistic prayer, everyone but the priest-celebrant is to kneel. The Federation of Diocesan Liturgical Commissions is pressuring the National Conference of Catholic Bishops to change this, claiming that "the people" are clamoring for the right to stand during the eucharistic prayer. The truth of the matter is that the people are not clamoring for this and in fact have never even been asked! This is the effort of a handful of self-appointed authorities who seek to undermine the sense of the sacred and to blur the distinction between the priesthood of the faithful and the ministerial priesthood.

In passing, I should also note that while many other countries do not kneel for the entire eucharistic prayer, all Catholics of the Latin Rite throughout the world — with no exceptions — kneel at least from the epiclesis (the invocation of the Holy Spirit) to the memorial acclamation. The FDLC does not want even that in place. I would suggest that readers do express their opinion on this important issue by writing to their bishops and letting them know that they have no problem with the current legislation and, as a matter of fact, enthusiastically support its maintenance.

The lectionary and Sunday Mass readings

Q. In my Thursday night Bible study group, we reflect on the readings for the upcoming Sunday Mass. We are often amazed at how most of the Scriptures are so skillfully selected for the liturgy. We sometimes joke about "the priest who lives in the basement of the Vatican" who can

*construct a theme by choosing the right verses on such a regular basis!
Seriously, who really does arrange the Sunday readings?*

A. The biblical readings are taken from the lectionary — a liturgical
book which sets forth the required readings for each day of the year and
for the various rites of the Church. The version we use now was
produced by a team of scholars in response to the call of the Fathers of
Vatican II to undertake the revision of the existing lectionary.

The Sunday lectionary as we have it now operates on a three-year
cycle of three readings. The First Reading usually comes from the Old
Testament and parallels the Gospel passage in theme, showing how the
Hebrew Bible prepared for the definitive revelation of the Gospel in
Christ. The Second Reading is generally taken from one of the epistles
or the Book of Revelation.

The Gospel pericopes or readings are arranged in such a way that in
the season throughout the year (Ordinary Time, the "green" season),
Cycle A relies on the Gospel according to St. Matthew; Cycle B, on
Mark; Cycle C, on Luke. St. John's Gospel is used in all three cycles and
especially during the Sundays in Lent during Cycle A. The weekday
readings are presented on a two-year cycle. Specific attention is given to
passages not covered on Sundays.

If a Catholic were to read no Scripture beyond the texts used for
Sunday Mass over the three-year period, that person would have been
exposed to more than 7,000 verses of the Bible — no mean
accomplishment. Of course, Bible reading has always formed the first
half of the Mass from apostolic times (as the New Testament itself
attests), but the lectionary revised since the Second Vatican Council
opened up even more of the Bible to Sunday-Mass Catholics.

The new lectionary is so extensive in its coverage of nearly the
entire New Testament and the most significant portions of the Old
Testament over the three years that most mainline Protestant
denominations have adopted it as well. In fact, if a Catholic attends daily
Mass, the percentage of Scripture proclaimed over a two-year span is
more than double that of the Sunday figure.

Unfortunately, Catholics have often labored under the
misperception that Protestants read more of the Bible than Catholics, but
that is not necessarily true — either quantitatively or qualitatively. Many
Protestant preachers select biblical passages according to the topic they
wish to handle for a given day. Thus, it is not unusual for them to have

favorite themes and key passages to which their congregations are treated on a recurring basis.

Fortunately, this kind of eclectic or selective Bible reading is not possible in the Catholic liturgy because the readings are assigned to a particular day. Hence, the homily must flow from the Word of God; the cleric's pet themes or interests do not determine the sections of the Word of God to be proclaimed. This is not an insignificant point to understand and appreciate in regard to the lectionary.

The ending 'Amen' of the Lord's Prayer

Q. Do you approve of dropping the Amen at the end of the Our Father in the Rosary? At the time when the Amen was eliminated from the Lord's Prayer at Mass, a priest said this was done because of the change in wording which followed. But he indicated this did not apply to the Our Father otherwise.

A. The priest in question is correct. The "Amen" was dropped from the Lord's Prayer at Mass because the "Deliver us, Lord" followed on its heels and continued its sentiments. To be correct, the "Amen" should not be dropped from the "Our Father" outside the Mass any more than it should be eliminated from the "Hail Mary" or any other prayer.

Traditionalists and the 'new' Mass

Q. Being a CYO (Catholic Youth Organization) moderator, I was confused as to what to tell my kids about the authenticity of the "new" Mass. A church I brought them to, for High Mass in Latin, passed out literature stating that it is a sin to attend any other Mass. I would like to comment on how reverent their celebration was.

A. The literature you sent me comes from a community of "traditionalist Catholics," not in union with the Holy See. I always feel very sorry for these folks because they must do great violence to their psyche by their actions. What I mean is this: To be a traditionalist obviously implies a fierce loyalty to Rome.

If, for example, Charles Curran or Hans Küng left the Church in a definitive manner, it should not cause them any great personal crisis because much of their approach is predicated on independence from Rome. For traditionalists, however, they believe that fidelity to the Tradition demands that they separate themselves from Rome — actually, they maintain that Rome left them!

Part of their contention is that the "new" Mass is not valid or at least grossly defective. Since I have dealt with that charge on numerous occasions in the past, I shall not go through all of that again. Their grievances are substantial in many instances and, regrettably, have not been taken seriously enough in several dioceses: liturgical aberrations which go unchecked; heterodox teaching and preaching; scandalous behavior on the part of clergy and Religious. In fact, some bishops who tend to ignore all the abuses from the left have come down on traditionalists like a ton of bricks. For all those reasons, I feel sorry for them. But leaving the unity of the Church is the wrong way to go, and rationalizing schismatic acts is no different from the theological sleight of hand performed by Curran, Richard McBrien, and others like them.

What's the solution? I think it's what is done by hundreds of thousands of faithful Catholics (clergy, Religious, and laity alike), who remain in the mainstream of Catholic life in this country, intent on bringing about the genuine renewal of the Church envisioned by the Second Vatican Council and temporarily derailed by the nonsense of the past fifteen to twenty years. I sincerely believe that the silly season is winding down (which is not to say that everything will be perfect within the next twelve months). But increasingly we find strong, orthodox bishops and young, courageous seminarians, priests, and Religious who are willing to provide the pastoral leadership for which lay people yearn. That process will take a good deal of prayer and no small amount of suffering, but if we love Christ's Church, it's worth it.

Children and eucharistic prayers

Q. The attached page accurately reports the wording from a pamphlet in our church sacristy. It is the justification for asking the grade-school children to respond during the eucharistic prayer during the weekly children's Mass. About ten times during the prayer, the priest interjects, "Let us pray to the Lord," and the assembly responds, "Lord, hear our prayer." Does this practice violate the following: "It is therefore an abuse to have some parts of the eucharistic prayer said by the deacon, by a lower minister, or by the faithful" (Inaestimabile Donum, n. 4)? Also, please advise if this text is currently approved in view of its provisional, temporary wording as of 1975. Does it have the approval of the United States bishops?

A. Eucharistic prayers for children were written with the good intention

212

of trying to provide texts which would (a) keep their attention and (b) teach them important truths of the Faith. Part of the psychology of those prayers is to involve children in giving acclamations at regular intervals during the prayer. The texts in the Sacramentary are approved by the Holy See for use in English-speaking lands.

Subsequent to their appearance, many people have questioned their advisability on several counts. First, many priests feel foolish using children's (and in some cases, childish) language to proclaim the eucharistic prayer. Second, educational psychologists generally do not think that the way to teach children to enter into an adult mystery is to give them a "dumbed down" text. After all, when Thomas Cranmer first came up with the Book of Common Prayer, it was undoubtedly "the King's English" and not that of the peasants. Gradually, however, the language of the BCP became not only familiar to the less educated but even found its way into their own speech.

My own experience seems to suggest that using the children's eucharistic prayers has fallen into disfavor in most quarters, as has the notion of a children's lectionary (even though such a volume has been approved by the National Conference of Catholic Bishops). In fact, from the very start, liturgists and specialists in early childhood learning recommended changing readings to simpler texts, rather than offering paraphrases.

A new 'lexicon'

Q. Will the NCCB be circulating a new, gender-neutral "lexicon"? Our parish priest says it's coming out soon, and that what he's doing is merely anticipating that directive.

A. It is not the task of the Church to write dictionaries; that belongs to grammarians and linguists. Our job is to take language as a given and use it to convey the truths of faith. One of the problems in the past few years is that of people in the Church getting into areas which are none of their concern. Over and above that, the question needs to be asked once more: "By what authority does a priest change liturgical and/or scriptural texts?"

The National Conference of Catholic Bishops will be coming out with a revised lectionary (on second thought, maybe this is the word your priest used and not "lexicon"), to incorporate the revisions in the New Testament of the New American Bible. The mandate by the NCCB to the committee working on the project says nothing about gender-neutrality for horizontal language (that is, among human beings) and specifically forbids the use of feminine titles in vertical language (that is, directed toward the Divinity). Now, some ideologies might get involved in the process and try to do violence to the integrity of the Word of God. But the bishops will need to watch out for that, as will the Holy See, which will be required to give its approval before the new lectionary can be used in the liturgy.

Deacons kneel for the consecration

Q. In [a recent] issue of TCA, in answering the question on "Deacons and the Celebration of the Mass," you stated, "Furthermore, the deacon should kneel from the epiclesis to the end of the consecration." However, n.134 of the General Instruction of the Roman Missal states, "During the eucharistic prayer, the deacon stands near the priest, but a little behind." Since the epiclesis is part of the eucharistic prayer and I cannot find any additional rubrics ordering a deacon to kneel. I am confused. Could you please clarify this?

A. You're doing your homework, and that's always a healthy sign. The difficulty is that you restricted yourself to the General Instruction of the Roman Missal; subsequent to its appearance was the Ceremonial of Bishops, which contains normative directives for all liturgical ministers. As a matter of fact, I understand that a volume based on it for parish liturgies is in the making. There one finds the following: "The deacons remain kneeling from the epiclesis to the elevation of the cup" (n. 155). The reason is that only the celebrant (or the concelebrants) should be standing at the time of the consecration, since he (they) alone is (are) acting *in persona Christi.*

Which preface for eucharistic prayer?

Q. In [a recent] issue on the overuse of certain eucharistic prayers, I agree that II is overdone. I disagree, however, with your statement on Eucharistic Prayer IV. Article 322e of the General Instruction says, "A eucharistic prayer which has its own preface may be used with that preface even when there is a proper seasonal preface" *(emphasis added).*

A. Thank you for your point, but I considered further clarification necessary because Article 322d, dealing specifically with Eucharistic Prayer IV, says this: "[It] has a fixed preface and provides a fuller summary of the history of salvation. It may be used *when a Mass has no preface of its own"* (emphasis added). The two articles seem to conflict, unless one should understand them to mean the following: If the Mass for a particular feast, for example, has its own preface. Prayer IV may not be used; if there is only a seasonal preface (e.g., Advent, Lent. etc.), Prayer IV may be used and always with its own preface. In point of fact, I have discovered that a later clarification was offered by the Congregation for Divine Worship, in which that interpretation is given. Thank you for raising the issue.

Holy Thursday repository and altar

Q. Some parishes are dismantling the Holy Thursday repository and its altar after the church closes on Holy Thursday night. The Sacrament is then locked somewhere (perhaps in the sacristy or a safe in the rectory), from which place It is then brought for Communion at the Good Friday liturgy. What is the correct procedure?

A. I guess the source of the confusion is that the first Roman Missal in English said that "after midnight all solemnity is removed," leading some to conclude that this obviously meant they should take away the repository. However, the 1985 edition is much clearer on this point, in noting that "there should be no solemn adoration after midnight." In other words, there is to be no public recitation of prayers or hymns at the repository after midnight on Holy Thursday; this is underscored by the "Circular Letter on Holy Week," issued in 1988 from the Congregation for Divine Worship and the Discipline of the Sacraments. In case anyone should yet be in doubt that the repository is envisioned as still being up, that same letter suggests that for veneration of the cross after the Solemn Liturgy of Good Friday and through the day on Holy Saturday, the veneration should be available to all and that the appropriate place for this to take place might well be the repository altar. If the altar is dismantled sometime after midnight on Holy Thursday, how could this be done at that very site less than twenty-four hours later?

So, to put it succinctly. I think the repository should remain up at least through the Liturgy of Good Friday, if for no other reason than to have a handy and dignified place in which to reserve the Blessed Sacrament and from which to bring It for the liturgy of that day.

Changes to prayers can damage unity

Q. I have just received the attached letter from the Carmelite Sisters in Indianapolis. Can these Breviary prayers be substituted for the approved Church Breviary?

A. For the benefit of readers, I should note that the texts are attempts at inclusive language. As has been said many times in this column, no one has the authority to alter official liturgical texts for any reason. The proper procedure is to have proposed revisions submitted to the Conference of Bishops, who vote on them; if that is favorable, then the texts are sent to the Holy See for final approval.

This kind of nonsense is going on in many seminaries and religious communities, and it has a destructive effect on any possibility of true Christian community. When one group imposes its will on everyone else, we are face to face with a totalitarian form of government. One Sister recently wrote me to say that the whole procedure is so bad in her community that she finds attendance at Mass and the Liturgy of the Hours so painful an experience that she just cannot wait to die. How sad that a woman who has given over sixty years of her life to God and the Church is not allowed to live out her days in peace. But this is the logical consequence of disobedience to the Church and the turning of all aspects of ecclesial life into ideological battles.

Eucharistic prayers from other countries

Q. Lately I've been hearing an unfamiliar eucharistic prayer in Masses said by a young Jesuit at Boston College. When I asked where it came from — he read it from a typed page — he said it came from the Canadian bishops and was used a lot in the Midwest. Do you know whether the Church has approved new eucharistic prayers for Canada? And is it legitimate to use them in other countries?

A. Some countries (e.g., Italy, Poland, Switzerland) have had additional eucharistic prayers approved by the Holy See; I would not be surprised if Canada is among them. However, what is permitted in Canada may not be imported into the United States, where the approved eucharistic prayers are limited to those in use in the universal Church.

Texts for the Latin Liturgy

Q. You have often spoken about the use of Latin in the liturgy, but it's so hard to find books for the people and choir. Do you have any suggestions?

A. The monks of Solesmes in France (those most committed to the restoration of Gregorian Chant in all its purity) have just published a magnificent volume, *Gregorian Missal*. It is a bilingual (Latin-English) work, containing all the Sunday Mass propers, as well as those for special feasts. The printing and binding are lovely, too. The American distributor is Paraclete Press, Box 1568, Orleans, MA 02653. Their toll-free number is: 800-451-5006. The cost of the book is $17.95.

Another valuable aid for the Latin Mass comes from Leaflet Missal Company in St. Paul, Minnesota. They produce a slim volume (bilingual also) of the entire Order of Mass, with the most common chants for the people's participation. They are available singly or in bulk at very reasonable rates.

It should be noted that both of the above are for use in the revised rites, not the preconciliar liturgy.

Sunday services that are not the Mass

Q. *Recently a new practice has been instituted in our parish. On Sundays when our pastor is unable to say Mass, three men from the parish take the place of the pastor. They say all the prayers of Mass and distribute Communion, but omit the consecration. I don't understand this change. Since I am elderly and don't drive, would it be a mortal sin not to attend Mass since I don't consider this practice at our church to be Mass?*
A. If this practice has been normative in your parish, as you suggest, something must be wrong. A Communion service, particularly in this country, should be the rare exception and not a normal event. You are correct in noting that this is not a Mass, and should never be thought of or spoken of as though it is. If there is no Mass available, one is obviously unable to fulfill the law of the Church binding one to attend, and hence the obligation ceases.

The Holy See has given permission for such Communion services where a priest is not able to be present in priest-poor areas. A pastor should never simply substitute a Communion service as a casual alternative to Sunday Mass. If the pastor is going on vacation, for instance, he has a serious duty to do everything in his power to secure a priestly replacement for himself. Separating the reception of Holy Communion from the offering of the Eucharistic Sacrifice is a serious problem from the viewpoints of sacramental theology and ecclesiology alike, only tolerable in the direst of situations.

The Rosary and the wake service

Q. When my mother died a few weeks ago, we had a Rosary at the wake; however, the funeral home had a letter from the bishop saying that we could not put "Rosary" in the paper. I was very upset at the wake when several people said they would have been there earlier if they had known that the Rosary was to be said. Why were we forbidden to mention the Rosary in the death notice?

A. The Church's pastoral care of the dead and their mourners takes place in a three-part rite: the service at the funeral home, the Mass in the church, and the graveside ceremony. The prayers for each part of the rite are spelled out in detail in a revised ritual that we have been using in this country for some years now. For about twenty years we were in a kind of limbo in regard to the prayers at the funeral home. Traditionally, the Rosary was done, and then in some places a biblical wake service was substituted. The definitive rite could be identified as more in line with that provisional biblical wake service. The reasons for this change are manifold: the postconciliar emphasis on Scripture; a desire to underscore the theme of resurrection and new life through appropriate prayers and readings; often the presence of many non-Catholics who cannot appreciate the Rosary; and, sadly enough, the difficulty of fallen-away Catholics who cannot even remember the basic prayers contained in the Rosary. However, I see no reason why a priest could not use the approved texts and then, if requested by the family, include the Rosary (or at least a decade).

One final remark: I hope that you are not saying that your friends absented themselves from the wake service because it was Scripture rather than the Rosary, for that would be a very poor attitude. After all, Our Lady was the believer who most reflected on the Word of God and put it into practice (cf. Lk 11:27).

Preaching during Benediction

Q. Recently at Benediction of the Blessed Sacrament, the priest covered the monstrance with a cloth after the "O Salutaris," before preaching. Is this allowed?

A. This is a throwback to a custom (sometimes a banner placed in front of the monstrance) that held sway in many parishes in the old days. The idea was that it was insulting to Our Lord in the Blessed Sacrament for the people to direct their attention to the preacher, rather than to the

Eucharist. Our theology of the Word and of preaching has evolved, so that we now see this action as one of worship, not in competition with eucharistic adoration but as an important part of it.

Celebrating the Hours with the Mass

Q. Recently, I attended Mass with the Liturgy of the Hours incorporated into it. I have never heard anything about this before. Could you please comment?

A. This is a completely acceptable practice, often found in religious communities or seminaries. For example, rather than have the liturgical hour of Morning Prayer, or Lauds, celebrated and then begin Mass, this option integrates the canonical hour into the celebration of the Mass. Thus, the psalms are worked into the Liturgy of the Word, with the Penitential Rite omitted; the general intercessions of Lauds become those of the Mass; the Gospel canticle is prayed as a kind of post-Communion thanksgiving. Clear directives are given for this in the General Instruction of the Liturgy of the Hours (cf. nos. 93-99).

This can also be done rather effectively in a parish. My own hesitancy would be to make this "regular fare," since the unique elements of both the Hours and the Mass could gradually be submerged into each other — and such an occurrence would be unfortunate.

First Friday Eucharist adorations

Q. Our pastor has eliminated our three-hour adoration of the Blessed Sacrament on the First Friday of each month. He says in the parish bulletin, which I have enclosed, that it is a violation of canon law to have this devotion. Is that true?

A. Your pastor reads canon law very differently from me. He cites canon 941 as dealing with short periods of eucharistic exposition and canon 942 for longer periods (like Forty Hours' Devotion). The first citation is indeed concerned with short-term exposition, and your three-hour adoration falls into that category. The second canon is directed toward either the Forty Hours' observance or something like perpetual adoration, because the canon makes clear a desire that this not be embarked upon unless there is an assurance that "a suitable gathering of the faithful is foreseen."

The revised norms for eucharistic worship outside Mass were designed to eliminate abuses which existed in earlier times. For example, it was common to have Benediction right after High Mass on Sundays, which could logically make one wonder what the point was, since everyone had just attended *the* peak of eucharistic liturgy in the celebration of the Mass and many had even received Our Lord in Holy Communion. Another incorrect procedure was exposing the Blessed Sacrament for only a few minutes, so as to justify blessing the people with the Eucharist. The new guidelines insist that exposition occur for a sufficiently long period, so that hymns, Scripture reading, and private prayer can take place — and only then may benediction (the blessing with the monstrance) be given.

As I understand your procedure, it is completely within the bounds of both the letter and the spirit of the law.

Devotion to the Sacred Heart

Q. When I was a child I heard so much about the First Friday devotions and the Sacred Heart of Jesus, but almost nothing in the past decade or so. What happened?

A. Of all the preconciliar devotions, the one to the Sacred Heart of Jesus may have been the most biblically based. Since the heart represents love, even in secular terms, the believer is brought to reflect on God's great love for His people, from the very beginning of time, especially His relationship with the Chosen People. The prophets, particularly Hosea, speak of God's unfathomable love in passionate language, often relying on the image of the heart. In the New Testament, St. John tells us that the heart of Christ was pierced on the cross, and from that wounded heart flowed blood and water, symbols of the basic Christian sacraments of Baptism and Eucharist, the means by which we are redeemed and continuously renewed (cf. John 19:26f).

The particular devotion so familiar to many Catholics before the Council was made popular due to the apparitions of Our Lord to St. Margaret Mary Alacoque, a French Visitation nun of the seventeenth century. No, the devotion is not dead, or at least it shouldn't be. For a very fine explanation of all this, I would recommend a book by Timothy T. O'Donnell, *The Heart of the Redeemer*, published by Trinity Communications in Manassas, Va.

The final blessing: a translation problem

Q. The English translation of the final blessing always irks me because it seems out of whack: "May almighty God bless you, the Father, and the

Son, and the Holy Spirit." Shouldn't the names of the Persons of the Trinity be modifying "God," instead of "you"?

A. Yes, I agree that the translation is defective. To avoid the problem you identify, many priests use the other English blessing: "May the blessing of almighty God, the Father, the Son, and the Holy Spirit descend upon you and remain with you forever." In that version, the modifiers are correctly placed, not leading one to imagine that "you" are "the Father, the Son, and the Holy Spirit"!

'Witness from silence'

Q. We have an ongoing argument in our convent about the proper way to begin and end the readings during Lauds and Vespers. Some sisters say there should be no introduction, while others say the readings should be done just as they are at Mass. What's correct?

A. The first answer to your question is the "witness from silence." There is no directive for the reader to say, "A reading from . . . This is the Word of the Lord," as there is in the lectionary used at Mass. Hence, the reader simply goes to the appropriate spot and begins the lesson, without introduction, and ends without a formal conclusion, followed by the responsory.

A confirmatory answer is also found in the 1971 decree *Novo Liturgiae Horarum*, from the Sacred Congregation for Divine Worship, which note that the reading ends without a *Deo gratias* ("Thanks [be] to God").

The general liturgical principle holds that when we're not told to do or say something, it should be omitted, not importing what is proper from one rite (in this case, Mass) to another rite (Liturgy of the Hours).

A difference in blessings

Q. What are the benefits of a priestly blessing to any object or person? When my children were babies, I used to receive Communion only from a priest so that my child could receive his blessing. Now I see lay men and women giving their "blessing" to children accompanying their parents to Communion. Does their "blessing" have any significance?

A. Lay people should not be giving blessings, as you describe. In many cultures, for example, it is customary for parents to make the Sign of the Cross on the foreheads of their children before sleep each night; that is a fine acknowledgement of the home as a domestic Church. In a church building, however, that function belongs to the priest.

May lay people confer blessings? The new Book of Blessings envisions certain circumstances under which a lay blessing would be given to objects, in the absence of a priest. The form, however, is different; namely, there is no Sign of the Cross over the thing being blessed, and the minister prays that God would bless the object ("May this . . . be blessed"), rather than asserting that it is blessed by oneself as would be said by a priest ("I bless you. . .").

Exaggeration in devotionals

Q. I am enclosing a prayer book which, I think you will agree, has lovely prayers, but some of the other material in it — with exaggerated promises and almost superstitious claims and threats — concerns me. Can you imagine if a non-Catholic got hold of this? Why does the Church allow such things to be printed and distributed to the faithful, particularly unsuspecting ones?

A. It is important to mention at the outset that the prayer book in question has no ecclesiastical approval. My first piece of advice, then, is to be sure that even your devotional materials are in accord with official Church teaching.

Sometimes devotional writers can get carried away by exaggerated fervor, and thus overstate their cases. What might be able to be excused as poetic license in some contexts cannot be tolerated when something is in print and thus able to lead a life of its own, apart from further explanation. I have always maintained that we do Our Lord, His Blessed Mother, and the other saints no favor by making outlandish claims which can be misunderstood by simplistic souls within the Church or people outside the Church. In fact, that kind of approach usually does more harm than good to the Catholic Faith in general and the devotional life in particular.

Keeping the Sacred Host overnight

Q. May an extraordinary minister who is assigned to take Holy Communion to shut-ins accept the Host, take it home and keep It until the next morning?

A. No one — priest, deacon, or extraordinary minister — may keep the Sacred Host on his person beyond the time absolutely necessary to bring

Communion to the sick. Any Hosts which remain are to be brought back to the church as soon as possible and returned to the tabernacle. "As soon as possible" does not mean after one goes shopping or until a more convenient moment; the glove compartment of the car is not a substitute tabernacle and should not be treated as one.

Lay ministers going to the tabernacle

Q. I am enclosing a copy of [a recent] issue of The Catholic Answer, highlighting your response to the question, "Who may go to the tabernacle?" I have always prepared my eucharistic ministers to go to the tabernacle, and your response seemed to put that procedure in doubt. I therefore wrote to our Archdiocesan Director for the Office of Divine Worship to clarify this point and am enclosing his response. Please readdress the question of "who may go to the tabernacle?" in some future issue of The Catholic Answer and state an answer that is more consistent with the opinion of the Bishops' Committee on the Liturgy.

A. I have read the response from your diocesan worship office and disagree with it and the national office's answer as well. The best indicator of the validity of my reply can be found by referring to Appendix V of the Roman Missal, in which one finds the rite of commissioning of an extraordinary minister of Holy Communion. There we are told that "when the priest has himself received Communion in the usual way, he gives Communion to the minister of the Eucharist. Then he gives him/her the paten or other vessel with the hosts. They then go to give Communion to the people." As I noted in my earlier answer, such a procedure is consistent, at the sign level, with the theological notion that extraordinary ministers operate by way of delegation and not by right.

Extraordinary ministers — again

Q. I know you said you don't want to discuss eucharistic ministers for some time, but I have a problem because of your column. I mentioned at our parish-council meeting that you said the proper title for these people is "extraordinary ministers of Holy Communion," but the nun said that in this diocese, that is not correct. The council members asked me to check it out, so I hope you'll oblige.

A. You force me to renege on my promise.

The official English translation of the Code of Canon Law,

published by the Canon Law Society of America, says the following: "The ordinary minister of Holy Communion is a bishop, a presbyter, or a deacon. The *extraordinary minister* of Holy Communion is an acolyte or other member of the Christian faithful deputed in accord with Can. 230.3" (Canon 910, emphasis added).

As should be clear, the text does not speak of "eucharistic ministers" or "special ministers" or anything else. It should also be noted that diocesan policy cannot contravene universal law; and a change in name here would seem to be intended to change the focus of the legislation, so that "extraordinary" wouldn't be taken to mean "to be used in extraordinary circumstances" when, of course, that is precisely what the law has in mind.

Readers report eucharistic abuses

Q. Last week after Mass, I noticed a Host on the floor near where the eucharistic minister was giving out Communion. I think It must have been consecrated, so I told the woman, who put It on the floor of the tabernacle since she said she didn't know what else to do and would tell the pastor.

Q. Last Sunday, as I was distributing Holy Communion, I noticed that a junior-high CCD girl had not consumed the Host after taking It in the hand. When she said, rather audibly, that she didn't like the taste and wouldn't be consuming It, I left my Communion station and retrieved It. Very shaken by the experience, I announced upon my return to my station that I would only give Communion-on-the-tongue. After Mass, I was berated and told I had no right to say or do what I did. Ironically enough, right after that incident I found a Host floating in the holy water font. What is a priest to do?

Q. I found a Host in the pew after Mass on Sunday. Everyone was gone already, so I wrapped It up in a handkerchief and took It home, but now don't know what else to do. Other parishioners have found Hosts in the holy water font, the confessional and even the poor box! How come this is happening?

A. What these three writers describe is not infrequent. In all honesty, I refrain from responding to these complaints more often because Communion-in-the-hand has become such a "sacred cow" in certain quarters that even to question it sets one up for charges of all kinds.

In my judgment, Communion-in-the-hand is a faulty pastoral

practice because it leads to just the types of abuses mentioned above. Can these same things happen with Communion-on-the-tongue? Only with great difficulty, and the fact that we never heard reports of them in the former situation would seem to argue strongly for the fact that they were not occurring. When the Church abandons a practice, she usually does so for good reason, and that was certainly the case with Communion-in-the-hand. If people wish to reintroduce a jettisoned practice, they must be able to ensure that the abuses which led to the suppression either no longer exist or can be obviated; that has not happened.

As far as the Host in your possession, bring It to church as soon as possible and give It to your priest. No one should have the Blessed Sacrament on his person or in his possession; It belongs in the tabernacle and may only be elsewhere when being brought to the sick, with remaining Hosts returned immediately to the church.

And to save us all time, please do not write in to tell me that my suggestion is denying you your right to receive in the hand. No one has a right to receive in the hand; rather, the priest has the prior obligation to determine that Communion administered in that way will not become the object of desecration or neglect. Only then may he, in good conscience, allow someone to exercise this option. Secondly, Communion-in-the-hand is not a right because it is an indult, which is a reluctant permission of the Holy See for local practice to deviate from universal law.

Laypersons may distribute Host

Q. Is it permissible for an extraordinary minister to distribute the Host while the priest administers the chalice with the Precious Blood for the Communion of the faithful?

A. Inasmuch as Christ is fully present under both forms or under either form alone, one who ministers a chalice is just as truly giving Christ to the faithful as one who distributes the Sacred Host. That having been said, I know of situations in which a priest deliberately ministers the chalice to force people to receive the Host from a layperson or else to receive under the form of wine. Playing games like that is, in my judgment, immature and unchristian, especially since it is using the liturgy as a tool for advancing a political agenda.

Extraordinary ministry limited

Q. I was an extraordinary minister in my old parish and brought a letter from my parish priest stating this to my new parish. I was told that the list of extraordinary ministers had already been sent to the Bishop for the current year. Does that mean that a person who wishes to be a part of that ministry must wait until the next year or is this just a formality?

A. The point you make is an important one, namely, that a person is commissioned as an extraordinary minister for only one institution, and that does not apply to anywhere else in the diocese or in the world. This is one more way the Church has of reminding everyone that this work is indeed to be viewed in the most extraordinary terms.

'Leftover' hosts

Q. I am an extraordinary minister of the Eucharist in my parish. A part of my duties involves bringing the Eucharist to nursing homes and shut-ins. It is almost impossible to determine the number of hosts to take on these visits because the patients vary in number. As a result, I usually return any excess hosts to the tabernacle, purify the pyx there, and then go home. A retired priest in the parish suggested that I give the last communicant several hosts to eliminate the necessity of returning the hosts to the tabernacle. I have not done this. Was his advice sound?

A. I would not give the last communicant several hosts, but I would not hesitate to consume the last few myself, presuming they are only a few. However, there is certainly nothing wrong with going back to the church to place the remaining hosts in the tabernacle, and that would actually be preferable.

Washing women's feet

Q. My parish has been washing women's feet on Holy Thursday, and my protests that it is forbidden by the Holy See were ignored. I was informed that the Bishops' Committee on the Liturgy has been in dialogue with Rome on this issue, and that Rome is satisfied with the American practice. I have enclosed for you a copy of the letter I received from Father Ronald Krisman at the NCCB's Secretariat for the Liturgy. What shall I do now?

A. I have read very carefully the detailed letter you received from the Bishops' Committee on the Liturgy. Father Krisman correctly quotes the appropriate Roman document which calls for *viri selecti* (chosen males) to be "led by the ministers to the chairs prepared in a suitable place." What is astonishing is that Father Krisman then goes on to argue that although this is what is clearly stated, it *does not explicitly exclude women from the footwashing*" (emphasis his). If it doesn't, then what does it mean? He himself admits three lines later that "all would honestly have to conclude that to include women in the washing of the feet goes beyond the literal meaning of the text." Yes, indeed, which is the whole point of the controversy. If we cannot trust "the literal meaning of the text," no document has any value.

Ash Wednesday and young children

Q. At our parish on Ash Wednesday it was announced that ashes would not be distributed to any child under the "age of reason." I thought that all people could receive ashes. Please explain why young children should not be allowed to receive them.

A. I have never heard of that. I imagine that the rationale for this would be that below the age of reason (normally given as seven years of age) one cannot commit serious sin and thus would not come under the obligation to repent. Absent any directive from the Church along these lines, however, I would not impose such a rigid and legalistic approach to the use of this sacramental.

Why suppress Tenebrae service?

Q. It is stated in the "Catholic Encyclopedia" that "the Tenebrae custom is technically suppressed in the present edition of the Liturgy of the Hours." The Tenebrae service is a beautiful and moving experience. Why, would/should it be suppressed?

A. The history of liturgy is the history of additions to and deletions from the official worship of the Church. Tenebrae was not very well-attended in the preconciliar period, and I suppose that was part of the rationale for dropping it from the liturgical rites per se. Interestingly enough, however, it has had a revival in many places without being formally designated as liturgical. My own parish community very much looks forward to it each year. Inasmuch as liturgy generally grows and develops in response to the needs of the people, Tenebrae may once more find itself included in the Church's official ritual, as opposed to being merely a devotional exercise at present.

General Index, Volume II

(For this *Catholic Answer Book* only)

Abortion, Abortionists, 22, 25, 51, 52, 63, 79, 102-104, 109, 112, 123, 124, 128, 134, 138, 139, 142, 143

Absolution, see General Absolution

Abuse, 158, 205, 212

Acolytes, see Altar Boys

Academic Freedom, 13

Acronym, 17

Act of Penance, 102, 156; See also Penance

Acts of the Apostles, 92

Adam, A. and Eve, 53, 54, 71, 84, 94, 106

Adult Education, 13; see also Education

Afterlife, 25, 90

Altar Boys, Servers, 181, 182, 197

"Altar Girls," see Female Servers

Anglo-Catholic, 65, 66; see also Church of England

Annulment, 98, 107, 117, 118, 121

Anointing of the Sick, 148

Anti-Catholic, 22, 25, 28, 132

Antichrist, 28, 59

Apostles, 60, 63, 85, 86

Apostolic Succession, 63

Aquinas, see Thomas, St.

Aramaic, 95

Artificial Birth Control, Contraception, 22, 105, 106, 112-113, 131, 134, 137-138, 140, 147. A. Candle, 184-185.

Ash Wednesday, 227

Attire, 33, 37, 38

Augustine of Hippo, St., Bishop, Doctor, Father, 127-128, 202

Baptism, 30-32, 46, 49-51, 65, 69, 71, 78, 94, 97, 102, 123, 142, 147, 148, 156-158, 170, 172, 188, 198, 220. Mormon B., 50. Valid B., 50, 157, 158

Baptismal, 29, 30, 32, 49, 70, 156, 158. B. Font, 29-30

Baptized, Baptizing, 8, 32, 45, 49-50, 157-158, 65, 69, 78, 98, 102, 117, 120, 123, 146, 147, 153, 154, 156-158

Base Communities, 64

Bayside "Apparitions," 27, 61, 62

Bells, 173, 191, 192

Benediction of the Blessed Sacrament, 218-220

Bible, 2, 27, 28, 73, 74, 77, 78, 85, 87-89, 91-97, 209-211, 213; see also Gospel, Scripture

Biretta, 168

Bishop, 5, 7, 8, 10, 11, 15, 22, 30, 34-36, 37, 39, 46, 48, 51, 53, 55, 58-65, 66, 67, 69, 70, 72, 77, 81, 82, 89, 112, 128, 139, 143, 147, 148, 150, 152, 155, 157, 159, 162, 165, 175, 177, 181-184, 187, 189, 192, 193, 195, 197, 202, 212-214, 216, 218, 223, 224, 226

Bishop's Ring, 36

"Black Mass," 29

Blessed Mother, 21, 52, 53, 89, 222; see also Mary

Blessed Salt, 25, 26

Blessing, 30, 71, 75, 84, 119, 160, 166, 171, 184, 189, 197, 220, 221, 222

Blood of Christ, 176, 179

Body and Soul, 54, 96

Both Species, 175, 179; see also Eucharist, Holy Communion, etc.

Bowing, 48, 191, 192; see also Kneeling

Bugnini, Archbishop Annibale, 151, 152

Byzantine Rite, Catholic, 66, 67, 160

Cannibalism, 49

Canon Law, 7, 10, 14-16, 30, 35, 47, 67, 99, 126, 128, 147, 148, 157, 165, 181, 183, 186, 187, 199, 208, 219, 223, 224

Cantor, 166, 174, 175, 178

Capital Punishment, 102, 103

Capitalization, Capitalizing, 18, 125

Catechesis, Catechetics, Catechism, 6, 7, 27, 31, 53, 68, 118, 121, 170, 179, 192-193, 203-204

Catholic Colleges, 28; see also Education. C. Form of Marriage, 129, 153, 178; see also Marriage. C. Funeral, 33. C. Hospitals, 14, 15, 109. C. Practices, 6-48 *passim*.

Catholics, Catholicism, 1-3, 5-7, 9-18, 20-26, 28-35, 39, 42, 49, 51, 53, 54, 55-69, 71, 72-78, 88, 89, 94, 100-104, 106-112, 114, 115-117, 119-125, 129-134, 138-143,

146, 151, 152, 153-155, 157, 164, 169, 170, 172, 174, 176, 177, 178, 180, 181, 188, 189, 193, 194, 198, 201, 202, 209-213, 222, 223, 227

Catholic Schools, 11-13, 101, 124, 189; see also C. Colleges, Education

Celebrant, 48, 81, 145, 149, 152, 159, 160, 164-167, 169-171, 179, 189, 194, 196-199, 201, 202, 205, 209, 214

Centering Prayer, 20; see also Prayer

Change, 11, 16, 30, 59, 64, 70, 77, 81, 82, 84, 123, 135, 156, 159, 166, 168, 170, 171, 190, 197, 202, 203, 206, 209, 211, 213, 217, 218, 224

Chaplain, 10, 11

Charismatics, 6, 26, 70, 74

"Chasu-Alb," 167

Chasuble, 167

Child, Children, 11-13, 30, 31, 32, 36, 49-52, 64, 66, 84, 91, 100-103, 107, 110, 111, 112, 113, 120, 122, 124, 127, 134, 135, 137, 138-140, 141, 147, 156-158, 158-160, 179, 189, 201, 205, 212, 213, 220, 221, 227

Christ, *passim*

Christian, 2, 5, 9-12, 17, 26, 28, 29, 41, 43, 46, 47, 50-52, 59, 62-65, 68, 72-74, 81, 82, 85, 89, 91, 95, 97-103, 108, 111-115, 118, 123, 129, 131, 132, 136, 137, 138, 140, 143, 146, 150, 172, 176, 189, 193, 194, 195, 216, 220, 224

Christmas, 87, 88, 133, 159, 169, 173

Church, Churches, 5, 6, 10, 13, 14, 16, 18-33, 35-38, 40, 41, 43, 44, 46, 47-72, 74-80, 82-86, 89, 90, 94, 95, 97-102, 104, 106, 108, 109, 111, 112, 114-132, 134, 137, 138, 139-146, 148-165, 167, 169-173, 175-182, 184, 186, 187-195, 197-201, 203, 204, 206, 210-213, 215, 216, 217, 218, 222, 223, 225-227

Church Decor, 187

Church History, 28

Church of England, 57, 58

Civil Divorce, 111, 112; see also Divorce and Remarriage

231

General Index, Volume I

(For the original *Catholic Answer Book*)

233